Benjamin Stillingfleet, Carl von Linn

Miscellaneous Tracts

Relating to Natural History husbandry and physick - To which is added The calendar

of flora

Benjamin Stillingfleet, Carl von Linn

Miscellaneous Tracts
Relating to Natural History husbandry and physick - To which is added The calendar of flora

ISBN/EAN: 9783337272883

Printed in Europe, USA, Canada, Australia, Japan

Cover: Foto ©Andreas Hilbeck / pixelio.de

More available books at **www.hansebooks.com**

MISCELLANEOUS TRACTS

RELATING TO

NATURAL HISTORY,

HUSBANDRY,

AND

PHYSICK.

To which is added the

CALENDAR of FLORA.

By BENJ. STILLINGFLEET.

THE SECOND EDITION,

Corrected and augmented with additional Notes
throughout, particularly on some of the English
Grasses, which are illustrated by Copper Plates.

LONDON, Printed:
And sold by R. and J. DODSLEY, in Pall-Mall;
S. BAKER, in York-Street, Covent-Garden;
And T. PAYNE, at the Muse Gate.

MDCCLXII.

TO THE

RIGHT HONORABLE

George, Lord Lyttelton,

Baron of FRANKLEY.

MY LORD,

BESIDES private motives of respect and honor, there is another of a public nature, which makes me desirous to inscribe the following sheets to Your Lordship. I mean the zeal which You shewed in Parliament for securing to this Country that noble collection of natural curiosities now reposited in the British Museum; which cannot fail

DEDICATION.

in time to produce many good effects, and prove the truth of what
Your Lordſhip obſerved, that the
reputation and intereſt of the nation
were highly concerned in that pur-
chaſe. I am, with the greateſt regard,

My Lord,

Your Lordſhip's moſt Obliged

and Humble Servant,

PREFACE

OF THE

TRANSLATOR.

THE following pieces were selected from many others published by several ingenious members of that great, and hitherto unrivalled school of natural history, the university of Upsal in Sweden, under the presidence of Linnæus[a]. They

A 3 were

---

[a] Linnæus Phil. Bot. p. 9. has these words, vid. dissert. nostra de ficu. Now there is a piece in Amœn. Acad. vol. 1. on this subject, in which the matter referred to is contained. This piece goes under the name of Cornelius Hegardt, tho' Linnæus plainly quotes

it

were felected not as the only, or even the
moft valuable, but as anfwering beft the
intention of the tranflator ; which was
to make known more generally how far
all mankind is concerned in the ftudy of
natural hiftory, and thereby to incite fuch
as are properly qualified to profecute, and
encourage that branch of knowledge, and
fpread, as far as the nature of the thing
is capable of, amongft all orders of men in
this nation, the improvements made in it
by the excellent Linnæus. His name, it
muft be confeffed, has been for fome time
paft in the mouths of people, but his
works, i imagine, are little known except
to a few vertuofi who have a more than
ordinary curiofity, and ardor to look into
the minute parts of nature. It cannot indeed be otherwife. For to underftand him
and to make ufe of his method, requires

it as his own. How far that may be the cafe of all the
other pieces in the Amæn. Acad. i cannot pretend to fay.
But it is moft likely from the practice in foreign univerfities in relation to thefes held for degrees, that they
muft in great part be attributed to him, as prefident.

more

more patience and time than are likely to fall to the fhare of the generality of the world. My defign therefore is not to exhort people indifcriminately to ftudy his works; but, as i obferved before, to give them fome idea how ufefull his purfuits are likely to become in many refpects. There will appear, i imagine, fuch great and extenfive views in relation to hufbandry, phyfic, and the general œconomy of human life in the few fpecimens i have given, that in this age and nation, where every art and fcience, that can be of any ufe to the public, are fure to meet with generous encouragers, there will be found many who will readily promote any rational endeavour to pufh thefe difcoveries farther, or put in practice fuch hints, as may feem to bear a probable appearance of fuccefs.

I can fcarcely condemn mankind for treating with contempt a vertuofo whom they fee employed in poring over a mofs or an infect day after day, and fpending his life in fuch feemingly unimportant and barren fpeculations. The firft and moft natu-

ral reflections that will arife on this occafion muft be to the difadvantage of fuch
purfuits.   Yet were the whole fcene of nature laid open to our views, were we admitted to behold the connections and dependencies of every thing on every other,
and to trace the œconomy of nature thro'
the fmaller as well as greater parts of this
globe, we might perhaps be obliged to own
we were miftaken; that the Supreme Ar-
chitect had contrived his works in fuch a
manner, that we cannot properly be faid to
be unconcerned in any one of them; and
therefore that ftudies which feem upon a
flight view to be quite ufelefs, may in the
end appear to be of no fmall importance to
mankind.   Nay, were we only to look
back into the hiftory of arts and fciences,
we muft be convinced, that we are apt to
judge over haftily of things of this nature.
We fhould there find many proofs, that he
who gave this inftinctive curiofity to fome
of his creatures, gave it for good and great
purpofes, and that he rewards with ufefull
difcoveries all thefe minute refearches.

It

It is true this does not always happen to the fearcher, or his contemporaries, nor even, fometimes to the immediate fucceeding generation; but i am apt to think that advantages of one kind or other always accrue to mankind from fuch purfuits. Some men are born to obferve and record what perhaps by itfelf is perfectly ufelefs, but yet of great importance, to another who follows and goes a ftep farther ftill as ufelefs. To him another fucceeds, and thus by degrees; till at laft one of a fuperior genius comes, who laying all that has been done before his time together brings on a new face of things, improves, adorns, exalts human fociety.

All thofe fpeculations concerning lines and numbers fo ardently purfued, and fo exquifitely conducted by the Grecians; what did they aim at? or what did they produce for ages? A little arithmetic, and the firft elements of geometry were all they had need of. This Plato afferts, and tho' as being himfelf an able mathematician and remarkably fond of thefe fciences, he

re-

recommends the study of them, yet he makes use of motives that have no relation to the common purposes of life.

When Kepler, from a blind and strong impulse merely to find analogies in nature, discovered that famous one between the distances of the several planets from the sun, and the periods in which they compleat their revolutions; of what importance was it to him or to the world?

Again; when Galileo, pushed on by the same irresistible curiosity, found out the law by which bodies fall to the earth, did he or could he foresee that any good would come from his ingenious theorems, or was any immediate use made of them?

Yet had not the Greeks pushed their abstract speculations so far; had not Kepler and Galileo made the above mentioned discoveries; we never could have seen the greatest work that ever came from the hands of man. Every one will guess that i mean Sir Isaac Newton's Principia.

Some obscure person, whose name is not so much as known, diverting himself idly as a ftander-by would have thought, with trying experiments on a feemingly contemptible piece of ftone, found out a guide for mariners on the ocean, and fuch a guide as no fcience, however fubtile and fublime its fpeculations may be, however wonderful its conclufions, would ever have arrived at. It was bare curiofity that put Sir Thomas Millington upon examining the minute parts of flowers; but his difcoveries have produced the moft perfect, and moft ufefull fyftem of botany that the world has yet feen.

Other inftances might be produced to prove, that bare curiofity in one age is the fource of the greateft utility in another. And what has frequently been faid of chymifts, may be applyed to every other kind of vertuofi. They hunt perhaps after chimæras and impoffibilities, they find fomething really valuable by the bye. We are but inftruments under the Supreme Director, and do not fo much as know in many cafes what is of moft importance for us to fearch after. But we may be fure

of

of one thing, viz. that if we ftudy and
follow nature, whatever paths we are led
into, we fhall at laft arrive at fomething
valuable to ourfelves and others, but of
what kind we muft be content to remain
ignorant.

I am fenfible that after all i have faid, or
can fay, many people will not be perfuaded
to allow that the ftudy of fome parts of natural hiftory can be worthy of a rational
creature. They will never vouchfafe to
look on moffes and infects in this light.
Yet why may not the ftudy of thefe likewife have its ufe in future times ? It ought
to be confidered that the number of the
latter is immenfe, that it is but lately that
any great attention has been paid to them,
that one of them is and has been long the
means of cloathing thoufands and feeding
more, that another affords us honey, another a fine dye, not to mention fome few
befides, of acknowledged benefit to mankind. Laftly, that they are capable of
doing us the greateft mifchief, and that it
is poffible that a more thorough knowledge
of

of them may inftruct us how to fecure ourfelves againft their attacks. Whether this
be poflible we can never know, till proper
encouragement has been given to this
branch of natural hiftory. Something to
the fame purpofe might be faid concerning moffes, but as the intent of one of the
following pieces is principally to take off
fuch objections as i have been confidering,
i fhall dwell no longer on this fubject;
but proceed to give a fhort account of what
Linnæus has done towards the improvement
of natural hiftory, that the reader, who is
unacquainted with his works, may form
fome idea, tho' very imperfect, of this
great man. Firft then, he has invented a new fyftem of botany, founded on
the male and female organs of generation
in plants, a fyftem which has thrown a
new light over botany. He has defined
about 10,000 plants, ranged them into
claffes, genera and fpecies, given new and
regular generical names to many inftead of
thofe barbarous and uncouth ones which
prevailed till his time, and added fpecifical

names

names to all, fhort, eafy, and oftentimes
fignificant, a thing never fo much as attempted before. He has brought into
botany, a precifion, concifenefs and elegance, that were very much wanted. He
has obferved and given names to fome parts
of plants not taken notice of by any other
botanift, parts which in fome cafes are fufficient as well as neceffary to diftinguifh
the genus and the fpecies.

The Philofophia botanica [b] of this author
affords throughout inftances of this reformation. Had he wrote no other book
but this, he would have deferved the
higheft praife from all lovers of botany.
For befides the improvements juft mentioned it comprehends in a fhort compafs fome-

[b] In the year 1750. when he was writing this book,
as he tells us in the preface to it, he was hindered from
going on by a terrible fit of the gout, that broke the
ftrength of his mind as well as body. In the year 1755,
he fays, Flor. Suec. article 450. that he had been freed
from the gout for fome years by eating great quantities
of frefh ftrawberries. He adds that this fruit diffolves
the tartar of the teeth, that it is remarkably good for
people afflicted with the ftone or gout, and that it may
be fafely eaten in abundance.

thing

thing of confequence in every branch of that part of natural hiftory, and affords hints for various difcoveries, hints that muft, if purfued, produce many confiderable improvements in phyfic, hufbandry, and œconomy.

He has publifhed a Materia medica fo far as relates to plants, in which he has undertaken to determine many fpecies commonly ufed but not fufficiently afcertained, adding throughout in the fhorteft manner poffible what he has found to be ufelefs or efficacious, and as he affures us never highly recommends any without being thoroughly convinced of their vertues by his own experience in the hofpitals where he prefided. Some of thefe medicines have not yet, i believe, been received into our fhops, but they may poffibly deferve confideration.

In the laft edition of his Syftema naturæ he has mentioned above 1500 fpecies of infects, has claffed them all, divided them into genera and fpecies, defcribed them as to the minuteft parts fo far as was neceffary to diftinguifh them, marked the places

where

where they are to be found, the plants
they feed upon, their transformations, cited
the authors who have treated on them, given
them claffical, generical, and trivial or fpecifical names; has done the fame by birds,
fifhes, and all other known animals; has
ranged all the foffils, minerals and ftones,
to ufe his language, in a manner partly bor-
rowed, and partly founded on his own obfervations. But what improvements and
additions he has lately made to this part of
natural hiftory, as well as that of plants, we
cannot fay till the other part of his new edition of the Syftem of nature comes out,
which is expected daily. However what
we fee he has done in relation to animals,
leaves us no room to doubt but that it will
all together be the moft extraordinary book
that was ever publifhed in this or almoft
any other way.

Befides his writings, of which i have
mentioned but a fmall part, this indefatigable man, born to be nature's hiftorian,
has travelled over Lapland, all Sweden,
part of Norway, Denmark, Germany,

I   Holland,

Holland, England, and France, in fearch of knowledge. That part of his travels which is publifhed in Latin has many curious and ufeful obfervations relating to the purpofes of common life. Of thofe which are written in his own tongue i cannot give any other account, but that by fome quotations from them to be found in the writings of his difciples it appears, that they very well deferve to be communicated to the world in a language more generally underftood.

Befides thefe labours of his own, the world will be one day obliged to him for what others have done. Incited by his example and perfuafion, C. Ternftrom went into Afia; P. Kalmius to Penfilvania and Canada; L. Montin into one part of Lapland; D. Selander into another; F. Haffelquift into Ægypt and Paleftine; O. Toren to Malabar and Surat; P. Ofbech to China and Java; P. Loefling to Spain and America; P. J. Berg to Gothland; M. Koehler to Italy and Apulia; and D. Rolander to Surinam and St. Euftacia; all

thefe

thefe with a view to the promotion of natural hiftory. When we confider him in
this light of a mafter of fuch difciples as
thefe, and many others, fome of whofe
works make up the following book, he
muft appear like Homer at the head of the
poets, Socrates at the head of Greek mo-
ralifts, and our Newton at the head of the
mathematical philofophers. Among all
thefe extraordinary qualifications there appear throughout his writings fpirit, candor,
a due regard for others, and proper mo-
defty and diffidence of himfelf.

I will give a fhort fpecimen of his way
of thinking in relation to the degree of human knowledge hitherto attained by man
on the fubject of natural hiftory. A fubject on which it was very natural for a lefs
extenfive genius to be vain, as he has had
fo great a fhare himfelf in the advancement
of it. The paffage is taken out of the introduction to the new edition of his Syftem
of nature, and is to this effect. ' How
' fmall a part of the great works of nature
' is laid open to our eyes, and how many
‘ things

' things are going on in fecret which we
' know nothing of! How many things are
' there which this age firft was acquainted
' with! How many things that we are ig-
' norant of will come to light when all
' memory of us fhall be no more! For
' nature does not at once reveal all her fe-
' crets. We are apt to look on ourfelves as
' already admitted into the fanctuary of her
' temple, we are ftill only in the porch. I
' have entered, adds he, into the thick and
' fhady woods of nature, which are every
' where befet with thorns and briars. I
' have endeavored as much as poffible to
' keep clear of them, but experience has
' taught me that there is no man fo circum-
' fpect as never to forget himfelf, and there-
' fore i have born with patience the fneers of
' the malevolent, and the buffoneries of thofe
' whofe vivacity is exerted only to mo-
' left and give offence to others. I have in
' fpite of thefe infults, kept on fteadily in
' my old path, and have finifhed the courfe
' I was deftined for.'

The latter part of this paffage, fhews that

he

he has not been without his enemies, and that he hath fuffered in the fame way that all the moft curious enquirers into nature have done in all ages. The tartnefs of his expreffions, which is ftill ftronger in the original, plainly proves that they have not ufed fair arguments againft him, but like interefted rivals, or men of a fuperficial underftanding, have endeavored to fub-ject him and his labours to ridicule. But whatever has been his fate in his own countrey, as far as I know, his name is almoft univerfally mentioned with refpect in all other parts of Europe. It is true, objections have been made to his innova-tions in other places befides Sweden[c],

which

---

[c] Having fince the firft edition of thefe tracts met with Browellius' anfwer to Siegefbec, M. D. and botanical profeffor at Peterfburg; who wrote againft the fexual fyftem of Linnæus, i cannot omit quoting one of his objections, which i imagine will divert the reader at the fame time, that it may ferve as an inftance how far zeal for old notions will fometimes carry men. The ob-jection is, that the laws of nature are overturned by Linnæus, fince polygamy and adultery would be ac-cording to his fyftem allowed in the vegetable world;

for

which muſt unavoidably happen on many
accounts, but particularly becauſe thoſe
natural hiſtorians who had been brought
up and inured to other ſyſtems, who

for in ſome plants there are many filaments to one piſtil.
This is polygamy. In others there are female flowers,
which are impregnated by the duſt of male flowers,
which have other female flowers belonging to them,
i. e. which are already married. This is plainly adultery. Now according to profeſſor Siegeſbec, it is not
credible that ſuch confuſion and deteſtable pollution
ſhould be tolerated in nature.

Browellius rightly obſerves in his anſwer, that Siegeſbec had totally overlooked many inſtances of theſe
enormities in the animal kingdom, and even the immo-
rality of farmers and their wives, ſhepherds, jockies,
ſportſmen, nay even ladies of reputation, who in their
ways promote theſe immoral and indecent practices.

However it muſt be obſerved in favor of this very
ſcrupulous profeſſor, that ſyſtems of philoſophy, founded
on facts have, been anathematiſed, and the authors
and favorers of them condemned to the ſevereſt pu-
niſhments, for reaſons as little to the purpoſe as the
foregoing of Siegeſbec. To quote inſtances would be
endleſs, as every one the leaſt converſant in the hiſtory
of learning will eaſily recollect them. But ſo moderate
is the world now become, that I do not hear that the
Linnæan ſyſtem is looked on as heretical even at the
court of Rome, though the profeſſor has drawn ſome
ſhrewd arguments againſt it from the book of Geneſis.

had

had learned things by other names, and could not eafily attain the new ones, muft have ftrong prejudices arife on this occafion. This objection being perfonal i fhall not confider it any farther, but readily allow that great indulgence is due to fuch · people, and that their fate is to be pitied for coming into the world too foon to be enlightened farther on fubjects, that perhaps had employed the greateft part of their life. But there are prejudices of another fort which i cannot omit to confider more fully on this occafion.

In order to this it muft be premifed, that the ufe and intent of a claffical fyftem in any part of natural hiftory, is not to range things according to their natural connections in regard to their outward afpects, or effential qualities, or their medicinal or œconomical properties, but to range them in fuch a manner that upon a plant, mineral or animal being fhewn to a naturalift he may certainly, upon a due infpection of the object, give its true name according to fome fyftem.   He who goes

farther

farther than this is not barely a naturalift, but fomething more, viz. a phyfician,
a chymift, a farmer, a gardener, &c.
And he who cannot go thus far to a certain degree, does not deferve the name of a
naturalift, however fkillfull he may be in
the vertues and properties of bodies animate and inanimate.

The ufe then and intent of a claffical fyftem is nothing more than that of a dic-
tionary, where no one complains that
words totally unconnected in fenfe are put
near one another.   The queftion therefore
as to the fexual fyftem [d], v. g. in plants, is
not whether they be ranged naturally, but
whether in the beft manner poffible in order
to be known.   Nay farther, it matters not
whether the fexual fyftem be founded on
nature or not, i. e. whether there be any

---

[d] At the end of the preface i have endeavored to explain the meaning of thefe terms in fuch a manner, that
i think any curious perfon that will be at the pains to
compare my explication with nature, cannot fail to underftand perfectly what they mean in general. I thought
this method would be more agreeable to the reader than
to be referred to other books.

propagation

propagation by feeds without male and female organs of generation. The whole to be confidered is whether thofe parts which are called, and, i believe truly called fo, do really exift, and whether they they for the moft part exift fo uniformly, as to furnifh marks fufficient to diftinguifh the claffes, &c. by. Nor does it matter whether it be hard to diftinguifh thofe marks, but whether they can with proper care and patience be diftinguifhed, and whether we can furely diftinguifh plants, without obferving thofe nice and minute parts, and whether a fyftem has been found equally fure with the Linnæan without having regard to thofe parts. Thofe who think fo would do well to in- form the world of their difcovery, and not make objeftions that affeft only the ob- fcurity of nature, when they mean to con- demn a fyftem which is obfcure mere- ly from its confonancy to nature. If Providence has thought fit to write in cyphers, fhall he be blamed who endea- vors to give a key to its works, becaufe

fome

some men cannot distinguish one stroke from another in the cypher?

Those who have not learned to read the characters of nature for want of leisure, patience, or any other cause, ought not to complain that Linnæus cannot make them skillfull in a part of knowledge they are not qualified for. If a man unacquainted with the learned languages wants to know the meaning of a Greek word, will he complain of the lexicon, because he cannot find it? certainly not. Neither ought we to complain of Linnæus in a similar case.

This i think is a full answer to all the objections that have or can be made to his system in general. What errors he has committed according to his own principles in relation to particulars is quite another question. I am one of those who think him not free from errors. Nor is it wonderfull that he should fall into some, but it is truly wonderfull that one man should be able to invent and carry so far so nice and extensive a system, especially when we consider not only what he has done in botany, but what he has done in all the branches of

natural

natural hiftory befides, and fome of them almoft entirely neglected before his time. I fhould therefore wifh that thofe who are fond of this part of knowledge would, inftead of making frivolous objections, try by an accurate and diligent examination to rectify his miftakes, and thereby help to perfect a fyftem which deferves the utmoft attention, and commendation.

Tho' i faid above that it matters not whether the fexual fyftem be founded on nature or not; yet it was natural for the inventor of it to endeavor by all proper means to vindicate it as likely to be fo, and this he has done to the fatisfaction of the moft curious obfervers; and i will venture to add, that it is natural for others likewife to embrace with zeal a fyftem, that puts the works of Providence in fo new and beautiful a light by continuing the analogy from the animate to the inanimate creation. It feems as if Providence intended to lead men to this difcovery by ftriking our fenfes fo intenfely and fo agreeably with thofe very parts which contain the clue of this fyftem. Yet fuch is the inattention and

in-

inaccuracy of man on certain points, that even a tolerable conjecture concerning the ufe of thofe parts was not made till the year 1676.

Having finifhed all that I think neceffary to fay concerning Linnæus and his works, i fhall now come to what relates immediately to myfelf only. Firft then as to the tranflation, I have endeavored to avoid making it too literal, and fervile, but yet i hope without taking any undue liberties, or deviating from the fenfe of the originals.

The part which is likely to prove leaft agreeable to the reader, is that which was moft troublefome to the tranflator. I mean the names of things not generally known. Some of thefe i have been obliged to leave in Latin, not being able to find any Englifh names for them. I will not pretend to have avoided all miftakes on this head, but it is certain i fhould have committed more, as well as have had much more trouble, had it not been for the affiftance of the ingenious Mr. Hudfon, whofe fkill in all the branches of natural hiftory, and particularly

cularly thofe relating to his profeffion as an apothecary, cannot fail to recommend him to the favor of the public.   To him i like-wife owe the afcertaining of fome of the graffes, one of which, viz. the fmall bent grafs which i had in my collection, but knew not where i found it, he difcovered to be the gramen minimum anglo-bri-tanum, mentioned in the indiculus plan-tarum dubiarum at the end of Ray's Synopfis.

I muft not omit alfo on this occafion to acknowledge my obligation to that excel-lent botanift Dr. Watfon, for favoring me with the perufal of his collection of graffes, which was of no fmall fervice to me.

But to return to the tranflation ; I faid that i did not pretend to have avoided all miftakes in relation to the names of things, i will now extend this farther, and own my fufpicions that i may have made fome in re-lation to other particulars, but i hope they are of fuch a kind only as may be looked on with indulgence by the learned, efpecially when they confider the great variety of fub-

jects

jects treated on in thefe pages, of none of
which fubjects i profefs to be a mafter, and
therefore do not undertake to teach fuch
readers; but on the contrary fhall always be
ready and even defirous to receive inftruc-
tions from them.   I beg they will alfo confider that i do not aim at letting the unlearned into the myfteries of this part of
knowledge, or even teaching them the elements of it.   My bufinefs is only to excite
curiofity, and therefore fmall errors can be
of no confequence.   What I have farther
to fay will be found in notes.

Res fummas initio deberi parvo ac debili
experientia omnium temporum teftatur.
Amænit. Acad. vol. 2. p. 266. §. 2.

End of the P R E F A C E.

IN

IN order to explain the fexual fyftem, i fhall make ufe of the lilly, as that plant is almoft every where to be found, and as the parts of generation are in that more obvious, than perhaps in any other flower. Upon opening the flower leaves there will appear in the very center, at the bottom, an oblong thickifh fubftance with fix furrows along its fides. This cuntains the feeds, and is called the

The germen or germ.

On this ftands a fmall kind of pillar called

The ftyle.

Which is terminated by a thickifh triangular head, called

The ftigma.

Thefe all together from the female part of the flower, and are called by one name,

The piftil.

Round this piftil grow fix long thready fubftances, called

The filaments,

Each terminated by an oblong body, that plays as on a pivot, upon the leaft motion

tion being given to the flower, and is called

The anthera.

This anthera contains the male duft, which when ripe is fcattered about by every breath of air, and what happens to fall on the ftigma, or upper part of the piftil, is fuppofed to enter thro' the ftyle into the germ, and there impregnate the feed.

This plant is called an hermaphrodite, becaufe the male and female organs of generation are contained within one flower. Moft plants are hermaphrodites, like this, and have fomething analogous to what i have defcribed above. Some plants have the male and female parts feparate on the fame individual; others have male parts on one plant and female on another.

The part of the flower that contains honey is called

The nectary.

Only a few plants have this part, the lilly; has it but as the knowledge of it is not neceffary for underftanding the following pieces, i fhall not trouble the reader with a defcription of it.

C O N-

CONTENTS.

BENEFIT

OF

TRAVELLING, &c.

B

Miſcellaneous Tracts, &c.

An ORATION concerning the neceſſity of travelling in one's own
countrey, made by Dr. LINNÆUS
at Upſal, Oct. 17, anno 1741, when
he was admitted to the royal and
ordinary profeſſion of phyſic.

Amænitat. Academ. vol. ii,

MOST honorable and moſt learned auditors of all orders, i am going to undertake a province, allotted to me by the favor of
our moſt auguſt, and moſt potent monarch,
whoſe will it is that i preſide over, and direct
the ſtudy of phyſic in this Univerſity; and
that i do my utmoſt to advance the glory of
this illuſtrious body. May his choice be
crowned with ſucceſs, and may the great and
good God favor my undertaking.

As by cuſtom, delivered down by our fore-
fathers, and preſcribed by the laws of our aca-

demy,

demy, i am obliged upon undertaking this province to fay fomething before fo illuftrious a circle of fathers and citizens; i confefs that all thofe circumftances, each of which is apt to ftrike terror into the mind of man, offer themfelves together in a croud before my eyes on this occafion. For whether i confider the amplenefs of the place, or the dignity of the audience, or the multitude of chofen people, or laftly my little talents in the arts of fpeech; all thefe circumftances, i ingenuoufly confefs, throw me into no fmall confufion.

For if the moft eloquent men, when they come to fpeak in public, have been known to tremble, and become incapable of uttering a fingle word; what muft i feel who have none of the common advantages, either from art or nature, in the readinefs and elegance of fpeech?

However, fince i am under a neceffity of faying fomething, i muft fly for refuge to that favor, and humanity, which you never refufe to thofe who fpeak on thefe occafions; and thus i doubt not but. that, however deficient i may be from want of talents, or want of exercife, i fhall not wholly fail of the end i aim at. I fhall therefore, moft honorable auditors, undertake to treat on a fubject neither unfuitable to the

the prefent occafion, nor to the office i am going to enter into, nor to that employment which i was lately engaged in by the will, and fuffrage of the high, and mighty ftates of this kingdom; and from which i am now once again brought back to this feat of the mufes. Nay fo far is the fubject, i am about to treat on, from being unfuitable to any of thefe circumftances, that it feems to me particularly adapted to every one of them. The fubject is concerning the neceffity of travelling in one's own countrey, and the advantages that may thence accrue, efpecially to phyficians. I fhall treat it in a plain and popular manner; and endeavor to manage it fo, that the meannefs of my language may be compenfated by the dignity of the matter, and the brevity of my expreffions.

All human knowledge is built on two foundations; reafon and experience.—Thefe two joyned together are neceffary to make a good phyfician.

We muft confefs indeed, that the bufinefs of reafoning may be carried on with equal fuccefs in our clofets, as in travelling, fuppofing we have an opportunity of converfing with men truly learned.

But

But it was experience, that fovereign miftrefs without which a phyfician ought to be afhamed to open his lips; it was experience, i fay, that confecrated to immortality fo many of the antients, and amongft the reft that divine old man Hippocrates, whofe writings were publifhed many ages before chriftianity. The writings of this wonderful man alone, among fo many ingenioufly contrived fyftems, remain to this day, and will for ever remain firm, unmoved, unfhaken, untouched by any decay, by any change. It is experience that has adorned with laurels the heads of fo many celebrated phyficians in all times, and even now adorns. And hence it is that the chief and moft honorable title of phyfician is to be called a man of experience. Experience ought to go firft; reafoning fhould follow. The former furnifhes the materials of knowledge; the latter holds her confultations on the given phænomena; and when fhe has weighed with judgment every circumftance, fhe difcovers truth, and concludes, orders, and determines rightly about the point in queftion. Experience ought to be animated by reafon in all phyfical affairs; without this fhe is void of order, void of energy, void of life. On the other hand reafon

with-

without experience can do nothing ; being nothing, but the mere dreams, phantafms, and meteors of ingenious men who abufe their time. The antients certainly did not, any more than we, bring experience into the world with them. There is need of much diligence and labor, before man can be thoroughly inftructed. Diofcorides confeffes, that he undertook many journies in order to increafe experience ; and the other fathers of phyfic in their writings frequently make mention of their travels either exprefsly or tacitly.

Academies were inftituted to the end, that men well verfed in all kinds of literature, and enriched befides by much experience, might be invited thither, and that the youth, who were ambitious of becoming learned, might flock together to thofe feats ; and have the advantage of improving no lefs by the experience, than by the erudition of the profeffors ; and thefe qualifications combined together, which is of all alliances the moft pleafing, very juftly deferve the utmoft veneration and refpect.

Vaft and fumptuous libraries are erected in academies ; in which the obfervations of the learned, like fo many legacies, and donations, are preferved; that they who diligently give themfelves up to ftudy, may become endued with learning, polifhed, and confirmed by experience. Thefe libraries are the repofitories of wifdom, and their ftores are laid open to every ingenious candidate.

Hofpitals are founded that the candidates of phyfic may learn thofe things at the patients bed fide, which cannot be learned from books; for here practice, and experience fhew their force by means of the eyes, and hands; as he paints any object moft accurately, who paints from the idea, which his own eyes afford him, and not from that, which he gets by the relation of another.

Anatomy fchools are erected, that we may behold in another's body, as it were in a glafs, the nature, and conftitution of our own; as thofe conceive more clearly the fituation of countries, diftricts, and cities, and the manners, rites, and cuftoms of their inhabitants, who themfelves have been there, and have feen what is remarkable amongft them with their own eyes, than he who relies folely upon the vague and imperfect maps, and relations of travellers.

Phyfic

Phyfic gardens are here cultivated ; where the plants of various kinds are collected from all parts of the globe, that we may by this means behold, as it were, the great in the little world.

Hither inftruments for experimental philofophy are brought together, that the abftrufe forces of the elements, which otherwife would efcape our fenfes, may be made manifeft, and that fo we may fuccefsfully be let into the very receffes of nature ; as far as human penetration will admit of.

All thefe things are inftituted in academies, that the youth may arrive at knowledge by experience ; all tend to this end, that tho' we be confined to one fpot, one corner of the earth, we may examine the great and various ftores of knowledge, and therein behold the immenfe domains of nature, and get acquainted with fuch things, as otherwife muft be fought for, and oftentimes in vain, over the whole globe.

In my opinion therefore ftudying at academies ought by no means to be neglected, but rather fhould be looked on as neceffary to thofe, who are ambitious of attaining wifdom, fupported by experience. And thofe who endeavor

deavor to inftill into the minds of young people a contempt for univerfities, and to with-
draw the ftudious from thefe feats of learning,
fuggeft very pernicious advice ; not confidering that in thefe ftorehoufes of knowledge
much greater, and more excellent things may
be attained by means of experience in a very
fhort fpace of time, than by the moft multifa-
rious, moft indefatigable, and moft extenfive
reading at home all one's life.

If i may be allowed to fpeak what is really
fact, this our univerfity may contend with any
foreign one whatever for true, and folid learning in all thofe parts of knowledge, which i
have enumerated, owing to our noble, and
exemplary inftitutions. For we begin to excell in botanical gardens, in hofpitals, in apparatus's for experimental philofophy, in ana-
tomical preparations, and other helps for arts
and fciences, and to excell fo much that we
are likely in time, by the blefling of the almighty, to be inferior to no univerfity.

Although fome univerfities excell others on
account of certain advantages peculiar to
themfelves ; for in proportion as one kind of
knowledge in this, or that nation is held
in greater, or lefs efteem, and is therefore

more

more or lefs cultivated, fo the profeffors of
it will be more or lefs fkillful; as at this
time the hofpitals at London both for
number and goodnefs exceed all others, at
Paris chirurgical operations, at Leyden, ana-
tomical preparations, at Oxford botanical collections; tho', i fay, this may be the cafe, yet
i cannot think, that thofe act prudently, or
enough confult the good of themfelves, and
countrey, who feek for that abroad, which may
be had at home, and who travel to foreign univerfities, before they have laid a fufficient
foundation in their own countrey.   And there
is no doubt but that they who do fo will at
laft repent of their error.   He, who goes
abroad raw, and ignorant, feldom returns more
learned.   Whereas, he, who has fpent his time
well at his own univerfity, will never find reafon to repent.   Whoever has employed himfelf properly in the ftudy of the arts, and fciences will become an ufefull, and folid man in
every branch of bufinefs.   Whoever, before he
fets out to vifit regions warmed by other funs,
has laid the firft foundations of his ftudies in
his native countrey, will be moft likely to bring
back materials of far greater price, than we
ufually fee amongft the greateft part of our

tra-

travellers, who feldom return home laden with
any thing, but fine founding, and empty words
collected out of the European languages. What
do they learn, but to prate about theatres, and
plays, and the modes of drefs amongft the Ita-
lians, the Spaniards, the Germans, and above
all the French? If they were well advifed they
would not ftir a foot out of their own countrey; that they might not deftroy their fortunes, their time, their health, nay their very
life itfelf by luxury, and voluptuoufnefs. They
would not then return, as too frequently happens, entirely ufelefs to themfelves, an countrey, and a burthen upon the face of the earth,
But whither am i hurried?

My defign was, in the little time allotted me,
to fpeak to you, gentlemen, not of the peculiar
advantages of univerfities, or of fojourning at
this, rather than any foreign one; but chiefly
of travelling in one's own countrey, thro' its
fields, and roads; a kind of travelling, i confefs, hitherto little ufed, and which is looked upon as fit only for amufement. I once more, moft
honorable auditors, beg your patience, and that
i may not forfeit all right to your favor, and
benevolence, i promife to be as fhort as poffible.
You know what the poet fays,

The

The farmer talks of graffes and of grain,
The failor tells you ftories of the main.

You ought not therefore to wonder, that i choofe to make travelling in one's own countrey the fubject of my difcourfe. Every one thinks well of what belongs to himfelf, and every one has pleafures peculiar to himfelf. I have travelled about, and paffed over on foot the frofty mountains of Lapland, have climbed up the craggy ridges of Norland, and wandered along its fteep hills, and almoft impenetrable woods. I have made large excurfions into the forefts of Dalecarlia, the groves of Gothland, the heaths of Smoland, and the unbounded plains of Scania. There is fcarcely any confiderable province of Sweden, which i have not crawled thro' and examined; not without great fatigue of body and mind. My journey to Lapland was indeed an undertaking of immenfe labor; and i muft confefs, that i was forced to undergo more labor, and danger in travelling thro' this one tract of the northern world, than thro' all thofe forreign countreys put together, which I have ever vifited; tho' even thefe have coft me no fmall pains, and have not a little exhaufted my vigor. But love to truth, and gratitude towards the fu-

preme

preme being oblige me to confefs, that no
fooner were my travels finifhed, but, as it were,
a Lethæan oblivion of all the dangers, and
difficulties came upon me ; being rewarded by
the ineftimable advantages, which i reaped
from thofe devious purfuits. Advantages, the
more confpicious for that i became daily more
and more fkillful, and gained a degree of experience, which I hope will be of ufe to myfelf, and others; and, what i efteem above all
other confiderations ; as it comprehends in one
all other duties, and charities ; to my countrey, and the public.

Good God! how many, ignorant of their
own countrey, run eagerly into forreign regions, to fearch out and admire whatever curiofities are to be found; many of which are
much inferior to thofe, which offer themfelves
to our eyes at home. I have yet beheld no
forreign land, that abounds more with natural
curiofities of all kinds, than our own. None
which prefents fo many, fo great, fo wonderfull works of nature ; whether we confider the
magazines of fnow heaped up for fo many ages
upon our Alps, and amongft thefe vaft tracks
of fnow green meadows, and delicious vallies
here and there peeping forth, or the lofty
                                                        heads

heads of mountains, the craggy precipices of rocks, or the fun lying concealed from our eyes for fo many months, and thence a thick Cimmerian darknefs fpread over our hemi-fphere, or elfe at another feafon darting his rays continually along the horizon.   The like to all which in kind, and degree, neither Hol-land, nor France, nor Britain, nor Germany, nor laftly any countrey in Europe can fhew ; yet thither our youth greedy of novelty flock in troops.   But it was not my intent to fpeak of thefe things at prefent.   I come now clofer to my purpofe, being about to fhew by in-ftances, that the natural philofopher, the mi-neralogift, the botanift, the zoologift, the phy-fician, the farmer, and all others, initiated in any part of natural knowledge, may find in travelling thro' our own countrey things, which they will own they never dreamed of before. Nay things which to this day were never dif-covered by any perfon whatever.   Laftly fuch things, as may not only gratify, and fatiate their curiofity ; but may be of fervice to them-felves, their countrey, and all the world.

To give a few examples.   The fagacious fearcher after nature will find here, wherewith-all to fharpen, and exercife his attention in be-

holding the top of mount Swucku, of fo immenfe a height, that it reaches above the
clouds. The wonderfull ftructure of mount
Torfburg, the horrid precipices of the rock
Blakulla in an ifland of that name, fituated near
Oeland, and that prefents by its name, ftill
ufed among the Suegothic vulgar, no lefs than
by its difmal afpect, an idea of the ftupidity,
and fuperftition of that antient people.

Befides the wonderfull vaults, and caverns of
the Skiula mountains, the high plains of the
ifland Carolina, the unufual form and ftructure
of the Kierkerfian fountains in Oeland; to pafs
over numberlefs other ftrange works of nature,
the like to which perhaps are no where to be
met with.

Where can we have greater opportunities,
than in this Suegothic tract, of confidering the
intenfe rigor, and vehemence of winter, the
incredible marble-like ftrength of ice ? And
yet in this inclement climate grain of all forts
is obferved to fpring forth fooner, grow quicker, and ripen in lefs time than in any other part
of the world.[a]

[a] Vid. a treatife concerning the foliation of trees publifhed in this collection, and the prolegomena to the Flora
Lapponica of this author, where he fays that at Purkyaur
in Lapland anno 1732. barley fown May 31. was ripe
July 28. i. e. in 58 days; and rye fown May 31. was
ripe, and cut Aug. 5. i. e. in 66 days.

Whoever defires to contemplate the ftupendous metamorphofes of fea, and land, will
fcarcely find any where a more convenient opportunity, than in the fouth, and eaft parts of
Gothland; where the rock-giants, as they are
called, feem to threaten heaven, and where
the epocha's of time, the ages, the years, if
i may fo fay, are as it were carved out in a
furprifing feries upon the fea-fhore, and the
ground above the fhore.

The philofopher will find room to exercife
his ingenuity fufficiently in the Oeland-ftone,
by trying to difcover how to overcome its moift
nature, and quality, which whoever could ac-
complifh would do no fmall fervice to his
countrey, and above all would infinitely oblige
the inhabitants of that place.

I fhall fay no more than what is known, and
confeffed by all the world, when i fay that
there is no countrey in the habitable part of
the globe, where the mineralogift may make
greater progrefs in his art, than in this our
countrey. Let any one, that can, tell me, in
what regions, more rich, and ample mines of
metal are found, than in Sweden, and where
they dig deeper into the bowels of the earth
than here.

C   Let

Let the mines of Norburg, the ridge of Taburga, the pits of Dannemore, Bitſberg, Grengia, and laſtly the immenſe treaſures of Salbergen, and Fahluna be my witneſs, which exceed all in the known world.

Where do the poſſeſſors ſuffer forreigners more freely to approach their furnaces, and obſerve their operations? where are there men more ready to communicate their knowledge? Strangers are received by us with civility, and even preſſed to ſtay.

Who would not ſhudder on beholding thoſe forges, vomiting forth immenſe clouds of fire and ſmoak, where our iron ores are melted? who would not behold with pleaſure the ſimple countreyman in the thick pine-groves of Dalecarlia, without furnace, without any apparatus, extracting an iron ſo very ſo fit for uſe, that it yields to no other, tho' prepared with the fierceſt fires, and greateſt expence?

Who ten years ago would have imagined, that the *lapis calaminaris* was to be had in Dalecarlia? or mines of the very beſt kind of *gold* in Smolandia?

You will perhaps ſcarce believe me when i tell you, that there are whole mountains full of *petroleum* in Dalecarlia. Yet doubt not. This
thing

thing hitherto unheard of, unſeen, i myſelf ſaw with theſe eyes, and was ſurpriſed.

We admire the abundance of *coral* on the Indian ſhores, yet the port of Capellus in Gothland alone equals, nay exceeds thoſe riches of the eaſt. I have ſeen deep ſtrata of *corals* extending many furlongs, many miles along its ſhores.

Botaniſts, who have travelled over the greateſt part of the globe in ſearch of the treaſures of the vegetable kingdom, have yet left many plants for us and our poſterity to diſcover in theſe our regions. For there is ſcarce any where a greater variety of *moſſes*, *lichens*, *fuci*, and *fungi*, than with us; and the moſt curious botaniſts are now diligently employed in contemplating theſe minute plants.

Whoever beheld, or deſcribed our *diapenſia?* who the *blaſia* unleſs Micheli alone? Theſe two kinds of plants grow with us, and the latter eſpecially is found in great plenty about Fahluna. What traveller, that is not totally ignorant in botany, does not go from Paris to Fontainebleau to ſee thoſe very rare *orchis's,* ſome of which repreſent helmets, others knats, others flies; all of them ſo exactly, ſo wonderfully, that there ſeems nothing

C 2 want-

wanting to make them the very animals themfelves, but noife, and motion? Who imagined
thefe flowers grew in our countrey, and in fuch
plenty in Oeland, than they are to be met with
in every field ?

Who would ever have thought of looking
in our countrey for the following exotics. The
winged pea, the *great burnet*, the *perennial lettuce*, the *dwarf carline thiftle*, the *middle fleabane*, the *black hellebore*, the Illyric *crowfoot*,
much lefs the *riccia*, and herb *terrible*, and
efpecially the *fcorpion fena*, that moft beautiful
fhrub, which in winter is carefully guarded
againft the frofts in the ftoves of our botanifts;
yet all thefe have lately been obferved to grow
in Oeland and Gothland.

We ufed to purchafe at a great price from
forreigners the following medicinal plants, *vervain*, *moneywort*, &c. which all are natives of
Sweden, and yet ten years ago nobody knew
this.

What expences have we been at yearly to
get the *glafs-wort*, of whofe afhes and falt,
glafs is made. The *dyers weed* and *woad* were
purchafed yearly at a very high price; plants
that we have at laft found grow every where
about our provinces.

Lapland

Lapland alone furnifhed me fome time ago with a hundred rare plants. I have gathered lately as many in the iflands of the Baltic, and in Scania as many more, never before obferved in Sweden. Nor can it be doubted, but that our other provinces conceal in their unfrequented corners other new plants, valuable for ufe or beauty, tho' hitherto overlooked, if a diligent and acute inquirer be not wanting. I will not fay with the poet, " Happy the rural inhabitant," but " happy " the Swedifh inhabitant if he knew but what " good he is poffeffed of [h]."

The zoologift will no where meet with a place more delightful, and more fuitable to his views, than that where flocks of all kinds of birds in fpring time, and fummer, gather

---

[h] Our countrey has been fearched by fo many able botanifts for plants, that what is faid here cannot be applied to us. But a curious traveller might be of great fervice in relation to plants even here, by obferving, and making generally known what plants are peculiarly cultivated in fome countries. Thus for inftance they fow *lotus*, 13. Linn. *birdsfoot trefoil*, *Ray fyn.* 334 in Herefordfhire, which grows all over England on dry paftures, and is found very good for fheep, tho' every where elfe, as far as i know, neglected. Again they make great ufe of the *common vetch* in Glocefterfhire, chiefly for horfes, feeding them with it upon the fpot, and eating it up time enough for turneps the fame year.

toge-

together to breed. This is the cafe in the woody, and mountainous parts of Sweden, more than in any other fpot of the earth; the Lapland *plover* called *pago*, the Norland *pied chaffinch*, the Oeland *tringa* called *alwar-grim*, the Gothland *duck* called *eider*, the artic *duck* of he ifland Carolina called *torde*, the Ottenbyenfian *cobler's awl* called *fierfloecha*, the *picus tridactylus* of the Darlecarlians are all more rare in other countries than pheafants are with us. I may venture to affirm that no countrey upon the face of the earth abounds more with birds and infects, than Sweden. Wild *rein-deer*, *flying fquirrels*, and the Norway *rat* that pours down in troops from the mountains into the plains below are unknown, and perhaps happily unknown, any where elfe.

Foreigners come into the Dalecarlian mountains to catch *falcons*, as is well known.

In the ifland Farô, fituated near Gothland, *whale* and *falmon* fifhery is very conveniently carried on, and no where with greater profit.

How many fpecies of fifhes furnifh our tables very common in Sweden, efpecially of the foftmouthed kind; fuch as the *afp*, the *wimba*, the *faren*, the *biorkna*, the *mudd*, and others,

others, unknown, undefcribed, unfeen in forreign countries. Who ever diffected, examined, defcribed thofe minute *red ferpents* called *afps*, or *æfpingar* by the fouthern Swedes,
whofe bite communicates a deadly poifon ?

It would be tedious were i to defcend to
the fpecies of infects. The great Reaumur,
who has fhewn a fagacity, and accuracy, before him unknown, in examining infects, upon feeing my collection of Swedifh infects
owned ingenuoufly, that my countrey alone
contained more fpecies of thofe animals, than
any other known in the world.

The curious diætetic, whofe bufinefs it is
to inquire into the various ways of living
among men, will fcarcely find any place,
where there are fo many different kinds of
food, as here. Here men vary in their food,
as they vary in fortune, fituation, and condition. And what is very remarkable, the inhabitants of this northern world have their
peculiar cuftoms, and rules of eating in every
province, and territory. In Lapland they
live without corn, or wine, without falt or
any made liquor. Water, and flefh, and preparations of thefe are their only fuftenance.

C 4   In

In fome places the countreyman lives in his fmoaky, and footy ftove on the *coregonus* when ftinking; and bread made of the roots of the *calla*, or of the hufks, and beards of grain pounded.

In fome places they live upon ftinking *herring*, and *ropy* whey called *fyra*; in other places on a food called *affu*, and *artfau*, and ftinking *fifh*; and yet they undergo much labor. In fome places their food is *turneps*, and their drink made of *juniper berries*. Some live upon *peas*, others on *buck wheat*, others grow fat upon *whale's* flefh, to the aftonifhment of ftrangers.

In travelling thro' other countries you will hardly ever fee fo many different ways of living in this refpect, as in the Swedifh dominions, and where confequently the diætetic philofopher may have fo many opportunities of making his experiments.

The pathologift, who inquires into the caufes of diftempers, will not lofe his time in travelling into thefe countries; as in every dif-

---

* A general name of fifhes, fome fpecies of which are known in England and Wales, as the *fhelley*, the *grayling*, the *gwiniad*, &c. Vid. Artedi ichthyolog.

ferent

ferent province men are fubject to peculiar
difeafes, which arife in a great meafure from
the different kinds of food, that prevail among
them. He will no doubt hence be empower-
ed to affign the true caufes ; why the Norlan-
der is infected with the fcurvy, and why the
Laplander on the contrary is free from it :
why the fame Laplander is fubject to thofe terrible gripes, called by them *ullem* ; why the
Gothlander is chiefly afflicted with the hypo-
chondriacal colic ; why the Weft-Bothnians,
who are more prolific than any other people
in our part of the world, lofe moft of their
children in the cradle ; why fo many people
are liable to the epilepfy in the territory of
Verns, for the caufe is flight in appearance,
but very fingular in its nature.

Why almoft all the males in Orfobæa dye
of confumptions before the age of 30.

To enumerate all the things, which we have
particular opportunities of obferving in relation to thefe affairs in our countrey, would require no fhort treatife.

I am fully perfuaded that it is abfolutely neceffary for the young phyfician to travel thro'
his own countrey, were it only for this reafon, that relying upon his own ftrength he
might

might daily become more diligent, gain experience, without which there can be no fkill in
phyfic, and bring the art which he profeffes
to fome degree of perfection. For it happens
amongft us, and perhaps no where fo frequently, that our common people have confidence in their phyficians, and run in crouds
to confult any one, that is known to have taken
a doctor's degree; in other countries they will
fcarcely truft a young phyfician with a favorite dog.

By following this courfe, and entering into
practice, the young phyfician will perceive,
whether medicines, oftentimes celebrated beyond all bounds of moderation, have that effect upon the patient, which we find mentioned in practical books. He will hear of many
domeftic remedies, unknown elfewhere, in ufe
among the countrey people, that are looked
upon as fpecifics, and preferred to the moft
coftly prefcriptions; for during the confulta-
tion, the patient may reveal the fecret, if the
phyfician is prudent, and makes ufe of a
little art.

What are thofe famous exotic remedies
brought from either Indies, and purchafed
at fo great a price. v. g. *farfaparilla*, a
fpe-

species of *smilax*, *ipecacuanha*, a species of *honey-suckle*, *acmella*, a species of *hemp agrimony*, *contrayerva* of *dorstenia*, and *simoruba* of *pistacia*, which in some diseases are reckoned specifics? what are all these, I say, but remedies approved by long use amongst the vulgar? and are not innumerable remedies used among our own countrey people of the same nature? were not all those I have enumerated found out by [d] barbarians, and when experience had shewn, that they were useful, and efficacious in many diseases, were they not thought worthy to be communicated to the rest of mankind? Let our young physician then learn,

[d] Vid. *Vires plantarum Amænitat. academ.* vol. i. p. 403. where Brunnerus is quoted for saying, that barbarians have done more towards the advancement of physic, than the learned of all ages. In the same passage the following words of Tournefort are quoted, *que tout le travail des hommes n'a encore rien produit de si assuré que deux ou trois drogues que les sauvages trouvent dans les bois.* The author subjoins to these quotations a list of twenty medicines with an &c. taken from barbarous nations, now used in our shops.

The curious reader may find in Dampier's voyages a very extraordinary instance of the skill of the savages of America in the chirurgical way. Wafer there gives an account of a cure performed upon himself by these people, and his testimony is the stronger, as he was a surgeon himself.

not to contemn, but accurately to remark thofe remedies, which are cried up amongft the common people. For he who boafts of knowing more of the virtues of fimples, than what ᶜ tafte, fmell, ᶠ fructification, and experiments will fuggeft, vehemently deceives, or is deceived.

Ye who intend one of thefe days to cultivate your native foil with advantage, and profit, may be affured that you will find nothing in all the books of hufbandry, that will be of fuch affiftance to you in that art, as travelling thro' the different provinces of this kingdom. In fome parts, and thofe the moft barren, you

---

ᶜ Vid. *Amænit. academ.* vol. 2. p. 371. in an exprefs treatife on this fubject the author quotes feveral eminent phyficians both ancient and modern, who maintained the fame opinion as to taftes. And vol. 3. p. 183. where the affiftance to be had from fmell is confidered, and the effects of odors amply treated on.

ᶠ Fructification. The reader perhaps may be at a lofs to underftand this. The meaning of it is, that plants which agree in the genus and even in the clafs agree alfo in their vertues. Thus the leaves of all the graffes are good for cattle, the leffer feeds for fmall birds, the greater for man, and this without exception. The ftellated plants of Ray are diuretic, the rough-leaved plants of the fame author are aftringent and vulnerary. Plants with a pea-flower are all wholefome for cattle and man, &c. Vid. a curious treatife on this fubject, in the *Academ.* vol. 1. p. 389.

will

will fee very confiderable crops produced by the force of fkill, and induftry. In others, tho' by nature extremely fertile, you will fcarcely fee any appearance of crops ; and the inhabitants live poorly, and in a miferable condition, merely from careleffnefs, and indolence. You may obferve how far the Cuprimontani exceed all others in the management of hay, and grafs, and the Gothlanders in relation to cattle, and particularly fheep.

You will have an opportunity of noting the different ways in different places of ploughing, manuring, harrowing, fowing, reaping, gathering, drying, and threfhing, from whence a prudent traveller may judge which way is beft.

It would be abfurd indeed to apply to our lands forreign methods of hufbandry in every particular, v. g. forreign grafs feed would not fucceed fo well as our own. Yet i will venture to fay one could fcarcely travel a day in any of our countries without learning fomething of ufe in œconomy. Many things that will occur, may appear trifling at firft fight, which yet upon a more mature confideration, you will own may be turned to very great advantage ; fuch as the various ways of cloathing, preparing victuals,

tuals, feeding cattle, not to mention the manners, commerce and numberless other particulars.

Lastly, however necessary and incumbent
upon us it may be to take a view of our countrey, it will be in vain to undergo this trouble,
if we do not lay the foundation of our studies
at the university, as to natural philosophy,
natural, and medical history; without which
preparation for travelling to advantage every
thing that occurs, will appear trite, common,
and not worth our attention. The traveller
however, above all men, ought to keep in
mind that famous principle of Descartes, viz.
to doubt about every thing. He must also be
very cautious not to suffer his mind, from too
eager a desire of knowledge, to be overwhelmed at the beginning by the number of
things to be observed[c]. * * * * * *
* * * * * * * * * * * * *

We ought to travel in the flower of our age,
while the mind, and body are in vigor, while
our strength is unimpaired, and alacrity at its
height; before a family, houshold affairs,

[c] Here follow some few lines in the original, which not
understanding i have omitted.

and conjugal tyes have engroffed our affections.

When by this method you have laid the firft
foundation of travelling in your own countrey,
you will then be qualified to go farther, and
become ferviceable to yourfelves, and the public, by learning thofe things abroad, which
could not be learned at home ; and thus, having made a fair examination, you may be enabled to judge, whether our own cuftons may
be improved by the help of forreign ones, and
how far ; and thus you will not be apt rafhly
to imagine, that every fafhion which prevails
at Paris, is fit to be introduced into our cottages ; laftly, thus you will not be better acquainted with the manners and cuftoms in
France, England, Germany, and other countries, than with thofe of your own ; i. e. you
will not, as the proverb fays, for want of common fenfe,

Invert all order, and become

Lynxes abroad, mere moles at home.

But not to abufe your patience any longer,
i here break off the thread of my difcourfe,
that what time remains may be employed by
me in expreffing my wifhes and thanks. Firft,
to thee, O omnipotent God, i humbly offer

up

up my thankfgiving, for the immenfe benefits, that have been heaped upon me thro' thy gracious protection, and providence.   Thou from my youth upwards haft fo led me by the hand, haft fo directed my footfteps, that i have grown up in the fimplicity, and innocence of life, and in the moft ardent purfuit after knowledge.   I give thee thanks for that thou haft ever preferved me in all my journies thro' my native and forreign countries, amidft fo many dangers, that furrounded me on every fide. That in the reft of my life, amidft the heavieft burthens of poverty, and other inconveniences, thou waft always prefent to fupport me with thy almighty affiftance. Laftly that amidft fo many viciffitudes of fortune, to which I have been expofed, amongft all the goods, i fay, and evils, the joyfull and gloomy, the pleafing, and difagreeable circumftances of life, thou endowedft me with an equal, conftant, manly, and fuperior fpirit on every occafion.

To our moft auguft, and potent prince Frederick the firft, as becomes a dutifull, and obedient fubject, i give moft humble thanks for his favorable kindnefs in beftowing upon me this honorable poft.   May the almighty grant, that his majefty, and his moft ferene confort,

thofe

thofe fhining ftars of the north, may long,
very long illuminate, and adorn this region
with the brightnefs of their rays.

To thee, moft mighty count Gyllenbourg,
illuftrious chancellor of this univerfity, to thee,
though abfent, i return the moft fincere, and
humble thanks for the great, and even endlefs benefits beftowed upon me; amongft
which, exceeding all number, this muft not be
reckoned the leaft, that, when I was called
hither by this academy, you recommended me
in the moft indulgent manner to our great
monarch. It fhall be my conftant care that
you may never repent of this favor, and by
reverence, refpect, and duty, to teftify my
gratitude to my lateft breath.

To the moft reverend the archbifhop, to the
vice-chancellor, to the magnificent rector, and
to you illuftrious and celebrated profeffors, i
return alfo moft grateful acknowledgments, who
honored me by your unanimous votes, and af-
fifted in bringing me to this chair. As this
your benevolence laid me under the greateft
obligation to you, to employ every office of
regard and friendfhip towards you, fo by the
grace of God i fhall omit no opportunity of
fhewing i am not unworthy of your favor.

D   What

Whilft i am thus employed in teftifying the
feelings of a grateful mind, i ought not to forget your name, moft illuftrious Roberg, my
predeceffor highly worthy of the utmoft veneration. As i am one of thofe who have had the
happinefs of being educated in your fchool, i
fhould be the moft ungratefull of men, if i
were ever to fuffer the remembrance of fuch
a benefit to flip out of my mind.

It has been your lot, venerable fir, to fur-
vive all your brethren ; and you may juftly
boaft, what every phyfician now in Sweden
will gratefully confefs, that to you, as to their
faithful inftructor, they owe the beginning,
the increafe, and the finifhing of their art.
Nay not only the faculty at Upfal, but the
whole circle here prefent ought to falute, and
reverence you as fuperior to them all in age.

Suffer then at laft your difciple to eafe
you of that burthen, which for forty years,
and more, you have fuftained, with honor; that now, time having laid his heavy
hand upon you, you may enjoy that reft, which
his facred majefty has kindly granted to your
wifhes. My fincere prayers are not wanting
to the almighty, that he may grant you a
chearfull, and vigorous old age, and that
every

every thing may fucceed to the utmoft of your defires.

Nor is it fit, ye florifhing and chofen youth, that on this folemn occafion i fhould pafs you over in filence. I have been long fenfible of your regard for me, by many, and undoubted proofs; i have been long fenfible, i fay, and i gratefullyacknowledge it. Many of you defired, ardently defired to have me in this ftation, though perhaps never feen by you before. For this alone, i know, i am called hither, that i may be ufeful to you. On you therefore my fortune turns. My induftry, my ftudies, my labors, my watchings, i willingly, and chearfully confecrate to your fervice, and by the affiftance of God, i will exert the utmoft of my power to fatisfy your expectations, that you may not be difappointed in the hopes you have conceived of me.

THE
OECONOMY
OF
NATURE.

THE
OECONOMY
OF
NATURE.

BY

ISAAC J. BIBERG.

Upsal, 1749. *March* 4.

Amænitat. Academ. vol. ii.

Æternæ funt vices rerum. Sen. nat. 3. 1.

§. I.

BY the Œconomy of Nature we underftand the all-wife difpofition of the Creator in relation to natural things, by which they are fitted to produce general ends, and reciprocal ufes.

All things contained in the compaſs of the univerſe declare, as it were, with one accord the infinite wiſdom of the Creator. For whatever ftrikes our fenfes, whatever is the object

of

of our thoughts, are so contrived, that they concur to make manifest the divine glory, i. e. the ultimate end which God proposed in all his works. Whoever duly turns his attention to the things on this our terraqueous globe, must necessarily confess, that they are so connected, so chained together, that they all aim at the same end, and to this end a vast number of intermediate ends are subservient. But as the intent of this treatise will not suffer me to consider them all, i shall at present only take notice of such as relate to the preservation of natural things. In order therefore to perpetuate the established course of nature in a continued series, the divine wisdom has thought fit, that all living creatures should constantly be employed in producing individuals; that all natural things should contribute and lend a helping hand to preserve every species; and lastly, that the death and destruction of one thing should always be subservient to the restitution of another. It seems to me that a greater subject than this cannot be found, nor one on which laborious men may more worthily employ their industry, or men of genius their penetration.

I am

I am very fenfible, being confcious of my own weaknefs, how vaft and difficult a fubject it is, and how unable i am to treat it as it deferves ; a fubject which would be too great a tafk for the ability of the moft experienced and fagacious men, and which properly performed would furnifh materials for large volumes, My defign therefore is only to give a fummary view of it, and to fet forth to the learned world, as far as i am able, whatever curious, worthy to be known, and not obvious to every obferver occurs in the triple kingdom of nature. Thus if what the induftry of others fhall in future times difcover in this way be added to thefe obfervations, it is to be hoped, that a common ftock may thence grow, and come to be of fome importance. But before i examine thefe three kingdoms of nature, it will not, i think, be amifs to fay fomething concerning the earth in general, and its changes.

§. 2.

The world, or the terraqueous globe, which we inhabit, is every where furrounded with elements, and contains in its fuperficies the three kingdoms of nature, as they are called; the *foffil,*

fil, which conftitutes the cruft of the earth, the *vegetable*, which adorns the face of it, and draws the greateft part of its nourifhment from the *foffil* kingdom, and the *animal*, which is fuftained by the *vegetable*. kingdom. Thus thefe three kingdoms cover, adorn and vary the fuperficies of our earth. It is not my defign to make any inquiry concerning the center of the terraqueous globe. He, who likes hypothefes, may confult Defcartes, Helmont, Kircher, and others. My bufinefs is to confider the external parts of it only, and whatever is obvious to the eye.

As to the *ftrata* of the earth and mountains, as far as we have hitherto been able to difcover, the upper parts confift of *rag-ftone*, the next of *flate*, the third of *marble* filled with petrifactions, the fourth again with *flate*, and laftly the loweft of *free-ftone*. The habitable part of the earth, though it is fcooped into various inequalities, yet is every where high in comparifon with the water, and the farther it is from the fea, it is generally higher. Thus the waters in the lower places are not at reft, unlefs fome obftacle confines them, and by that means form lakes, and marfhes.

The fea furrounds the continent, and takes up the greateft part of the earth's fuperficies,

as geography informs us. Nay, that it once
spread over much the greateſt part, we
may be convinced by its yearly decreaſe, by
the rubbiſh left by the tides, by *ſhells*, *ſtrata*,
and other circumſtances.

The ſea-ſhores are uſually full of dead teſta-
ceous animals, wrack, and ſuch like bodies,
which are yearly thrown out of the ſea. They
are alſo covered with ſand of various kinds,
ſtones, and heaps of other things not very
common. It happens moreover, that while
the more rapid rivers ruſh through narrow vallies, they wear away the ſides, and thus the
friable, and ſoft earth falls in, and its ruins
are carried to diſtant, and winding ſhores;
whence it is certain, that the continent gains
no ſmall increaſe, as the ſea ſubſides.

The clouds collected from exhalations,
chiefly from the ſea, but likewiſe from other
waters, and moiſt grounds, and condenſed in
the lower regions of the atmoſphere, ſupply
the earth with rain; but ſince they are at-
tracted by the mountainous parts of the earth,
it neceſſarily follows, that thoſe parts muſt
have, as is fit, a larger ſhare of water than
the reſt. Springs, which generally ruſh out
at the foot of mountains, take their riſe from

this

this very rain water, and vapours condenfed, that trickle through the holes, and interftices of loofe bodies, and are received into caverns.

Thefe afford a pure water purged by ftrain-ing, which rarely dry up in fummer, or freeze in winter, fo that animals never want a whole-fome and refrefhing liquor.

The chief fources of rivers are fountains, and rills growing by gradual fupplies into ftill larger and larger ftreams, till at laft, after the conflux of a vaft number of them, they find no ftop, but falling into the fea with leffened ra-pidity, they there depofit the united ftores they have gathered, along with foreign mat-ter, and fuch earthy fubftances, as they tore off in their way. Thus the water returns in a circle, whence it firft drew its origin, that it may act over the fame fcene again.

Marfhes arifing from water retained in low grounds are filled with moffy tumps, which are brought down by the water from the higher parts, or are produced by putrifyed plants.

We often fee new meadows arife from marfhes dryed up. This happens fooner when the ᵍ *fphagnum* F. S. 864.* has laid a founda-

ᵍ A kind of mofs.

* This refers to the firft Edition of the *Flora Suecica.* It is 958 in the fecond Edition.

tion ;

tion ; for this in procefs of time changes into a very porous mould, till almoft the whole marfh is filled with it. After that the *rufb* ftrikes root, and along with the *cotton graffes* conftitutes a turf, raifed in fuch a manner, that the roots get continually higher, and thus lay a more firm foundation for other plants, till the whole marfh is changed into a fine and de-lightfull meadow ; efpecially if the water hap-pens to work itfelf a new paffage.

Hillocks, that abound in low grounds, oc-cafion the earth to increafe yearly, more than the countreyman would wifh, and feem to do hurt : but in this the great induftry of nature deferves to be taken notice of. For by this means the barren fpots become fooner rich meadow, and pafture land. Thefe hillocks are formed by the ant, by ftones, and roots, and the trampling of cattle ; but the principal caufe is the force of the winter cold, which in the fpring raifes the roots of plants fo high above the ground, that being expofed to the air they grow, and perifh ; after which the *golden maidenhairs* fill the vacant places.

Mountains, hills, vallies, and all the ine-qualities of the earth, though fome think they take away much from its beauty, are fo far

from

from producing fuch an effect, that on the contrary they give a more pleafing afpect, as well as great advantages. For thus the terreftrial fuperficies is larger; different kinds of plants thrive better, and are more eafily watered, and the rain-waters run in continual ftreams into the fea, not to mention many other ufes in relation to winds, heat and cold. Alps are the higheft mountains, that reach to the fecond region of the air, where trees cannot grow erect. The higher thefe Alps are, the colder they are *cæteris paribus*. Hence the Alps in Sweden, Siberia, Swifferland, Peru, Brafil, Armenia, Afia, Africa, are perpetually covered with fnow; which becomes almoft as hard as ice. But, if by chance the fummer heats be greater than ordinary, fome part of thefe ftores melts, and runs through rivers into the lower regions, which by this means are much refrefhed.

It is fcarcely to be doubted, but that the rocks and ftones difperfed over the globe were formed originally in, and from the earth; but when torrents of rain have foftened, as they eafily do, the foluble earth, and carried it down into the lower parts, we imagine it happens that thefe folid, and heavy bodies, being

laid

laid bare, ftick out above the furface. We might alfo take notice of the wonderfull ef-fects of the tide, fuch as we fee happen from time to time on the fea-fhore, which being daily and nightly affaulted with repeated blows, at length gives way, and breaks off. Hence we fee in moft places the rubbifh of the fea, and fhores.

The winter by its froft prepares the earth, and mould, which thence are broken into very minute particles, and thus, being put into a mouldering ftate, become more fit for the nourifhment of plants; nay by its fnow it covers the feeds, and roots of plants, and thus by cold defends them from the force of cold. I muft add alfo that the piercing froft of the winter purifies the atmofphere, and pu-trid waters, and makes them more wholefome for animals.

The perpetual fucceffion of heat and cold with us renders the fummers more pleafing; and though the winter deprives us of many plants, and animals, yet the perpetual fummer within the tropics is not much more agreeable, as it often deftroys men, and other animals by its immoderate heat; though it muft be confeffed

feffed that thofe regions abound with moft ex-
quifite fruits. Our winters, though very
troublefome to a great part of the globe, on
account of their vehement, and intenfe cold,
yet are lefs hurtfull to the inhabitants of the
northern parts, as experience teftifies. Hence
it happens, that we may live very conveniently
on every part of the earth, as every different
countrey has different advantages from nature.

The feafons, like every thing elfe, have
their viciffitudes, their beginnings, their progrefs, and their end.

The age of man begins from the cradle,
pleafing childhood fucceeds, then active youth,
afterwards manhood firm, fevere and intent
upon felf-prefervation, laftly old age creeps on,
debilitates, and at length totally deftroys our
tottering bodies.

The feafons of the year proceed in the fame
way. Spring, the jovial, playfull infancy of
all living creatures, reprefents childhood and
youth ; for then plants fpread forth their luxu-
riant flowers, fifhes exult, birds fing, every
part of nature is intent upon generation. The
fummer, like middle age, exhibits plants, and
trees every where cloathed with green ; it

gives

gives vigor to animals, and plumps them up, fruits then ripen, meadows look cheerfull, every thing is full of life. On the contrary autumn is gloomy, for then the leaves of trees begin to fall, plants to wither, insects to grow torpid, and many animals to retire to their winter quarters. The day proceeds with just such steps, as the year. The morning makes every thing alert, and fit for business ; the sun pours forth his ruddy rays, the flowers which had, as it were, slept all night, awake and expand themselves again; the birds with their sonorous voices, and various notes make the woods ring, meet together in flocks, and sacrifice to Venus. Noon tempts animals into the fields, and pastures ; the heat puts them upon indulging their ease, and even necessity obliges them to it. Evening follows, and makes every thing more sluggish ; flowers shut up, [h] and animals retire to their lurking

[h] Of such flowers as sleep by night some account is given by Linnæus in Philof. Botan. p. 88. where the curious may also find p. 274. a list of plants one or other of which shut their flowers at every hour of the day without regard to the weather. One plant is so remarkable for this property, that it is generally known in our countrey by the name of go-to-bed-at-noon. Its botanical name is tragopogon or goat's-beard. See a Differtation in the Amæn. acad. vol. 4. where this subject is treated at large.

E.   places.

places. Thus the spring, the morning, and youth are proper for generation; the summer, noon, and manhood are proper for preservation; and autumn, evening, and old age are not unfitly likened to destruction.

§. 3.

The fossil kingdom.

Propagation.

It is agreed on all hands, that stones are not organical bodies, like plants, and animals; and therefore it is as clear that they are not produced from an egg, like the tribes of the other kingdoms. Hence the variety of fossils is proportionate to the different combinations of coalescent particles, and hence the species in the fossil kingdom are not so distinct, as in the other two. Hence also the laws of generation in relation to fossils have been in all ages extremely difficult to explain; and lastly hence have arisen so many different opinions about them, that it would be endless to enumerate them all. We therefore for the present will content ourselves with giving a very few observations on this subject.

That

That clay is the fediment of the fea is fufficiently proved by obfervation, for which reafon it is generally found in great plenty along
the coafts.

The journals of feamen clearly evince, that
a very minute fand covers the bottom of the
fea, nor can it be doubted, but that it is daily
cryftallifed out of the water.

It is now acknowledged by all, that teftaceous bodies and petrifactions refembling
plants were once real animals or vegetables; [i]
and it feems likely that fhells being of a calcareous nature have changed the adjacent clay,
fand, or mould into the fame kind of fubftance.
Hence we may be certain that marble may be
generated from petrifactions, and therefore it
is frequently feen full of them.

Rag-ftone the moft common matter of our
rocks appears to be formed from a fandy kind
of clay, but this happens more frequently,
where the earth is impregnated with iron.

Freeftone is the product of fand, and the
deeper the bed, where it is found, the more
compact it becomes; and the more denfe the

---

[i] I have taken the liberty not to follow the original
text in this place. The learned will fee the reafon at firft
fight.

fand,

fand, the more eafily it concretes. But if an *alcaline* clay chances to be mixed with the fand, the *freeſtone* is generated more readily, as in the *freeſtone* called *cos friatilis, particulis argillo-glarenſis*, S. N. 1. 1.

The *flint*, S. N. 3. 1. is almoſt the only kind of *ſtone*, certainly the moſt common in *chalky* mountains. It feems therefore to be produced from *chalk*. Whether it can be reduced again to *chalk*, i leave to others to inquire.

Stalactites, S. N. 33. 1. or *drop-ſtone* is compofed of calcareous particles, adhering to a dry and generally a vegetable body.

The incruſtations S. N. 32. 5, 6, 7, 8. are often generated, where a vitriolic water connects claiey and earthy particles together.

Slate by the vegetables, that are often incloſed in it, feems to take its origin from a marſhy mould.

Metals vary according to the nature of the matrix, to which they adhere, e. g. the *pyrites cupri Fahlunenſis* contains frequently *fulphur, arſenic, iron, copper,* a little *gold, vitriol, alum,* fometimes *lead ore, filver* and *zinck.* Thus *gold, copper, iron, zinck, arſenic, pyrites, vitriol* come out of the fame vein. That very rich *iron* ore at Normark in Vermelandia, where it was cut tranfverfly by a vein of clay, was changed into a pure *filver*. The number therefore of fpecies, and varieties of *foffils*, each ferving for different purpofes, according to their different natures, will be in proportion, as the different kinds of earths and *ftones* are varioufly combined.

§. 4.

Prefervation.

As *foffils* are deftitute of life, and organifation, are hard, and not obnoxious to putrefaction; fo they laft longer, than any other kind of bodies. How far the air contributes to this duration it is eafy to perceive, fince air hardens many *ftones* upon the fuperficies of the earth, and makes them more folid, compact, and able to refift the injuries of time. Thus it is known from vulgar obfervation that *lime*, that has been long expofed to the air, becomes hardened. The *chalky marl*, which they ufe in Flanders for building houfes, as long as it continues in the quarry, is friable; but when dug up and expofed to the air, it grows gradually harder. In the fame way our old walls, and towers gain a firmnefs in procefs of time,

E 3   and

and therefore it is a vulgar miftake, that our anceftors excelled the modern architects in the art of building as to this point ᵏ.

However ignorant we may be of the caufe, why large rocks are every where to be feen fplit, whence vaft fragments are frequently torn off; yet this we may obferve, that fiffures are clofed up by water, that gets between them, and is detained there; and are confolidated by *cryftal* and *fpar*. Hence we fcarcely ever find *cryftal*, but in thofe *ftones*, which have for fome time in its chinks water loaded with ftony particles. In the fame manner *cryftals* fill the cavities in mines, and concrete into *quartz* or a debafed *cryftal*.

It is manifeft that *ftones* are not only generated, augmented, and changed perpetually

ᵏ Too great ftrefs ought not, I think, to be laid on this obfervation of our author, though it may be in part true; for without fuppofing that our anceftors had more fkill in building, we may fuppofe, what was likely to be the cafe, that they ufed more care in the choice of their materials, and had them wrought up with more labor; which muft add confiderably to the firmnefs of the cement. Where thefe circumftances have happened to be wanting, time alone has not been able to produce the fame effect. I have feen a houfe about fourfcore years old, where one might rub out the mortar from between the bricks without fcarcely ufing any force.

from

from incruftations brought upon mofs, but are alfo increafed by *cryftal* and *fpar*. Not to mention that the adjacent earth, efpecially if it be impregnated with iron particles, is commonly changed into a folid *ftone*.

It is faid, that the *marble quarries* in Italy, from whence fragments are cut, grow up again. *Ores* grow by little and little, whenever the mineral particles, conveyed by the means of water through the clefts of mountains, are retained there ; fo that adhering to the homogeneous matter a long while, at laft they take its nature, and are changed into a fimilar fubftance.

§. 5.

Deftruction.

Foffils, although they are the hardeft of bodies, yet are found fubject to the laws of deftruction, as well as all other created fubftances. For they are diffolved in various ways by the elements exerting their force upon them, as by water, air and the folar rays, as alfo by the rapidity of rivers, violence of cataracts, and eddies which continually beat upon and at laft reduce to powder the hardeft *rocks*. The agitations

E 4   tations

tations of the fea, and lakes, and the vehemence of the waves, excited by turbulent
winds pulverife *ftones*, as evidently appears by
their roundnefs along the fhore. Nay as the
poet fays,

The hardeft ftone infenfibly gives way

To the foft drops, that frequent on it play.
So that we ought not to wonder, that thefe
very hard bodies moulder away into powder,
and are obnoxious like others to the confum-
ing tooth of time.

Sand is formed of *freeftone*, which is deftroyed partly by froft, making it friable,
partly by the agitation of water, and waves;
which eafily wear away, diffolve, and reduce
into minute particles, what the froft had made
friable.

Chalk is formed of rough *marble*, which the
air, the fun, and the winds have diffolved, as
appears by Iter. Goth. 170.

The *flate* earth or *humus fchifti* Syf. Nat. 511.
owes its origin to *flate*, diffolved by the air,
rain and fnow.

Ochre is formed of metals diffolved, whofe
fæces prefent the very fame colours, which
we always find the *ore* tinged with, when
expofed to the air. *Vitriol* in the fame

man-

manner mixes with water from *ores* deftroyed.

The *muria faxatilis* Syf. Nat. 14. 6. a kind
of talky ftone yielding falt in the parts that
are turned to the fun, is diffolved into fand,
which falls by little and little upon the earth,
till the whole is confumed ; not to mention
other kinds of *foffils*. Laftly from thefe there
arife new *foffils*, as we mentioned before, fo
that the deftruction of one thing ferves for
the generation of another.

Teftaceous worms ought not to be paffed over
on this occafion, for they eat away the hardeft
rocks. That fpecies of *fhell fifh* called the *razor
fhell* bores thro' ftones in Italy, and hides itfelf
within them ; fo that the people who eat
them are obliged to break the ftones, before
they can come at them. The *cochlea* F. S.
1299. a kind of *fnail* that lives on craggy
rocks, eats, and bores through the chalky
hills, as worms do through wood. This is
made evident by the obfervations of the celebrated de Geer.

§. 6.

§. 6.

The Vegetable Kingdom.

Propagation.

Anatomy abundantly proves, that all *plants* are *organic*, and living bodies; and that all *organic* bodies are propagated from an egg has been sufficiently demonstrated by the industry of the moderns. We therefore the rather, according to the opinion of the skilfull, reject the æquivocal generation of *plants*; and the more so, as it is certain that every living thing is produced from an egg. Now the seeds of *vegetables* are called eggs; these are different in every different *plant*, that the means being the same, each may multiply its species, and produce an offspring like its parent. We do not deny, that very many *plants* push forth from their roots fresh offsets for two or more years. Nay not a few *plants* may be propagated by branches, buds, suckers and leaves fixed in the ground, as likewise many trees. Hence their stems being divided into branches, may be looked on as roots above ground; for in the same way the roots creep under ground;

and

and divide into branches. And there is the more reafon for thinking fo, becaufe we know that a tree will grow in an inverted fituation, viz. the roots being placed upwards, and the head downwards, and buried in the ground; for then the branches will become roots, and the roots will produce leaves, and flowers. The *lime-tree* will ferve for an example, on which gardeners have chiefly made the experiment. Yet this by no means overturns the doctrine, that all *vegetables* are propagated by feeds; fince it is clear that in each of the foregoing inftances nothing vegetates but what was part of a plant, formerly produced from feed, fo that, accurately fpeaking, without feed no new *plant* is produced.

Thus again *plants* produce feeds, but they are entirely unfit for propagation, unlefs fœcundation precedes, which is performed by an intercourfe between different fexes, as experience teftifies. *Plants* therefore muft be provided with *organs* of generation; in which refpect they hold an analogy with *animals*. Since in every *plant* the flower always precedes the fruit, and the fœcundated feeds vifibly arife from the fruit; it is evident that the *organs* of generation are contained in the flower, which

which *organs* are called *antheræ*, and *ſtigmata*, and that the impregnation is accompliſhed within the flower. This impregnation is performed by means of the duſt of the *antheræ* falling upon the moiſt *ſtigmata*, where the duſt adheres, is burſt, and ſends forth a very ſubtle matter, which is abſorbed by the *ſtyle*, and is conveyed down to the rudiment of the ſeed, and thus renders it fertile. When this operation is over, the *organs* of generation wither and fall, nay a change in the whole flower enſues. We muſt however obſerve, that in the *vegetable kingdom* one, and the ſame flower does not always contain the *organs* of generation of both ſexes, but oftentimes the male *organs* are on one *plant*, and the female on another. But that the buſineſs of impregnation may go on ſuccefsfully, and that no plant may be deprived of the neceſſary duſt, the whole moſt elegant *apparatus* of the *antheræ* and *ſtigmata* in every flower is contrived with wonderful wiſdom.

For in moſt flowers the *ſtamina* ſurround the *piſtills*, and are about the ſame height; but there are many *plants*, in which the *piſtill* is longer than the *ſtamina*, and in theſe it is wonderfull to obſerve, that the Creator

has

has made the flowers recline, in order that the dust may more easily fall into the *stigma*, e. g. in the *campanula, cowslip* [1], &c. But when the fœcundation is compleated the flowers rise again, that the seeds may not fall out before they are ripe, at which time they are dispersed by the winds. In other flowers on the contrary the *pistill* is shorter, and there the flowers preserve an erect situation, nay when the flowering comes on they become erect; tho' before they were drooping, or immersed under water. Lastly, whenever the male flowers are placed below the female ones, the leaves are exceedingly small, and narrow, that they may not hinder the dust from flying upwards, like smoak; as we see in the *pine, fir, yew, sea-grape, juniper, cyprefs*, &c. and when in one and the same species one plant is male, and the other female, and confequently may be far from one another, there the dust, without which there is no impregnation, is carried in abundance by the help

[1] This curious phænomenon did not escape the poetical eye of Milton, who was so very much struck with the beauty of it, that he thought it worth describing in the following enlivened imagery,

With cowslips *wan that hang the pensive head.*

of

of the wind from the male to the female; as in the whole *dioicous* [m] clafs. Again a more difficult impregnation is compenfated by the longævity of the individuals, and the continuation of life by buds, fuckers and roots, fo that we may obferve every thing moft wifely difpofed in this affair. Moreover we cannot without admiration obferve that moft flowers expand themfelves when the fun fhines forth, whereas when clouds, rain, or the evening comes on, they clofe up, left the genital duft fhould be coagulated, or rendered ufelefs, fo that it cannot be conveyed to the *ftigmata*. But what is ftill more remarkable and wonderfull! when the fœcundation is over, the flowers neither upon fhowers, nor evening coming on clofe themfelves up. Hence when rain falls in the flowering time, the hufbandman and gardener foretell a fcarcity of fruits. I could and would iluftrate all this by many remarkable inftances, if the fame fubject had not lately been explained, in this very place [n] in a manner equal to its

[m] i.e. where one plant bears male flowers, and the other female ones.

[n] I fuppofe the author here alludes to a treatife publifhed in Amœn. academ. vol. 1. entitled, *Sponfalia plantarum*, in which are contained fo many proofs of the reality of the different fexes of plants, that to me there feems to remain no room for doubt.

im-

importance. I cannot help remarking one particular more, viz. that the organs of generation, which in the animal kingdom are by nature generally removed from fight, in the vegetable are expofed to the eyes of all, and that when their nuptials are celebrated, it is wonderfull what delight they afford to the fpectator by their moft beautiful colours and delicious odors. At this time bees, flies, and other infects fuck honey out of their nectaries, not to mention the humming bird ; and that from their effete duft the bees gather wax.

§. 7.

As to the diffemination of feeds, after they come to maturity, it being abfolutely neceffary; fince without it no crop could follow; the Author of nature has wifely provided for this affair in numberlefs ways. The ftalks and ftems favor this purpofe, for thefe raife the fruit above the ground, that the winds, fhaking them to and fro, may difperfe far off the ripe feeds. Moft of the [n] *pericarps* are fhut at

[n] Whatever furrounds the feeds is called by botanical writers a *pericarpium*, and as we want an Englifh word to exprefs this, i have taken the liberty to call it a pericarpy.

top,

top, that the feeds may not fall, before they
are shook out by stormy winds. Wings are
given to many *feeds*, by the help of which
they fly far from the mother plant, and oftentimes spread over a whole countrey. These
wings confift either of a down, as in moft of
the compofite flowered plants, or of a membrane, as in the *birch*, *alder*, *ash*, &c. Hence
woods, which happen to be confumed by fire,
or any other accident, will soon be reftored
again by new plants, diffeminated by this
means. Many kinds of fruits are endued with
a remarkable elafticity, by the force of which,
the ripe *pericarps* throw the *feeds* to a great
diftance, as the *wood-forrel*, the *fpurge*, the
phyllanthus, the *dittany*. Other *feeds* or *pericarps* are rough, or provided with hooks; fo
that they are apt to ftick to animals, that pafs
by them, and by this means are carried to their
holes where they are both fown, and manured
by nature's wonderfull care; and therefore the
plants of thefe *feeds* grow, where others will
not, as *hounds-tongue*, *agrimony*, &c.

Berries and other *pericarps*, are by nature
allotted for aliment to animals, but with this
condition, that while they eat the pulp they
fhall fow their *feeds*; for when they feed upon

it

it they either difperfe them at the fame time, or, if they fwallow them, they are returned with intereft; for they always come out unhurt. It is not therefore furprifing, that if a field be manured with recent mud or dung not quite rotten, various other plants, injurious to the farmer, fhould come up along with the grain, that is fowed. Many have believed that *barley*, or *rye* has been changed into *oats*, altho' all fuch kinds of metamorphofes are repugnant to the laws of generation, not confidering that there is another caufe of this phænomenon, viz. that the ground perhaps has been manured with horfe-dung, in which the *feeds* of *oats*, coming entire from the horfe, lye hid and produce that grain. The *mifletoe* always grows upon other trees, becaufe the thrufh that eats the feeds of it, cafts them forth with its dung, and as bird-catchers make their bird-lime of this fame plant, and daub the branches of trees with it, in order to catch the thrufh, the proverb hence took its rife;

The thrufh, when he befouls the bough,
Sows for himfelf the feeds of woe.

It is not to be doubted, but that the greateft part of the *junipers* alfo, that fill our woods,

F are

are fown by thrufhes, and other birds in the
fame manner; as the berries, being heavy,
cannot be difperfed far by the winds. The
crofs-bill that lives on the fir-cones, and the
hawfinch that feeds on the pine-cones, at the
fame time fow many of their *feeds*, efpecially
when they carry the *cone* to a ftone, or trunk
of a tree, that they more eafily ftrip it of its
fcales. Swine likewife, by turning up the
earth, and moles by throwing up hillocks,
prepare the ground for feeds in the fame manner, as the ploughman does.

I pafs over many other things, which might
be mentioned concerning the fea, lakes, and
rivers, by the help of which oftentimes *feeds*
are conveyed unhurt to diftant countries; nor
need I mention in what a variety of other
ways nature provides for the diffemination of
plants, as this fubject has been treated on at
large in our illuftrious prefident's oration concerning the augmentation of the habitable
earth. ᴾ

§. 8.

ᴾ As there is fomething very ingenious, and quite new
in the treatife here referred to, i will for the fake of thofe,
who cannot read the original, give a fhort abftract of it.
His defign is to fhew that there was only one pair of all
living things, created at the beginning. According to the
account

§. 8.

Prefervation.

The great Author and Parent of all things,
decreed, that the whole earth fhould be covered with plants, and that no place fhould be
F 2   void,

account of Mofes, fays the author, we are fure, that this
was the cafe in the human fpecies ; and by the fame account we are informed that this firft pair was placed in E-
den, and that Adam gave names to all the animals. In
order therefore that Adam might be enabled to do this, it
was neceffary that all the fpecies of animals fhould be in
paradife ; which could not happen unlefs alfo the fpecies
of vegetables had been there likewife. This he proves
from the nature of their food, particularly in relation to
infects, moft of which live upon one plant only. Now
had the world been formed in its prefent ftate, it could
not have happened that all the fpecies of animals fhould
have been there. They muft have been difperfed over all
the globe, as we find they are at prefent, which he thinks
improbable for other reafons which I fhall pafs over for the
fake of brevity. To folve all the phænomena then he
lays down a principle, that at the beginning all the earth
was covered with fea, unlefs one ifland large enough to
contain all animals and vegetables. This principle he en-
deavors to eftablifh by feveral phænomena which make it
probable, that the earth has been and is ftill gaining upon
the fea, and does not forget to mention *foffil fhells*, and
plants every where found, which he fays cannot be accounted for by the deluge. He then undertakes to fhew
how

void, none barren. But since all countries
have not the same changes of seasons, and
every soil is not equally fit for every plant, He
therefore, that no place should be without

how all vegetables and animals might in this island have a
soil and climate proper for each, only by supposing it to be
placed under the æquator, and crowned with a very high
mountain.   For it is well known that the same *plants* are
found on the Swifs, the Pyrenean, the Scotch alps, on
Olympus, Lebanon, Ida, as on the Lapland and Green-
land alps.   And Tournefort found at the bottom of mount
Ararat the common plants of Armenia, a little way up
those of Italy, higher those which grow about Paris, afterwards the Swedish plants, and lastly on the top the
Lapland *alpine plants* ; and i myself, adds the author, from
the plants growing on the Dalecarlian alps could collect
how much lower they were than the alps of Lapland. He
then proceeds to shew how from one plant of each species
the immense number of individuals now existing might
arise.   He gives some instances of the surprising fertility of
certain plants, v. g. the elecampane, one plant of which
produced 3000 seeds, of spelt, 2000, of the sunflower
4000, of the poppy 3200, of tobacco 40320.   But supposing any annual plant producing yearly only two seeds,
even of this after 20 years there would be 1,048,576 individuals.   For they would increase yearly in a duple proportion, viz. 2, 4, 8, 16, 32, &c. He then gives some instances of plants brought from America, that are now
become common over many parts of Europe.   Lastly he
enters upon the subject for which he is quoted in the
text, where the detail he gives of the several methods
which nature has taken to propagate vegetables is extremely curious, but too long to insert in this place.

                                            some,

some, gave to every one of them such a nature, as might be chiefly adapted to the climate; so that some of them can bear an intense cold, others an equal degree of heat; some delight in dry ground, others in moist, &c. Hence the same plants grow only where there are the same seasons of the year, and the same soil.

The *alpine* plants live only in high, and cold situations, and therefore often on the *alps* of Armenia, Switzerland, the Pyreneans, &c. whose tops are equally covered with eternal snows, as those of the Lapland *alps*, plants of the same kind are found, and it would be in vain to seek for them any where else. It is remarkable in relation to the *alpine* plants, that they blow, and ripen their *seeds* very early, otherwise the winter would steal upon them on a sudden, and destroy them.

Our northern plants, altho' they are extremely rare every where else, yet are found in Sibiria, and about Hudson's bay, as the *arbutus, Flor.* 339. *bramble* 412. *winter-green*, &c.

Plants impatient of cold live within the torrid zones; hence both the Indies tho' at such a distance from one another have plants in com-

mon,

mon. The Cape of Good Hope, i know not from what caufe, produces plants peculiar to itfelf, as all the *mefembryanthema*, and almoft all the fpecies of *aloes*. *Graffes*, the moft common of all plants, can bear almoft any temperature of air, in which the good providence of the Creator particularly appears; for all over the globe they above all plants are neceffary for the nourifhment of cattle, and the fame thing is feen in relation to our moft common grains.

Thus neither the fcorching fun, nor the pinching cold hinders any countrey from having its vegetables. Nor is there any foil, which does not bring forth many kinds of plants; the *pond-weeds*, the *water-lily*, *lobelia* inhabit the waters. The *fluviales*, *fuci*, *confervæ* cover the bottoms of rivers, and fea. The *fphagna* [q] fill the marfhes. The *brya* [r] cloath the plains. The dryeft woods and places fcarce ever illuminated by the rays of the fun are adorned with the *hypna*. Nay ftones and the trunks of trees are not excepted, for thefe are covered with various kinds of *liverwort*.

The defart, and moft fandy places have their peculiar trees, and plants; and as rivers or

[q] Kind of mofs.   [r] Kind of mofs.

brooks

brooks are very feldom found there, we cannot without wonder obferve that many of them diftill water, and by that means afford the greateft comfort both to man, and beafts that travel there. Thus the ' *tillandfia*, which is a *parafitical plant*, and grows on the tops of trees in the defarts of America, has its leaves turned at the bafe into the fhape of a pitcher, with the extremity expanded ; in thefe the rain is collected, and preferved for thirfty men, birds, and beafts,

The *water-tree* in Ceylon produces cylindrical bladders, covered with a lid ; into thefe is fecreted a moft pure, and refrefhing water, that taftes like nectar to men, and other animals. There is a kind of *cuckow-pint* in New-France, that if you break a branch of it, will afford you a pint of excellent water. How wife, how beautiful is the agreement between the plants of every countrey, and its inhabitants, and other circumftances.

' A kind of *mifletoe.*

§. 9.

Plants oftentimes by their very ſtructure contribute remarkably both to their own preſervation, and that of others. But the wiſdom of the Creator appears no where more, than in the manner of growth of *trees*. For as their roots deſcend deeper, than thoſe of other *plants*, proviſion is thereby made, that they ſhall not rob them too much of nouriſhment ; and what is ſtill more, a ſtem not above a ſpan in diameter often ſhoots up its branches very high ; theſe bear perhaps many thouſand buds, each of which is a *plant* with its *leaves, flowers* and *ſtipulæ*. Now if all theſe grew upon the plain, they would take up a thouſand times as much ſpace, as the *tree* does, and in this caſe there would ſcarcely be room in all the earth for ſo many *plants*, as at preſent the *trees* alone afford. Beſides *plants* that ſhoot up in this way are more eaſily preſerved from cattle by a natural defence, and farther their leaves falling in autumn cover the *plants* growing about againſt the rigor of the winter, and in the ſummer they afford a pleaſing ſhade, not only to animals, but to *plants*, againſt the intenſe heat of the ſun. We may add that

trees

trees like all other *vegetables* imbibe the water from the earth, which water does not cir-
culate again to the root, as the ancients imagined [t]; but being difperfed, like fmall rain,
by the tranfpiration of the leaves, moiftens the
plants that grow about. Again, many *trees*
bear flefhy fruits of the *berry* or *apple* kind,
which, being fecure from the attack of cattle,
grow ripe for the ufe of man, and other animals, while their feeds are difperfed up and
down after digeftion. Laftly the particular
ftructure of *trees* contribute very much to the
propagation of infects; for thefe chiefly lay
their eggs upon their leaves, where they are
fecure from the reach of cattle.

Ever-green trees, and *fhrubs* with us are chiefly found in the moft barren woods, that they
may be a fhelter to animals in the winter. They
lofe their leaves every third year, as their feeds
are fufficiently guarded by the *moffes,* and do
not want any other covering. The *palms* in
the hot countries perpetually keep their leaves,
for there the feeds ftand in no need of any
fhelter whatever.

[t] See *Vegetable Statics* by that great philofopher Dr.
Hales, where this fubject is treated in a mafterly way.

Many

Many *plants*, and *ſhrubs* are armed with
thorns, e. g. the *buck-thorn*, *ſloe*, *carduus*, *cot-*
ton-thiſtle, &c. that they may keep off the animals, which otherwiſe would deſtroy their fruit.
Theſe at the ſame time cover many other
plants, eſpecially of the annual kind, under
their branches ". So that while the adjacent
grounds are robbed of all *plants* by the voraci-
ty of animals, ſome may be preſerved, to ripen
flowers and fruit, and ſtock the parts about
with ſeeds, which otherwiſe would be quite extirpated.

All *herbs* cover the ground with their leaves,
and by their ſhade hinder it from being totally
deprived of that moiſture, which is neceſſary
to their nouriſhment. They are moreover an
ornament to the earth, eſpecially as leaves
have a more agreable verdure on the upper,
than the under ſide.

The *moſſes*, which adorn the moſt barren
places, at the ſame time preſerve the leſſer
plants, when they begin to ſhoot, from cold
and drought. As we find by experience in our

" This obſervation may be extended farther; for it is
conſtantly ſeen upon commons, where *furze* grows, that
wherever there was a buſh left untouched for years by the
commoners, ſome *tree* has ſprung up, being ſecured by the
prickles of that *ſhrub* from the bite of the cattle.

gardens, that *plants* are preferved in the fame way. They alfo hinder the fermenting earth from forcing the roots of *plants* upwards in the fpring; as we fee happen annually to trunks of trees, and other things put into the ground. Hence very few *moffes* grow in the warmer climates, as not being fo neceffary to that end in thofe places.

The Englifh *fea mat-weed* or *marran* will bear no foil but pure fand, which nature has allotted to it. Sand the produce of the fea, is blown by winds oftentimes to very remote parts, and deluges, as it were, woods and fields. But where this grafs grows, it frequently fixes the fand, gathers it into hillocks, and thrives fo much, that by means of this alone, at laft an entire hill of fand is raifed. Thus the fand is kept in bounds, other *plants* are preferved free from it, the ground is increafed [w],

---

[w] This obfervation is found in Linn. Flor. Lapp. p. 62. where he fays the Dutch fow this grafs on their fand banks, that the fand may not overwhelm the neighboring parts. I do not fee why this experiment fhould not be tryed on the barren fands in Norfolk, where I am affured by credible witneffes, that the fmall cottages are fometimes totally buried under fand during high winds. This grafs grows plentifully along the fea fhores in England. Vid. Ray, 393. 1.

and

and the fea repelled by this wonderful difpofition of nature.

How folicitous nature is about the prefervation of graffes is abundantly evident from
hence, that the more the leaves of the perennial graffes are eaten, the more they creep by
the roots, and fend forth off-fets. For the
Author of nature intended, that *vegetables* of
this kind, which have very flender, and erect
leaves, fhould be copious, and very thick-fet,
covering the ground like a carpet; and thus
afford food fufficient for fo vaft a quantity of
grazing animals. But what chiefly increafes
our wonder is, that although the graffes are
the principal food of fuch animals, yet they
are forbid, as it were, to touch the flower, and
feed-bearing ftems; that fo the feeds may
ripen and be fown.

The *caterpillar* or *grub* of the *moth*, Faun.
Sue. 826. called *graefmafken*, although it feeds
upon graffes, to the great deftruction of them,
in meadows; yet it feems to be formed, in order to keep a due proportion between thefe
and other plants; for graffes, when left to
grow freely, increafe to that degree, that they
exclude all other plants; which would confequently be extirpated, unlefs this infect fometimes

times prepared a place for them, Hence always more fpecies of *plants* appear in thofe places where this caterpillar has laid wafte the paftures the preceding year, than at any other time.

§. 10.

Deftruction.

Daily experience teaches us, that all *plants* as well as all other living things, muft fubmit to death.

They fpring up, they grow, they florifh, they ripen their fruit, they wither, and at laft, having finifhed their courfe, they die, and return to the duft again, from whence they firft took their rife. Thus all black mould, which every where covers the earth, for the greateft part is owing to dead *vegetables*. For all roots defcend into the fand by their branches, and after a *plant* has loft its ftem the root remains; but this too rots at laft, and changes into mould. By this means this kind of earth is mixed with fand, by the contrivance of nature, nearly in the fame way as dung thrown upon fields is wrought into the earth by the induftry of the hufbandman. The earth thus

pre-

prepared offers again to *plants* from its bo-
fom, what it has received from them. For
when feeds are committed to the earth, they
draw to themfelves, accommodate to their
nature, and turn into *plants*, the more fubtile parts of this mould by the co-operation
of the fun, air, clouds, rains, and winds; fo
that the talleft tree is, properly fpeaking, nothing but mould wonderfully compounded
with air, and water, and modified by a vertue communicated to a fmall feed by the
Creator. From thefe *plants*, when they die,
juft the fame kind of mould is formed, as
gave birth to them originally; but in fuch a
manner, that it is in greater quantity than
before. *Vegetables* therefore increafe the black
mould, whence fertility remains continually uninterrupted. Whereas the earth could
not make good its annual confumption, unlefs it were conftantly recruited by new fupplies.

The cruftaceous *liverworts* are the firft foundation of *vegetation*, and therefore are *plants*
of the utmoft confequence in the œconomy
of nature, though fo defpifed by us. When
rocks firft emerge out of the fea, they are fo
polifhed by the force of the waves, that

fcarce

scarce any herb can find a fixed habitation upon them ; as we may obferve every where near the fea. But the very minute cruftace-ous *liverworts* begin foon to cover thefe dry rocks, although they have no other nourifh-ment, but that fmall quantity of mould, and imperceptible particles, which the rain and air bring thither. Thefe *liverworts* dying at laft turn into a very fine earth; on this earth the ˣ imbricated *liverworts* find a bed to ftrike their roots in. Thefe alfo dye after a time, and turn to mould; and then the various kinds of moffes, e. g. the *hypna*, the *brya*, *politricha* find a proper place, and nourifhment. Laftly thefe dying in their turn, and rotting afford fuch a plenty of new formed mould, that herbs and fhrubs eafily root, and live upon it.

That trees when they are dry or are cut down may not remain ufelefs to the world, and lye, as it were, melancholy fpectacles, nature haftens on their deftruction in a fingular way: firft the *liverworts* begin to ftrike root in them; afterwards the moifture is drawn out of them;

ˣ I have ufed this word becaufe we have no Englifh one of the fame meaning unlefs it be the word *fcaly*, that i know of. However imbricated means parts lying over parts like tiles, as in the cup of the *thiftle flower*.

I

whence putrefaction follows. Then the *mush-room* kinds find a fit place for nourishment on them, and corrupt them still more. The *beetle* called the *dermestes*, next makes himself a way between the bark, and the wood. The *musk-beetle*, the *copper talc beetle*, and the *caterpillar* or *cossus* 812. bores an infinite number of holes through the trunk. Lastly the *woodpeckers* come, and while they are seeking for insects, wear away the tree, already corrupted; till the whole passes into earth. Such industry does nature use to destroy the trunk of a tree! Nay trees immersed in water would scarcely ever be destroyed, were it not for the worm that eats ships, which performs this work ; as the sailor knows by sad experience.

Thistles, as the most usefull of plants, are armed, and guarded by nature herself. Suppose there were a heap of clay, on which for many years no plant has sprung up ; let the seeds of the *thistle* blow there, and grow, the *thistles* by their leaves attract the moisture out of the air, send it into the clay by means of their roots, will thrive themselves, and afford a shade. Let now other plants come hither, and they will soon cover the ground. St. Bjelke.

All

All fucculent plants make ground fine, of a good quality, and in great plenty, as *fedum*, *craffula*, *aloe*, *algæ* [y]. But dry plants make it more barren, as *ling* or *heath*, *pines*, *mofs*; and therefore nature has placed the fucculent plants on rocks, and the dryeft hills.

§. 11.

The animal kingdom.

Propagation.

The generation of animals holds the firft place among all things, that raife our admiration, when we confider the works of the Creator; and that appointment particularly, by which he has regulated the conception of the *fœtus*, and its exclufion, that it fhould be adapted to the difpofition, and way of living of each animal, is moft worthy of our attention.

We find no fpecies of animals exempt from the ftings of love, which is put into them to the end, that the Creator's mandate may be executed, *increafe and multiply*; and that thus

[y] A kind of *grafs wrack*.

the

the egg, in which is contained the rudiment of the *fœtus* may be fœcundated ; for with-out fœcundation all eggs are unfit to produce an offspring.

Foxes and *wolves*, struck with these stings, every where howl in the woods ; crowds of *dogs* follow the female ; *bulls* shew a terrible countenance, and very different from that of *oxen*. *Stags* every year have new horns, which they lose after rutting time. Birds look more beautifull than ordinary, and warble all day long through lascivioufnefs. Thus *small birds* labour to outsing one another, and *cocks* to outcrow. *Peacocks* spread forth again their gay, and glorious trains. *Fishes* gather to-gether, and exult in the water ; and *grashop-pers* chirp, and pipe as it were, amongst the herbs. The *ants* gather again into colonies, and repair to their citadels ². I pass over many other particulars, which this subject affords, to avoid prolixity.

² See this subject treated with great spirit in Thom-son's Spring and in Virgil's Georgics.

§. 12.

The fœcundated egg requires a certain, and proportionate degree of heat for the expanfion of the *ftamina* of the *embryo*. That this may be obtained, nature operates in different manners, and therefore we find in different claffes of animals a different way of excluding the *fœtus*.

The females of *quadrupeds* have an *uterus*, contrived for eafy geftation, temperate and cherifhing warmth, and proper nourifhment of the *fœtus*, as moft of them live upon the earth, and are there fed.

Birds, in order to get fubfiftence, and for other reafons, are under a neceffity of fhifting place ; and that not upon their feet but wings. Geftation therefore would be burthenfome to them. For this reafon they lay eggs, covered with a hard fhell. Thefe they fit upon by a natural inftinct, and cherifh till the young one comes forth.

The *oftrich* and *caffowary* are almoft the only birds, that do not obferve this law ; thefe commit their eggs to the fand, where the intenfe heat of the fun excludes the *fœtus*.

Fifhes

Fishes inhabit cold waters, and moft of them have cold blood ; whence it happens that they have not heat fufficient to produce the *fœtus*. The all-wife Creator therefore has ordained, that moft of them fhould lay their eggs upon the fhore ; where, by means of the folar rays, the water is warmer, and alfo fitter for that purpofe ; becaufe it is there lefs impregnated with falt, and confequently milder ; and alfo becaufe water-infects abound more there, which afford the young fry a nourifhment.

Salmons in the like manner, when they are about to lay their eggs, are led by inftinct to go up the ftream, where the water is frefh and more pure.

The *butterfly fish* is an exception, for that brings forth its *fœtus* alive.

The *fishes of the ocean*, which cannot reach the fhores by reafon of the diftance, are alfo exempt from this law. The Author of nature to this kind has given eggs that fwim ; fo that they are hatched amidft the fwimming *fucus*, called *fargazo*. Flor. Zeilon. 389.

The *cetaceous* fifh have warm blood, and therefore they bring forth their young alive, and fuckle them with their teats.

Many

Many *amphibious* animals bring forth live *fœtuses*. As the *viper*, and the *toad*, &c. But the species that lay eggs, lay them in places, where the heat of the sun supplies the warmth of the parent.

Thus the rest of the *frog* kind and the *lizard* kind, lay their eggs in warm waters; the common *snake* in dunghills, and such-like warm places, and give them up to nature, as a provident nurse, to take care of them. The *crocodile*, and *sea tortoises* go ashore to lay their eggs under the sand, where the heat of the sun hatches them.

Most of the *insect* kind neither bear young nor hatch eggs; yet their tribes are the most numerous of all living creatures; insomuch that if the bulk of their bodies were proportionate to their quantity, they would scarce leave room for any other kinds of animals. Let us see therefore with what wisdom the Creator has managed about the propagation of these minute creatures. The females by natural instinct meet and copulate with the males; and afterwards lay their eggs, but not indiscriminately in every place; for they all know how to choose such places as may supply their offspring in its tender age with nourishment, and

other

other things neceſſary to ſatisfy their natural wants; for them other, ſoon after ſhe has laid her eggs, dyes, and were ſhe to live ſhe would not have it in her power to take care of her young.

Butterflies, *moths*, ſome *beetles*, *wevils*, *bugs*, *cuckow-ſpit inſeĉts*, *gall-inſeĉts*, *tree bugs*, &c. lay their eggs, on the leaves of plants, and every different tribe chooſes its own ſpecies of plant *. Nay there is ſcarce any plant, which does not afford nouriſhment to ſome inſeĉt; and ſtill more, there is ſcarcely any part of a plant, which is not preferred by ſome of them. Thus one inſeĉt feeds upon the flower; another upon the trunk; another up-on the root; and another upon the leaves. But we cannot help wondering particularly, when we ſee how the leaves of ſome trees, and plants, after eggs have been let into them, grow into galls; and form dwellings, as it were, for the young ones, where they may conveniently live. Thus when the *gall-inſeĉt* called *cynips*, Fn. 947. has fixed her eggs in the leaves of an oak, the wound of the leaf ſwells, and a knob like an apple ariſes, which includes and nouriſhes the embryo.

* Vid. Syſt. Nat. Edit. 10. Fauna Suecica; and Hoſpita Inſeĉtorum Flora Amœn. Academ. vol. 3.

When

When the *tree-bug*, Faun. Suec. 700. has depofited its eggs in the boughs of the fir tree, excrefences arife fhaped like peas. When another fpecies of the *tree-bug*, Fn. 695. has depofited its eggs in the *moufe-ear chickweed* or the *fpeedwell*, Fl. 12. the leaves contract in a wonderfull manner into the fhape of a head. The *water-fpider*, Fn. 1150. excludes its eggs either on the extremities of the *juniper*, which from thence forms a lodging, that looks like the *arrow-headed grafs*, or on the leaves of the *poplar*, from whence a red globe is produced. The *tree-loufe*, Fn. 1355. lays its eggs on the leaves of black poplar, Fl. 821. which from thence turn into a kind of inflated bag, and fo in other inftances. Nor is it upon plants only that infects live, and lay their eggs. The *knats*, Fn. 1116. commit theirs to ftagnating waters. The water infect called *monoculus*, Fn. 1182. often increafes fo immenfely on pools, that the red legions of them have the appearance of blood. Others lay their eggs in other places, e. g. the *beetle* in dunghills. The *dermeftes* in fkins. The *flefh fly* in putrifyed flefh. The *cheefe-maggot* in the cracks of cheefe, from whence the *caterpillars* iffuing forth oftentimes confume the whole cheefe,

and

and deceive many people, who fancy the worms are produced from the particles of the cheese itself, by a generation called æquivocal, which is extremely abfurd. Others exclude their eggs upon certain animals. The *mill-beetle* Fn. 618. lays its eggs betwen the fcales of fifhes. The *fpecies of glad-fly* Fn. 1024. on the back of cattle. The *fpecies* 1025 on the back of the rhen deer. The *fpecies* 1026 in the nofes of fheep. The *fpecies* 1028 lodges during the winter in the inteftinal tube, or the throat of horfes, nor can it be driven out till the fummer comes on. Nay *infects* themfelves are often furrounded with the eggs of other infects, infomuch that there is fcarcely an animal to be found, which does not feed its proper infect, not to fay any more of all the other places, where they depofit their eggs. Almoft all the eggs of *infects*, when laid, are ordained to undergo, by a wonderfull law of nature, various metamorphofes, e. g. the egg of the *butterfly* being laid in the cabbage firft of all becomes a *caterpillar*, that feeds upon the plant, crawls, and has fixteen feet. This afterwards changes into a *nymph*, that has no feet, is fmooth, and eats nothing ; and laftly this burfts into a *butterfly*, that flies, has variety of colours, is rough,

and

and lives upon honey. What can be more worthy of admiration, than that one, and the fame animal fhould appear on the ftage of life under fo many characters, as if it were three diftinct animals [a].

The laws of generation of *worms* are ftill very obfcure, as we find they are fometimes produced by eggs, fometimes by offsets, juft in the fame manner as happens to trees. It has been obferved with the greateft admiration, that the *polypus* or *hydra* S. N. 221. lets down fhoots and live branches, by which it is multiplied. Nay more, if it be cut into many parts, each fegment, put into the water, grows into a perfect animal ; fo that the parts which were torn off are reftored from one fcrap.

§. 13.

The multiplication of animals is not tyed down to the fame rules in all ; for fome have a remarkable power of propagating, others are

[a] Linnæus Amœn. academ. vol. 2. in a treatife on the wonders relating to infects, fays, " as furprifing as thefe " transformations may feem, yet much the fame happens " when a chicken is hatched, the only difference is, that " the chicken breaks all three coats at once, the butterfly " one after another,

con-

confined within narrower limits in this refpect. Yet in general, we find, that nature
obferves this order, that the leaft animals, and
thofe which are ufefull, and ferve for nourifhment to the greateft number of other animals,
are endued with a greater power of propagating than others [b].

Mites, and many other infects will multiply
to a thoufand within the compafs of a very few
days. While the *elephant* fcarcely produces
one young in two years.

The *hawk* kind generally lay not above two
eggs, at moft four, while the *poultry* kind rife
to 50.

- The *diver* or *loon*, which is eaten by few
animals, lays alfo two eggs, but the *duck* kind,
the *moor game*, *partridges*, &c. and *fmall birds*
lay a very large number.

If you fuppofe two *pigeons* to hatch nine
times a year, they may produce in four years
14672 young [c]. They are endued with this

[b] Herodotus fpeaking of the flying ferpents in Arabia
makes the fame reflection, and attributes this courfe of nature to the divine providence. Thal.

[c] I have given this paffage as it ftands in the original.
The numbers ought to have been 14760, or the expreffion
fhould have been altered ; for he includes the firft pair.

He fuppofes it generally known that pigeons hatch but
two eggs at a time, and that they pair.

remark-

remarkable fertility, that they may ferve for food, not only to man, but to hawks and other birds of prey *. Nature has made harmlefs and efculent animals fruitfull. Plin. Nature has forbid the *bird* kind to fall fhort of the number of eggs allotted to each fpecies, and therefore if the eggs which they intend to fit upon, be taken away a certain number of times, they prefently lay others in their room, as may be feen in the fwallow, duck, and fmall birds.

§. 14.

Prefervation.

Prefervation follows generation; this appears chiefly in the tender age, while the young are unable to provide for their own fupport. For then the parents, though otherwife ever fo fierce in their difpofition, are affected with a wonderfull tendernefs or fenfe of love towards their progeny, and fpare no pains to provide for, guard, and preferve them, and that not by an imaginary law, but one given by the Lord of nature himfelf.

Quadrupeds give fuck to their tender young and fupport them by a liquor, perfectly eafy of digeftion, till their ftomachs are able to digeft,

* Vid. Mufchenbr. Orat. de Sap. Divin.

and

and their teeth are fit to chew more folid food. Nay their love toward them is fo great, that they endeavour to repell with the utmoft force every thing, which threatens danger, or de-ftruction to them. The *ewe* which brings forth two *lambs* at a time, will not admit one to her teats, unlefs the other be prefent, and fuck alfo; left one fhould famifh, while the other grows fat.

Birds build their nefts in the moft artificial manner, and line them as foft as poffible, for fear the eggs fhould get any damage. Nor do they build promifcuoufly in any place; but there only, where they may quietly lye con-cealed and be fafe from the attacks of their enemies.

The *hanging bird*, Act. Bonon. vol. 2. makes its neft of the fibres of withered plants, and the down of the poplar feeds, and fixes it upon the bough of fome tree hanging over the water; that it may be out of reach.

The *diver*, Fn. 123. places its fwimming neft upon the water itfelf amongft the rufhes. I de-fignedly pafs over many other inftances of the like kind.

Again birds fit on their eggs with fo much patience, that many of them choofe to perifh

with

with hunger, rather than expofe the eggs to danger by going to feek for food.

The male *rooks* and *crows* at the time of incubation bring food to the females.

Pigeons, fmall birds, and other *birds,* which pair, fit by turns; but where polygamy prevails, the males fcarcely take any care of the young.

Moft of the *duck* kind pluck off their feathers in great quantity, and cover their eggs with them, left they fhould be damaged by the cold, when they quit their nefts for the fake of food; and when the young are hatched, who knows not how folicitous they are in providing for them, till they are able to fly, and fhift for themfelves?

Young *pigeons* would not be able to make ufe of hard feeds for nourifhment, unlefs the parents were to prepare them in their crops, and thence feed them.

The *eagle owl* makes its neft on the higheft precipices of mountains, and in the warmeft fpot, facing the fun; that the dead bodies brought there may by the heat melt into a foft pulp, and become fit nourifhment for the young.

The

The *cuckow* lays its eggs in the nest of other small birds, generally the *wagtail,* [d] or [e] *hedge-sparrow*, and leaves the incubation, and preservation of the young to them. But that these young, when grown up, degenerate into hawks, and become so ungratefull, that they destroy their nurses, is a mere vulgar error, for it is contrary to their nature to eat flesh.

Amphibious animals, *fishes* and *insects*, which cannot come under the care of their parents, yet owe this to them, that they are put in places, where they easily find nourishment, as we have observed.

[d] This custom of the cuckow is so extraordinary, and out of the common course of nature, that it would not be credible, were it not for the testimony of the most knowing and curious natural historians, such as Ray, Willughby, Gesner, Aldrovandus, Aristotle, &c.

Much has been said by the writers on birds about the fate of the young birds, in whose nest the cuckow is hatched, but as i find nothing but mere conjecture, it would not be worth while transcribing.

[e] Hedge sparrow. Linnæus seems to have taken the white-throat for the hedge-sparrow.

§. 15.

As soon as animals come to maturity, and want no longer the care of their parents, they attend with the utmoſt labor, and induſtry, according to the law and œconomy appointed for every ſpecies, to the preſervation of their lives. But that ſo great a number of them, which occur every where, may be ſupported, and a certain and fixed order may be kept up amongſt them, behold the wonderfull diſpoſition of the Creator, in aſſigning to each ſpecies certain kinds of food, and in putting limits to their appetites. So that ſome live on particular ſpecies of plants, which particular regions, and ſoils only produce. Some on particular animalcula, others on carcaſes, and ſome even on mud and dung. For this reaſon Providence has ordained, that ſome ſhould ſwim in certain regions of the watery element, others ſhould fly; ſome ſhould inhabit the torrid, the frigid, or the temperate zones, and others ſhould frequent deſarts, mountains, woods, pools or meadows, according as the food proper to their nature is found in ſufficient quantity. By this means there is no terreſtrial tract,

tract, no fea, no river, no countrey, but what contains, and nourishes various kinds of animals. Hence alfo an animal of one kind cannot rob thofe of another kind of its aliment; which, if it happened, would endanger their lives or health; and thus the world at all times affords nourifhment to fo many, and fo large inhabitants, at the fame time that nothing, which it produces, is ufelefs or fuperfluous.

I think it will not be amifs to produce fome inftances, by which it will appear, how providentially the Creator has furnifhed every animal with fuch cloathing, as is proper for the countrey where they live, and alfo how excellently the ftructure of their bodies is adapted to their particular way of life; fo that they feem to be deftined folely to the places, where they are found.

Monkies, _elephants_, and _rhinocerofes_ feed upon vegetables, that grow in hot countries, and therefore therein they have their allotted places. When the fun darts forth its moft fervid rays, thefe animals are of fuch a nature, and difpofition, that it does them no manner of hurt; nay with the reft of the inhabitants of thofe parts they go naked, whereas were

they

they covered with hairy skins they must perish with heat.

On the contrary the place of *rhen deer* is fixed in the coldest part of Lapland, because their chief food is the *liverwort*, Fl. 980. which grows no where so abundantly as there; and where, as the cold is most intense, the *rhen deer* are cloathed, like the other northern animals, with skins filled with the densest hair; by the help of which they easily defy the keenness of the winter. In like manner the *rough-legged partridge* passes its life in the very Lapland alps, feeding upon the seeds of the *dwarf birch*, and that they may run up and down safely amidst the snow, their feet are feathered.

The *camel* frequents the sandy, and burning desarts, in order to get the barren *camel's hay*. Mat. Med. 31. How wisely has the Creator contrived for him! he is obliged to go thro' the desarts, where oftentimes no water is found for many miles about. All other animals would perish with thirst in such a journey; but the camel can undergo it without suffering; for his belly is full of cells, where he reserves water for many days. It is reported by travellers, that the Arabians, when in travelling they want water, are forced to kill their camels; and take water out of their bellies, that is perfectly good to drink, and not at all corrupted.

The *pelican* likewise lives in defart, and dry places; and is obliged to build her neft far from the fea, in order to procure a greater fhare of heat to her eggs. She is therefore forced to bring water from afar for herfelf and her young; for which reafon Providence has furnifhed her with an inftrument moft adapted to this purpofe; v. g. fhe has a very large bag under her throat, which fhe fills with a quantity of water fufficient for many days; and this fhe pours into the neft to refrefh her young, and teach them to fwim. The wild beafts, lions, and tigers, come to this neft to quench their thirft, but do no hurt to the young.

Oxen delight in low grounds, becaufe there the food moft palatable to them grows.

Sheep prefer naked hills, where they find a particular kind of grafs called the *feftuca*, Fl. 95. which they love above all things.

Goats climb up the precipices of mountains, that they may browfe on the tender fhrubs, and in order to fit them for it, they have feet made for jumping*.

* Vid. Derham's Phifyco-Theol. p. 319. not 7.

Horſes chiefly reſort to woods, and feed upon leafy plants.

Nay, ſo various is the appetite of animals,
that there is ſcarcely any plant, which is not
choſen by ſome, and left untouched by others.
The *horſe* gives up the *water hemlock* to the
goat. The *cow* gives up the *long-leaved water hemlock* to the ſheep. The *goat* gives up
the *monks-hood* to the horſe, &c. for that
which certain animals grow fat upon, others
abhor as poiſon. Hence no plant is abſolutely
poiſonous, but only reſpectively. Thus the
ſpurge, that is noxious to man, is a moſt wholeſome nouriſhment to the *caterpillar*, Fn. 825.
That animals may not deſtroy themſelves for
want of knowing this law, each of them is
guarded by ſuch a delicacy of taſte and ſmell,
that they can eaſily diſtinguiſh what is pernicious from what is wholeſome ; and when it happens that different animals live upon the ſame
plants, ſtill one kind always leaves ſomething
for the other, as the mouths of all are not
equally adapted to lay hold of the graſs; by
which means there is ſufficient food for all.
To this may be referred an œconomical experiment well known to the Dutch, that when
eight cows have been in a paſture, and can no

longer

longer get nourifhment, two horfes will do very well there for fome days, and when no-thing is left for the horfes, four fheep will live upon it.

Swine get provifion by turning up the earth; for there they find the fucculent roots, which to them are very delicious.

The leaves and fruits of trees are intended as food for fome animals, as the floth ͬ, the

---

ͬ There is fo curious an account of this animal in Kir-cher's Mufurgia, that i think the reader will excufe my tranfcribing it. That author fays thus : ' The defcription of
' this animal i had from father Torus, provincial of the Jefuites
' in America, who had animals of this kind in his poffeffion,
' and made many experiments in relation to their nature
' and qualities. Its figure is extraordinary ; it is about the
' bignefs of a cat, of very ugly countenance, and has claws
' extended like fingers. The hinder part of the head and
' neck are covered with hair. It fweeps the ground with
' its fat belly, never rifes upon its feet, and moves fo
' flowly, that it would fcarce go the length of a bow-fhot
' in 15 days, tho' conftantly moving, and it is therefore
' called the Sloth. It is not known what it feeds upon,
' not being ever obferved to take any food. It lives gene-
' rally upon tops of trees, and employs two days to crawl
' up, and as many to get down again. Nature has doubly
' guarded this animal againft its enemies. Firft by giving
' it fuch ftrength in its feet that whatever it feizes, it holds
' fo faft, that it never can be freed from its claws, but muft
' there dye of hunger. Secondly in giving it fuch a moving
' afpeᵭ,

the fquirrel, and thefe laft have feet given . them fit for climbing.

Befides myriads of fifhes, the *caftor*, the *fea calf*, and others inhabit the water, that they may there be fed, and their hinder feet are fit

for

‘ afpect, when it looks at any man who fhould be tempted
‘ to hurt it, that it is impoffible not to be touched with
‘ compaffion ; befides that at the fame time it fheds tears,
‘ and upon the whole perfuades one, that a creature fo de-
‘ fencelefs, and of fo unhappy a body ought not to be tor-
‘ mented. To make an experiment of this, the above-
‘ mentioned father procured one of thefe animals to be
‘ brought to our college at Carthagena. He put a long
‘ pole under his feet, which it feized upon very firmly, and
‘ would not let it go again. The animal therefore thus voluntari-
‘ ly fufpended was placed between two beams along with the
‘ pole, and there it remained without meat, drink, or fleep,
‘ forty days; its eyes being always fixed on people that
‘ looked at it, who were fo touched, that they could not
‘ forbear pitying it. At laft being taken down they let loofe
‘ a dog on it, which after a little while the Sloth feized with
‘ his feet, and held him four days, till he dyed of hunger.
‘ This was taken from the mouth of the father. They add,
‘ continues Kircher, that this creature makes no noife but
‘ at night, but that very extraordinary. For by interrup-
‘ tions, that laft about the length of a figh or femipaufe
‘ it goes thro’ the fix vulgar intervals of mufic ut, re, mi,
‘ fa, fol, la. La, fol, fa, mi, re, ut, afcending and defcend-
‘ ing, and thefe perfectly in tune. So that the Spaniards,
‘ when they firft got poffeffion of this coaft, and heard thefe

H 3   ‘ notes,

for fwimming, and perfectly adapted to their manner of life.

The whole order, of the *goofe* kind, as ducks, merganfer, &c. pafs their lives in water as feeding upon water-infects, fifhes, and their eggs [g]. Who does not fee, that attends ever fo little, how exactly the wonderfull for-

‘ notes, they imagined that fome people brought up to our ‘ mufic, were finging. This animal is called by the na- ‘ tives Haut, certainly becaufe going thro’ thefe mufical ‘ intervals, it repeats, Ha, ha, ha, ha, ha, &c.

This account feems very wonderfull, and i leave it as it ftands without entering into any difcuffion about its credibility. I will only add, that Linnæus feems in the new edition of the Syft. Nat. to give credit to it. For he fays in his fhort way of defcription among other things, ‘ It utters ‘ an afcending hexacord. Its noife is horrible, its tears pi- ‘ teous.’ He quotes Mangrave, Clufius, Gefner, &c. But not having an opportunity of confulting thefe books i cannot tell how far thefe authors confirm the foregoing account; if it be true, it would furnifh fome obfervations, but this would not be a place for them.

[g] Many opinions, fays the author in the note, have been ftarted in order to account how it happens that fifhes are found in pools, and ditches, on high mountains and elfewhere. But Gmelin obferves that the *duck* kind fwallow the eggs of fifhes, that fome of thefe eggs go down, and come out of their bodies unhurt, and fo are propagated juft in the fame manner, as has been obferved of plants. Biberg.

Gmelin adds, that the Sibirians themfelves account for this phænomenon in the manner above mentioned.

mation

mation of their beaks, their necks, their feet, and their feathers fuit their kind of life, which obfervation ought to be extended to all other birds.

The way of living of the *fea-fwallow* Fn. 129. deferves to be particularly taken notice of ; for as he cannot fo commodioufly plunge into the water and catch fifh, as other aquatic birds, the Creator has appointed the *fea-gull* to be his caterer in the following manner. When this laft is purfued by the former, he is forced to throw up part of his prey, which the other catches ; but·in the autumn, when the fifhes hide themfelves in deep places, the merganfer, Fn. 113. fupplies the gull with food, as being able to plunge deeper into the fea. Act. Stock.

The chief granary of *fmall birds* is the *knot-grafs,* Fol. Suec. 322. that bears heavy feeds, like thofe of the *black bindweed.* It is a very common plant, not eafily deftroyed, either by the road fide by trampling upon it, or any where elfe, and is extremely plentifull after harveft in fields, to which it gives a reddifh hue by its numerous feeds. Thefe fall upon ,the ground, and are gathered all the year round by the fmall birds.

H 4   Thus

[h] Thus bountifull nature feeds the fowls of the air.

The Creator has taken no lefs care of fome *amphibious animals*, as the fnake and frog kind, which, as they have neither wings to fly, nor feet to run fwiftly, and commodioufly, would fcarcely have any means of taking their prey, were it not that fome animals run, as it were of their own accord, into their mouths. When the *rattle-fnake* a native of America, with open jaws fixes his eyes on a bird, fly, or fquirrel, fitting on a tree, they fly down his throat, being rendered ftupid, and giving themfelves up [i], as deftitute of all refuge. On the other hand we cannot but adore the Creator's great goodnefs towards man, when we

[h] To which we may add, that many fmall birds feed upon the feeds of *plantain*, particularly linnets. It is generally known that the goldfinch lives upon the feed of *thiftles*, from which he has its name in Greek, Latin and French.

[i] How dreadfull this ferpent is to other animals will appear by an account we have in a treatife intitled, Radix Senega. Where the author Amæn. academ. vol. 2. fays, one of thefe terrible ferpents got clandeftinely into the houfe of governor Blake at Cacolina ; where it would have long laid concealed, had it not been that all the domeftic animals, as dogs, hogs, turkies and fowls admonifhed the family by their unufual cries, equally fhewing their horrror and confternation, their hair, briflies and crefts ftanding up an end.

confider

confider the rattle which terminates this ferpent's tail. For by the means of that we have an opportunity of guarding againft this dreadfull enemy; the found warning us to fly, which if we were not to do, and we fhould be wounded by him, the whole body would be turned into a putrid corruption in fix hours, nay fometimes in half an hour.

The limits of this differtation will not permit me to produce more examples of this kind. But whoever will be at the pains to take ever fo flight a view of the wonderfull works of the Creator, will readily fee, how wifely the plan, order and fitnefs of things to divine ends are difpofed.

§. 16.

We cannot without the utmoft admiration behold how providently the Creator has acted as to the prefervation of thofe animals, which at a certain time of the year, are by the rigor of the feafon excluded from the neceffaries of life. Thus the *bear* in the autumn creeps into the *mofs*, which he has gathered, and there lies all winter; fubfifting upon no other nourifhment but his fat, collected during the fummer in the cellulous membrane, and which

without

without doubt, during his faſt, circulates thro'
his veſſels, and ſupplies the place of food ; to
which perhaps is added that fat juice which
he ſucks out of the bottom of his feet.

The *hedge-hog*, *badger* and *mole* in the
ſame manner fill their winter quarters with vegetables, and ſleep during the froſts.

The *bat* ſeems cold, and quite dead all
the winter. Moſt of the *amphibious animals* get
into dens, or to the bottom of lakes and pools.

In the autumn, as the cold approaches, and
inſects diſappear, *ſwallows* [k] ſeek for an aſylum
againſt the violence of the cold in the bottom

of

---

[k] I never had but one credible teſtimony that ſwallows
paſs the winter at the bottom of lakes or ponds ; and this
from a gentleman of character, who ſaw a ſwallow ſo found
brought to life by warmth. On the other hand, i know of
no author but Herodotus who mentions their being ſeen in
any country during the winter. He lib. 2. p. 109. edit.
Steph. ſays, that ſwallows and kites continue all the year about
the ſprings of the Nile. What he mentions concerning kites
deſerves ſome notice, viz. that they lye concealed in holes a few
days. Pliny ſays a few months. Geſner repeats the ſame, adding that they have been found in hollow trees ſomewhere in
Upper Germany, but he ſeems to relate this upon hearſay
only. Aldrovandus gives the ſame account as Geſner, and
adds that they winter in Ægypt, but whether upon the authority of Bellonius or any other credible writer, does not

appear.

of lakes amongft the reeds and rufhes; from whence by the wonderfull appointment of nature they come forth again. The periftaltic motion of the bowels ceafes in all thefe animals, while they are obliged to faft, whence the appetite is diminifhed, and fo they fuffer lefs from hunger. To this head may be referred the obfervation of the celebrated Lifter concerning thofe animals; that their blood, when let into a bafon, does not coagulate, as that of all other animals, and fo is no lefs fit for circulation than before.

The *moor-fowls* work themfelves out walks under the very fnow. They moult in the fummer, fo that about the month of Auguft they

appear. He quotes a paffage from that author concerning the appearance of a vaft number of kites at the mouth of the Bofphorus, but this happened at the latter end of May, and feems to prove nothing; for the time marked for their appearance by Calippus, who obferved near the Hellefpont, is the month of March. Willughby fays that kites are fuppofed to be birds of paffage, and then quotes from Bellonius the place abovementioned.

From what has been faid it appears evident, that nothing certain is known by the moderns about the difappearance of thefe remarkable birds, yet their coming was regularly noted by the antient writers, and coincided with that of fwallows, as appears by the old calendars of Geminus, and Ptolemy from the obfervations of Eudoxus, Euctemous, Calippus, and Dofitheus.

can-

cannot fly, and are therefore obliged to run into the woods ; but then the moor-berries and
bilberries are ripe, from whence they are
abundantly fupplied with food.   Whereas the
young do not moult the firſt fummer, and
therefore, tho' they cannot run fo well, are
able to efcape danger by flight.

The *reſt of the birds* who feed upon infeɛts
migrate every year to forreign regions, in order to feek for food in a milder climate; while
all the northern parts, where they live well in
the fummer, are covered with fnow.

Infeɛts in the winter generally lye hid within their cafes, and are nouriſhed by the fur-
rounding liquor like the fœtus of other animals, from whence at the approach of fpring
they awake, and fly forth to the aſtoniſhment
of every one.

However all animals which lye hid in winter, do not obferve thefe laws of faſting. Some
provide ſtore-houfes in fummer, and autumn,
from which they take what is neceſſary, as
mice, jays, fquirrels, bees.

§. 17.

What i have obferved in a few words concerning the migration of birds into forreign
coun-

countries, gives me an opportunity of illu-
ftrating this fubject farther by inftances.

The *ftarling*, Fn. 183. finding with us after the
middle of fummer worms in lefs plenty, yearly
goes inot Schonen, Germany and Denmark.

The *female chaffinches* every winter about
Michaelmas go in flocks to Holland ; but as the
males ftay with us, they come back the next
fpring, unlefs fuch as choofe to breed no
more.

In the fame manner the female *Caro-
line yellow-hammer* in the month of September,
while the rice, on which fhe feeds, is laid up
in granaries, goes towards the fouth, and returns in the fpring to feek her mate.

Our *aquatic birds* are forced by neceffity to
fly towards the fouth every autumn before the
water is frozen. Thus we know that the lakes
of Poland and Lithuania are filled with *fwans*
and *geefe* every autumn, at which time they
go in great flocks along many rivers as far as
the Euxine. But in the beginning of fpring, as
foon as the heat of the fun molefts them, they
turn back, and go again to the northern pools,
and lakes, in order to lay their eggs. For there,
and efpecially in Lapland, there is a vaft abundance of knats Fn. 1116. which afford them
excellent

excellent norifhment, as all of this kind live
in the water, before they get their wings.

The *woodcock* Fn. 141. lives in England in
winter, and departs from thence at the coming
on of fpring after they have paired.

The *fwallow-tail'd fheldrake* Fn. 96. croffes
Sweden in April, and does not ftop till fhe has
reached the White fea.

The *coblers awl* Fn. 137. goes every autumn
into Italy.

The *arctic driver* Fn. 121. goes into Germany
every fpring, and autumn.

The *miffel thrufh* Fn. 189. fills our woods in
the fpring, but leaves us in the winter.

The *pied chaffinch* Syf. Nat. 10. 97. 1. during
the winter, being obliged to leave the alps *,
haftens into Sweden, and often into Germany.

The *gulls* vifit Spain and Italy.

The *raven* [1] goes into Schonen.

By thefe migrations birds alfo become ufeful to many different countries, and are diftri-
buted over almoft all the globe. I cannot forbear expreffing my admiration here, that all

---

* The Author means the Northern alps.

[1] I have tranflated the word corvus by raven, becaufe
Linnæus does not mention the carrion crow at all, either in
the Faun. Succ. nor in the Syft Nat. before the late edition.

of them exactly obferve the times of coming and
going, and that they do not miftake their way.

There is a very large fhell-fifh in the Medi-
terranean called the *pinna*, blind as all of that
genus, but furnifhed with very ftrong calcareous valves. (Bell. aquat. 401. t. 401. Jonft.
exfang. t. 16. f. 5, 6. Gualt. ind. t. 79, 79.)
The *fcuttle-fifh* (Bell. aquat. 330. t. 331. Jonft.
exfang. t. 1. f. 1.) is an inhabitant of the fame
fea, and a deadly enemy to the former; as
foon as the *fcuttle-fifh* fees the *pinna* open its
fhell, he rufhes upon her like a lion, and devours her. The *pinnoteres* or *pinnophylax*
(Jonft. exfang. t. 20. f. 3.) is of the crab kind
naked, like the hermit, and very quick-fight-
ed. This *cancer* or *crab* the *pinna* receives
into her covering, and when fhe opens her
valves in queft of food, lets him out to look for
prey. During this the *fcuttle-fifh* approaches;
the *crab* returns with the utmoft fpeed and
anxiety to his hoftefs, who being thus warned
of the danger fhuts her doors, and keeps out
the enemy. That very fagacious obferver D.
D. Haffelquift in his voyage towards Paleftine
beheld this curious phænomenon, which tho'
well known to the antients had efcaped the
moderns. Arift. hift. lib. 5. c. 15. relates,
that

that the *pinna* kept a guard to watch for her.
That there grew to the mouth of the *pinna*
a fmall animal, having claws, and ferving as
a caterer, which was like a *crab*, and was called
the *pinnophylax*. Plin. lib. 9. 51. fays, the fmall-
eft of all the kinds is called the *pinnoteres*, and
therefore liable to injury ; this has the prudence
to hide itfelf in the fhells of *oyfters*. Again lib.
9. 66. he fays [m] the *pinna* is of the genus of
fhell-fifh ;: it is produced in muddy waters,
always erect, nor ever without a companion,
which fome call the *pinnoteres*, others the
pinnophylax. This fometimes is a fmall *fquill*,
fometimes a *crab*, that follows the *pinna* for
the fake of food. The *pinna* is blind, and

[m] This is taken out of Ariftotle, who feems to have
thought, that the pinna grew from that which really is its
beard, and which it throws out upon the adjoyning bodies
in order to fix itfelf. For he fays the pinna is produced
from the byffus, which is generally fuppofed to mean the
beard of this fhell-fifh, and to have been ufed for making
the fineft of ftuffs, frequently mentioned by antient writers
under the name of Byffine garments, and of which they
now in fome countries make ftockings as i am informed.
This notion of the pinna growing from the byffus or beard
is of the fame kind with that which prevailed formerly in
relation to the goofe tree, mentioned by many writers, of
whom a long lift may be feen in the tenth edition of the
Syft. Nat.

when

when upon opening its ſhell it expoſes itſelf
as a prey to the ſmalleſt kind of fiſhes, theſe
immediately aſſault her, and growing bolder
upon finding no reſiſtance venture in. The
guard watching its time gives notice by a bite;
upon which the *pinna* cloſing its ſhell, ſhuts in,
kills, and gives part of whatever happens to be
there to its companion.

The *pinna*, and the *crab* together dwell,
For mutual ſuccour in one common ſhell.
They both to gain a livelihood combine ;
That takes the prey, when this has given the ſign.
From hence this *crab* above his fellows famed,
By antient Greeks was *pinnoteres* named.

OPPIAN.

§. 18.

Deſtruction.

We have obſerved above that all animals
do not live upon vegetables, but that there
are ſome which feed upon certain animalcula.
Nay there are ſome which ſubſiſt only by ra-
pine, and daily deſtroy numbers of the peace-
able kind.

Theſe animals are deſtroyed, but in ſuch a

I   manner

manner that the weaker generally are infested by the stronger in a continued series. Thus the *tree-louse* lives upon plants. The fly called *musca aphidivora* lives upon the *tree-louse*. The *hornet* and *wasp fly* upon the *musca aphidivora*. The *dragon fly* upon the *hornet* and *wasp fly*. The *spider* on the *dragon fly*. The *small birds* on the *spider*. And lastly the *hawk* kind on the *small birds*.

In like manner the [n] *monoculus* delights in putrid waters, the *knat* eats the *monoculus*, the *frog* eats the *knat*, the *pike* eats the *frog*, the *sea calf* eats the *pike*.

The *bat* and *goat-sucker* make their excursions only at night, that they may catch the *moths* which at that time fly about in vast quantities.

The *wood-pecker* pulls out the *insects*, which lye hid in the trunks of trees.

The *swallow* pursues those which fly about in the open air.

The *mole* pursues the *worms*. The large fishes devour the small. Nay we scarcely know an animal, which has not some enemy to contend with.

---

[n] An insect that has no name in English as far as i can find.

Amongst

Amongst quadrupeds *wild beasts* are most remarkably pernicious and dangerous to others, as the *hawk* kind among birds. But that they may not, by too atrocious a butchery, destroy whole species; even these are circumscribed within certain bounds, Firft, as to the most fierce of all, it deferves to be noted how few they are in proportion to other animals. Secondly, the number of them is not equal in all countries. Thus France and England breed no *wolves*, and the northern countries no *tigers* or *lions*. Thirdly, these fierce animals fometimes fall upon, and deftroy one another. Thus the *wolf* devours the *fox*. The *dog* infefts both the *wolf* and *fox*; nay *wolves* in a body will fometimes venture to furround a *bear*. The *tiger* often kills its own male whelps. *Dogs* are fometimes feized with madnefs and deftroy their fellows; or with the mange deftroy themfelves.

Laftly, wild beafts feldom arrive at fo great an age as animals, which live on vegetables. For they are fubject from their alcaline diet to various difeafes, which bring them fooner to an end.

But although all animals are infefted by their peculiar enemies, yet they are often able to

elude

elude their violence by ftratagems and force.
Thus the *hare* often confounds the dog by her
windings.

When the *bear* attacks *fheep* and cattle,
they draw up together for mutual defence.
Horfes joyn heads together, and fight with
their heels. *Oxen* joyn tails, and fight with
their horns.

Swine get together in herds, and boldly op-
pofe themfelves to any attack, fo that they are
not eafily overcome; and it is worth while to
obferve, that all of them place their young, as
lefs able to defend themfelves, in the middle,
that they may remain fafe during the battle.

Birds by their different ways of flying oftentimes efcape the *hawk* If the *pigeon* had the
fame way of flying as the *hawk* fhe would
hardly ever efcape his claws °.

It deferves alfo to be remarked, how much
fome animals confult their fafety by night.
When *horfes* fleep in woods, one by turns remains awake, and, as it were, keeps watch.
When *monkies*, S. N. 2. 10. in Brafil fleep

upon

° As i have, when opportunities offered, meafured and
weighed.feveral kinds of birds, i fhall here fubjoyn a table
of fome of them with the proportions of the weight to the
fail. N. B. By fail i mean the extent of the wings and tail.

I do

upon trees, one of them keeps awake, in order to give the fign, when the *tiger* creeps towards them,

I do not pretend to accuracy, and i imagine it will not be expected on a fubject of this nature.

		Weight Avoidupois.		Proportion of fquare inches to the ounce.
		l.	oz.	
Turkey	——	8	8	$2\frac{1}{4}$
Pheafant	——	2	8	$2\frac{1}{4}$
Coot	——	2	8	$2\frac{1}{4}$
Black cock	——	2	6	$3\frac{1}{2}$
Puttock	——	1	14	18
Rook	——	1	3	$10\frac{1}{4}$
Partridge	——	1	1	3
Ivy owl	——	0	15	9
Ring-dove	——	0	14	10
Woodcock	——	0	10	6
Small hawk	—	0	$6\frac{3}{4}$	26
Wood-pecker	—	0	4	9
Cuckow	——	0	4	18
Miffel bird	——	0	4	14
Snipe	——	0	4	$9\frac{1}{4}$
Redfhank	——	0	4	9
Crofs bill	——	0	$1\frac{1}{2}$	$11\frac{3}{4}$
Houfe fwallow	—	0	1	18
Houfe fparrow	—	0	1	12
Wheat-ear	——	0	1	14
Linnet	——	0	$0\frac{1}{2}$	$20\frac{1}{4}$
Black cap	——	0	$0\frac{1}{2}$	18
Stone fmich	——	0	$0\frac{1}{2}$	25
Beccafigo	——	0	$0\frac{1}{2}$	24
White throat	—	0	$0\frac{1}{2}$	17
			grains.	
Long tailed titmoufe		0	95	25
Regulus criftatus		0	76	23

them, and in cafe the guard fhould be caught
afleep, the reft tear him to pieces*. Hence the
hunting of rapacious animals is not always fuc-
cefsfull, and they are often obliged to labor for
a whole day to no purpofe.   For this reafon the
Creator has given them fuch a nature, that they
can bear fafting a long time.   Thus the *lion*
lurks in his den many days without famifhing,
and the *wolf*, when he has once well fatisfied
his hunger, can faft many weeks without any
difficulty.

It appears by this table that the fmaller birds in general
have more fail in proportion than the larger of the efculent
kind, fuch as the pheafant, partridge, woodcock, ring-dove,
&c. and that it fhould be fo contrived appears reafonable on
more accounts than one.   Firft, becaufe fmall birds living,
many of them, amongft fhrubs and bufhes, are obliged to
make fhort and quick motions in hopping from bough to
bough, at which time they always make ufe of their wings;
fome of them live chiefly on worms and flies, which are not
to be caught without great nimblenefs, and frequent gardens
and houfes and are more liable to the attacks of cats and
other animals.   And thofe which live in the open fields are
expofed to the hawk, and were they not quick at turning
they would fcarcely ever efcape.
Again the different proportions of the bulk to the furface
in large and fmall birds is to the difadvantage of the latter,
on account of the greater proportional refiftance of the air,
and this wanted fome compenfation.
More might be added on this fubject, but i am afraid moft
readers will think what i have already faid is more than
enough.
   * Maregraf. Braf. 227. Biberg.

If

If we confider the end for which it pleafed the Supreme Being to conftitute fuch an order of nature, that fome animals fhould be, as it were, created only to be miferably butchered by others, it feems that his Providence not only aimed at fuftaining, but alfo keeping a juft proportion amongft all the fpecies; and fo prevent any one of them increafing too much, to the detriment of men, and other animals. For if it be true, as it is moft affuredly, that the furface of the earth can fupport only a cer-tain number of inhabitants, they muft all pe-rifh, if the fame number were doubled, or tripled, Derh. Phyf. Theol. p. 237.

There are fome viviparous *flies*, which bring forth 2000 young. Thefe in a little time would fill the air, and like clouds intercept the rays of the fun, unlefs they were devoured by birds, fpiders, and many other animals.

Storks, and *falcons* free Ægypt from *frogs*, which after the inundation of the Nile, cover all the countrey. The fame birds alfo clear Paleftine of *mice*. Bellonius on this fubject fays as follows. " The *ftorks* come to Ægypt
" in fuch abundance, that the fields, and mea-
" dows are white with them. Yet the Ægyp-
" tians are not difpleafed with this fight; as

* Mufchenbr.

I 4

" *frogs*

" *frogs* are generated in fuch numbers there,
" that did not the *ftorks* devour them, they
" would over-run every thing. Befides they
" alfo catch, and eat *ferpents*. Between Belba
" and Gaza the fields of Paleftine are often
" defert on account of the abundance of *mice*,
" and *rats*; and were they not deftroyed by the
" *falcons*, that come here, by inftinct, the in-
" habitants could have no harveft.

The *white fox* S. N. 8. 7. is of equal advantage
in the Lapland alps; as he deftroys the Norway
rats, F. N. 26. which are generated there in great
abundance; and thus hinders them from increafing too much in proportion, which would
be the deftruction of vegetables.

It is fufficient for us, that nothing is made
by Providence in vain, and that whatever is
made, is made with fupreme wifdom. For it
does not become us to pry too boldly into all the
defigns of God. Let us not imagine, when
thefe rapacious animals fometimes do us mifchief, that the Creator planned the order of nature according to our private principles of œconomy; for the Laplanders have one way of
living; the European hufbandman another;
the Hottentots and favages a third, whereas
the ftupendous œconomy of the Deity is one
through-

throughout the globe, and if Providence does not always calculate exactly according to our way of reckoning, we ought to confider this affair in the fame light, as when different feamen wait for a fair wind, every one, with refpect to the part he is bound to, who we plainly fee cannot all be fatisfied.

§. 19.

The whole earth would be overwhelmed with carcafes, and ftinking bodies, if fome animals did not delight to feed upon them. Therefore when an animal dyes, *bears, wolves, foxes, ravens*, &c. do not lofe a moment till they have taken all away. But if a *horfe* e. g. dyes near the public road, you will find him, after a few days, fwoln, burft, and at laft filled with innumerable *grubs* of carnivorous *flies*, by which he is entirely confumed, and removed out of the way, that he may not become a nufance to paffengers by his poifonous ftench.

When the carcafes of fifhes are driven upon the fhore, the voracious kinds, fuch as the *thornback*, the *hound fifh*, the *conger eel*, &c. gather about and eat them. But becaufe the flux, and reflux

reflux foon change the ftate of the fea, they themfelves are often detained in pits, and become a prey to the wild beafts, that frequent the fhores. Thus the earth is not only kept clean from the putrefaction of carcafes, but at the fame time by the œconomy of nature the neceffaries of life are provided for many animals. In the like manner many *infects* at once promote their own good, and that of other animals. Thus *knats* lay their eggs in ftagnant, putrid and ftinking waters, and the *grubs* that arife from thefe eggs clear away all the putrefaction; and this will eafily appear, if any one will make the experiment by filling two veffels with putrid water, leaving the *grubs* in one, and taking them all out of the other. For then he will foon find the water, that is full of *grubs*, pure and without any ftench, while the water that has no *grubs* will continue ftinking.

Lice increafe in a wonderfull manner in the heads of children, that are fcabby, nor are they without their ufe, for they confume the redundant humours.

The *beetle* kind in fummer extract all moift and glutinous matter out of the dung of cattle, ſo that it becomes like duſt, and is ſpread by the wind over the ground. Were it not for this, the vegetables that lye under the dung, would be ſo far from thriving, that all that ſpot would be rendered barren.

As the excrements of *dogs* is of ſo filthy and ſeptic a nature, that no *inſect* will touch them, and therefore they cannot be diſperſed by that means, care is taken that theſe animals ſhould exonerate upon ſtones, trunks of trees, or ſome high place, that vegetables may not be hurt by them.

Cats bury their dung. Nothing is ſo mean, nothing ſo little, in which the wonderfull order, and wiſe diſpoſition of nature does not ſhine forth.

§. 20.

Laſtly; all theſe treaſures of nature ſo art-fully contrived, ſo wonderfully propagated, ſo providentially ſupported throughout her three kingdoms, ſeem intended by the Creator for the ſake of man. Every thing may be made ſubſervient to his uſe, if not immediately, yet mediately, not ſo to that of other animals. By the help of reaſon man tames the fierceſt animals,

mals, purſues and catches the ſwifteſt, nay he is able to reach even thoſe, which lye hid in the bottom of the ſea.

By the help of reaſon he increaſes the number of vegetables immenſely, and does that by art, which nature, left to herſelf, could ſcarcely effeĉt. By ingenuity he obtains from vegetables whatever is convenient or neceſſary for food, drink, cloathing, medicine, navigation, and a thouſand other purpoſes.

He has found the means of going down into the abyſs of the earth, and almoſt ſearching its very bowels. With what artifice has he learned to get fragments from the moſt rocky mountains, to make the hardeſt ſtones fluid like water; to ſeparate the uſefull metal from the uſeleſs droſs, and to turn the fineſt ſand to ſome uſe! In ſhort when we follow the ſeries of created things, and conſider how providentially one is made for the ſake of another, the matter comes to this, that all things are made for the ſake of man; and for this end more eſpecially, that he by admiring the works of the Creator ſhould extoll his glory, and at once enjoy all thoſe things, of which he ſtands in need, in order to paſs his life conveniently and pleaſantly.

§. 20.

§. 21.

This fubject concerning the œconomy of nature, a very fmall part of which i have lightly
touched upon, is of fuch importance and dignity, that if it were to be properly treated in
all its parts, men would find wherewithal to
employ almoft all the powers of the mind. Nay
time itfelf would fail before even the moft
acute human fagacity would be able to difcover the amazing œconomy, laws, and ex-
quifite ftructure of the leaft infect, fince as
Pliny obferves, nature no where appears more
herfelf, than in her moft minute works. Every
fpecies of created beings deferves to engrofs one
examiner.

If according to grofs calculation we reckon
in the world 20000 fpecies of *vegetables*, 3000
of *worms*, 12000 of *infects*, 200 of *amphibious animals*, 2600 of *fifhes*, 2000 of *birds* P,
200 of *quadrupeds*; the whole fum of the fpecies of living creatures will amount to 40000.
Out of thefe our countrey has fcarcely 3000,

P How the author came to reckon 2000 fpecies of birds
in the world i cannot guefs, for in the Syft. Nat. Linn. edit.
6. there are only about 150 mentioned, and in the laft edition of that book not above 550.

for

for we have difcovered only about 1200 native plants, and about 1400 fpecies of animals. We of the human race, who were created to praife and adore our Creator, unlefs we choofe to be mere idle fpectators, fhould and in duty ought to be affected with nothing fo much as the pious confideration of this glorious palace. Moft certainly if we were to improve and polifh our minds by the knowledge of thefe things ; we fhould befides the great ufe which would accrue to our œconomy, difcover the more excellent œconomy of nature, and more ftrongly admire it when difcovered.

Omnium elementorum alterni recurfi funt,
Quicquid alteri perit in alterum tranfit.
                                     Senec. Nat. III. 10.

THE foregoing piece, though on a fubject often treated by learned and ingenious men, feems to me to contain many things new and curious, and to give a more comprehenfive and diftinct view, as it were in a map, of the feveral parts of nature, their connections and dependencies, than is any where elfe to be found. But exclufive of this or any other comparative merit, it certainly conveys an ufefull
lefson,

leſſon, and ſuch an one as the beſt of us often want to have inculcated.

From a partial conſideration of things, we are very apt to criticiſe what we ought to ad- mire ; to look upon as uſeleſs what perhaps we ſhould own to be of infinite advantage to us, did we ſee a little farther ; to be peeviſh where we ought to give thanks ; and at the ſame time to ridicule thoſe, who employ their time and thoughts in examining what we were, i. e. ſome of us moſt aſſuredly were, created and appointed to ſtudy. In ſhort we are too apt to treat the Almighty worſe than a rational man would treat a good mechanic; whoſe works he would either thoroughly examine, or be aſhamed to find any fault with them. This is the effect of a partial conſideration of nature ; but he who has candor of mind and leiſure to look farther, will be inclined to cry out :

How wond'rous is this ſcene! where all is form'd
With number, weight, and meaſure! all deſign'd
For ſome great end! where not alone the plant
Of ſtately growth ; the herb of glorious hue,
Or food-full ſubſtance ; not the laboring ſteed,
The herd, and flock that feed us ; not the mine
That yields us ſtores for elegance, and uſe ;

The

The fea that loads our table, and conveys
The wanderer man from clime to clime, with all
Thofe rolling fpheres, that from on high fhed
    down·
Their kindly influence·; not thefe alone,
Which ftrike ev'n eyes incurious, but each mofs;
Each fhell, each crawling infect holds a rank
Important in the plan of Him, who fram'd
This fcale of beings ; holds a rank, which loft
Wou'd break the chain, and leave behind a gap
Which nature's felf would rue. Almighty Being, .
Caufe and fupport of all things, can i view
Thefe objects of my wonder ; can i feel
Thefe fine fenfations, and not think of thee ?
Thou who doft thro' th' eternal round of time ;
Doft thro' th' immenfity of fpace exift
Alone, fhalt thou alone excluded be
From this thy univerfe ? Shall feeble man
Think it beneath his proud philofophy
To call for thy affiftance, and pretend
To frame a world, who cannot frame a clod ?—
Not to know thee, is not to know ourfelves —
Is to know nothing—nothing worth the care
Of man's exalted fpirit—all becomes
Without thy ray divine, one dreary gloom ;
WHERE lurk the monfters of phantaftic brains,
Order bereft of thought, uncaus'd effects,

                           Fate

Fate freely acting, and unerring Chance.
WHERE meanlefs matter to a chaos finks
Or fomething lower ftill, for without thee
It crumbles into atoms void of force,
Void of refiftance — it eludes our thought.
WHERE laws eternal to the varying code
Of felf-love dwindle. Intereft, paffion, whim
Take place of right, and wrong, the golden chain
Of beings melts away, and the mind's eye
Sees nothing but the prefent. All beyond
Is vifionary guefs — is dream — is death.

ON THE

FOLIATION of TREES.

.

.

K 2

XXXXXXXXXXXXXXXXXXXXXXXXX

ON THE

FOLIATION of TREES;

O R,

The time when they put out their leaves.

By *HARALD BARCK.*

Upsal, 1753. May 3.

Amæn. Acad. vol. iii.

§. I.

BOtanifts in every age have not only taken great pains to difcover and give names to plants, but have alfo defcribed them with all poffible accuracy. But this part of knowledge has been, till this prefent age, confined to narrower bounds than it deferved ; for an opinion has prevailed amongft almoft all the men of learning, that it is of no ufe out of the re-

K 3

gions

gions of medicine. From whence it has happened, that we find very few that have cultivated botany, but phyficians; nor have even
thefe carried their inquiries farther than to obtain a moderate knowledge of officinal plants.
But in our times fome, who are worthy of the
higheft regard from all true lovers of this ftudy,
have endeavoured to find out, and inveftigate
the vertues of plants with greater care, and
induftry. For thefe men befides medical ufes
have difcovered great, and remarkable advantages accruing from fuch refearches.

However i do not intend to give a catalogue of them here, but fhall content myfelf
with juft touching upon fome few things, that
have been done in this way, in our own univerfity. In the *Philofophia Botanica* our illuftrious prefident has fhewn, that every foil has
its own peculiar plants, which we fhould feek
for in vain any where elfe ; and that certain
plants keep, as it were, their watches, i. e.
expand their flowers and clofe them again at
ftated times [q]. The differtation on the *ef-
poufals of plants* has imparted to the learned
world the ufe of various phænomena, which

[q] Vid. Philof. Botan. p. 263. 273. Barck.   This curious
fubject is amply treated in Amæn. Acad. vol. 4.

occur

occur in the fœcundation of plants. The *Flora œconomica* has faithfully set forth the use of plants in private life. The differtation on the *buds of plants* has opened to us the caufe, why various trees cannot bear the fnows, and frofts of our part of the world. From the effay on the *efculent plants* of our countrey we find, that there are many plants growing with us, which are proper for food, hitherto over-looked. In the *Swedifh Pan* it is fhewn, that certain plants only are deftined for fuftenance to certain animals. From the *Hofpita Infecto-rum Flora* we are informed that certain vege-tables are eat by certain fpecies of infects.

It is now the fourth year fince our illuftrious prefident exhorted his countreymen to obferve with all care and diligence, at what time every tree expands its buds, and unfolds its leaves; imagining, and not without good reafon, that our countrey would fome time or other, from obfervations of this kind made in different places, reap fome new, and perhaps unexpected advantage. Upon this admonition, i at that time living in Smoland with that noble perfon G. A. Witting major, and knight of the mi-litary order, was incited to obferve for the fpace of three years, beginning from the year

1750, the days when different trees began to put out their leaves, when the countreymen fowed their fields, and how much time there paffed between feed time, and harveft. This i did with intent, if poffible, to find out fixed laws by which to regulate the proper feed-time in every province. But the few obfervations, which i was able to make, were not fufficient for this purpofe ; that the work therefore which i meditated might not reft upon too flight a foundation, our prefident communicated all the papers fent to him from different places for my examination. Such then is the defign of this effay, and i fubmit it to the candid reader, hoping that he will look upon it with an indulgent eye.

§. 2.

Our lands, which lye under a cold fky, are bound up with froft all the winter. Hence the roots of our plants oppreffed, as it were, with a drowfy fleep, are benummed, and many herbs, that remain above ground, dye [r]. But when

---

[r] We have had five winters remarkably fevere in Sweden, viz. 1665, $\frac{1681}{1684}$, $\frac{1708}{1709}$, $\frac{1739}{1740}$, and 1751. The cold of which laft Feb. 1. N S. was extremely intenfe, and fuch as has

when the fun by its mild rays at the beginning
of fpring refrefhes the earth, the fnows melt,
the

has fcarcely been known in this age, for the botanic thermometer funk to 32 degrees. Barck.

In that thermometer the freezing point is 0, and that of
boiling water 100. So that taking it for granted that the
author muft mean 32 below 0, this point would anfwer to 57
below 32 or the freezing point of Farenheit, which is a degree of cold never known in this countrey. I am affured
from good authority, that in the year 1739 the thermometer did not fink nine degrees below freezing point in England.
They who are curious to fee much more furprizing inftances
of cold than that in Sweden, may confult the preface to
Gmelin's Flora Sibirica, where they will find how very apt
philofophers are to fall into miftakes about the powers of
nature, when they truft to theory, inftead of confulting
experience. Monf. Maupertuis fays, that the mercury in
Reaumur's thermometer in Lapland funk to 37 degrees below
freezing point, which is equal to 67 degrees in Farenheit.

Perhaps, fays Linnæus in the Flora Lapponica, the
curious reader will wonder how the people in Lapland
during the terrible cold, that reigns there in winter, can
preferve their lives; fince almoft all birds, and even
fome wild beafts, defert it at that time. The Laplander
not only in the day, but thro' whole winter nights is
obliged to wander about in the woods with his herds of
rhen deer. For the rhen deer never come under cover, nor
eat any kind of fodder, but a particular kind of *liverwort*.
On this account the herdfmen are under a neceffity of living continually in the woods, in order to take care of their
cattle, left they fhould be devoured by wild beafts. The
Lap-

the ice gives way, the froft is diffolved, and a joyfull face of things returns. Immediately we

fee

Laplander eafily does without more light, as the fnow re-flects the rays that come from the ftars, and as the *aurora borealis* illuminates the air every night with a great variety of figures. The cold is fo great that forreigners are kept aloof, and even deterred from their moft happy woods. No part of our body is more eafily deftroyed by cold than the extremities of the limbs, which are moft remote from the fun of this microcofm, the heart. The kibes that happen to our hands, and feet, fo common in the northern parts of Sweden, prove this. In Lapland you will never fee fuch a thing, altho' were we to judge by the fituation of the countrey we fhould imagine juft the contrary, efpecially as the people wear no ftockings, as we do, not only fingle but double, and triple. The Laplander guards himfelf againft the cold in the following manner. He wears breeches made of rhen deer fkins with the hair on, reaching down to his heels; and fhoes made of the fame materials, the hairy part turned outwards. He puts into his fhoes *flender-eared broad-leaved cyperus grafs*, carex veficaria, Spec. Pl. that is cut in fummer and dryed. This he firft combs, and rubs in his hands, and then places it in fuch a manner, that it not only covers his feet quite round, but his legs alfo; and being thus guarded, he is quite fecured againft the intenfe cold. With this grafs they ftuff their gloves likewife in order to preferve their hands. As this grafs keeps off the cold in winter, fo in fummer it hinders the feet from fweating, and at the fame time preferves their feet from being annoyed by ftriking againft ftones, &c. for their fhoes are very thin, being made, not of tanned leather, but the raw hide. It

was

fee the vernal flowers begin to celebrate their nuptials, and the trees, one after another, open their buds, and cloath themfelves with leaves. It is a matter of wonder why the *wood plants*, as the *fpurge laurel*, the *wood anemone*, the *noble liverwort*, the *vernal vetch*, the *broom rape*, the *pafque flower*, the *colts-foot*, the *fage of Jerufa-lem*, *pilewort*, *violets*, &c. and the garden plants, as the *affara bacca*, *fnow drops*, *bulbous violet*, *vernal crocus*, &c. fhould flower in the very beginning of fpring; when we cannot by any pains, or care bring them to flower in the autumn, or after the fummer folftice. For it is remarkable that thefe plants, which are fo very patient of the cold in the fpring, are yet in the autumn fo tender, and weak, that they dye like the Indian plants upon the firft hoar froft [s], e. g. the

was difficult for me to find what particular kind of grafs they prefer for this purpofe, as not being every where the fame, tho' always one of the *cyperus graffes*, but i perceived at laft that it was what i mentioned above. Thus far Linnæus. I will add, that this grafs grows with us.

[s] The iron nights, as they are called in the Swedifh lan-guage, i. e. fharp nights, happen generally at Upfal be-tween the 19th and 3ft of Auguft. e. g. 1746 they began the 19th, 1748 the 17th, 1749 the ift of Sept 1750 the 20th of Auguft, 1751 the 27th, 1752 the 2cth. They feldom

the *blue mountain thiftle*, *touch-me-not*, &c. On the contrary we fee *fuccories* and *thiftles* never flower before the fame folftice, whence the hufbandman judges from their flowers, as from a calendar that cannot deceive, that the folftice is paft. From hence it is evident, that there is fomething elfe befides moifture and heat which promotes the fertility of plants,

§. 3.

In the fame manner trees obferve fixed laws, and a certain order in their leafing; fo that he, who is but moderately verfed in this affair,

seldom laft above three or four nights. After thefe barley does not grow, and about the time they come on, the gardeners do not venture to truft their green-houfe and other tender plants any longer to the open air. At that time the leaves of the *fig*, the *mulberry*, the *walnut*, the *vine*, the *toxicodendrum* and even of the *beech* are fhrivelled up. The Indian plants, fuch as the *kidney bean*, the *African marygold*, the *cucumber*, the *amaranth*, the *convolvulus*, the *tobacco*, the *thorn apple*, &c. dye. Nay fometimes even our native plants, as the *noli me tangere*, the *leffer burdock*, the *bryony*, the *vipers buglos*, the *pimpernel*, the *blue mountain fow-thiftle*, the *goofewort*, &c. wither. But before this happens, the *meadow faffron* puts forth its flowers, and that fometimes fooner, fometimes later, according as thefe iron nights come fooner or later. Barck.

may

may immediately know, when he fees one fpecies of trees in leaf, what fpecies will be next
in leaf. Nor do we hardly ever find this order
of Flora tranfgreffed. He who fhould imagine
he had found the true caufe of this phænomenon in the different depths of the roots of different trees would be miftaken; for then fhrubs
would always be in leaf before trees of one,
and the fame kind; which yet rarely happens.
This phænomenon therefore arifes without
doubt from fome other caufe, hitherto undif-
covered, and perhaps explicable only by the
different texture of the tree.

The order of the leafing of trees with us is
as follows.

1	*Red elder*	12	The *ofier*
2	*Honey fuckle*	13	*Alder*
3	*Goofeberry*	14	*Sea buckthorn*
4	*Red currant*	15	*Apple tree*
5	*Spiræa frutex*	16	*Cherry tree*
6	*Bird cherry*	17	*Water elder*
7	*Spindle tree*	18	*Birch*
8	*Shrub cinquefoil*	19	*Hafel*
9	*Common elder*	20	*Elm*
10	*Privet*	21	*Dog rofe*
11	*Quicken tree*	22	*Pear tree*

23 *Plum*

23 *Plum tree*   28 *Aria Theophrasti*
24 *Buckthorn*   29 *Asp*
25 *Berry-bearing alder* 30 *Maple*
26 *Lime tree*   31 The *oak*
27 *Beech*   32 The *ash* [t]

With the firſt ſoft breeze, ſays Pliny, the *cornelian cherry* puts forth its buds, next the *bay* a little before the æquinox. The *lime,*

---

[t] As i do not know that any thing of this kind has ever been publiſhed in England, i will ſubjoyn the order of the leafing of ſome trees and ſhrubs, as obſerved by me in Norfolk, Ann. 1755.

1 Honey ſuckle	Jan. 15	19 Marſh elder	Apr. 11
2 Gooſeberry	March 11	20 Wych elm	12
3 Currant	11	21 Quicken tree	13
4 Elder	11	22 Hornbeam	13
5 Birch	April 1	23 Apple tree	14
6 Weeping willow	1	24 Abele	16
7 Raſberry	3	25 Cheſnut	16
8 Bramble	3	26 Willow	17
9 Briar	4	27 Oak	18
10 Plumb	6	28 Lime	18
11 Apricot	6	29 Maple	19
12 Peach	6	30 Walnut	21
13 Filberd	7	31 Plane	21
14 Sallow	7	32 Black poplar	21
15 Alder	7	33 Beech	21
16 Sycomore	9	34 Acacia robinia	21
17 Elm	10	35 Aſh	22
18 Quince	10	36 Carolina poplar	22

the

the *maple*, the *poplar*, the *elm*, the *fallow*, the *alder*, the *filberd* and *hasel* are among the first that put out leaves; the *plane tree* also is very early. Nat. Hist. lib. 16. 25.

The foliation or leafing of the first four named trees, 1, 2, 3, 4, varies very much as to the time, and the day on which they break bud; for as the winter goes off sooner or later, so they are in leaf sooner or later. But this does not hold of the rest, e. g. in the year 1750, in which there was scarcely any winter-weather, but the whole was almost a perpetual spring, i observed towards the latter end of March, that the *currant* and *gooseberry* were in blow about Gripenberg; whereas the last year they did not blow till the middle of April. The *oak*, and the *ash* seldom shew their leaves before the night frosts are over[v]. For which reason gardeners do not venture to trust their house plants to the open air, till the leaves of the last trees give sign of a mild winter.

[v] This agrees with lord Bacon's observations, Nat. Hist. p. 146. that a long winter makes the earlier and later flowers come together. This i observed was the case in the year 1755, when the spring was very backward. The author says in a note, that it has been observed for above ten years past, that the oak has been always in leaf before the end of May, in Upland.

3

§. 4.

§. 4.

The prudent hufbandman will above all things watch with the greateft care the proper time for fowing ; becaufe this with the Divine affiftance produces plenty of provifions, and lays the foundation of the public welfare of the kingdom, and of the private happinefs of the people. The ignorant farmer being more tenacious of the ways, and cuftoms of his anceftors, fixes his fowing feafon generally to a month, and to a day ; whether or no the earth be prepared to receive the feed he little cares. From whence it frequently happens, that the fields do not return what might be expected, and that what the fower fowed with fweat, the reaper reaps with forrow. Wife œconomifts therefore in all ages have endeavored to their utmoft to fix a certain time for fowing ; but hitherto their labor has proved fruitlefs. There have been fome, who have tryed to difcover the qualities of the land neceffary for this purpofe, by tafte and fmell ; nor have there been wanting to others, who were perfuaded, that the fmell of the earth, and the *fila divæ virginis* *, were infallible figns of feed-time. All

* I do not underftand the meaning of thefe words.

which,

which, although perhaps they are not wholly
without foundation, are yet infufficient for ob-
taining the end we aim at. For the experience
of many years has taught us, that the feeds of
one and the fame fpecies fown in the fame
ground at different times do not produce equal
crops. We have feen even a great difference
between what was fown in the morning, and
the afternoon, Thus alfo while one plant is
vigorous and florifhes, another of the fame
nature, and raifed in the fame foil withers, and
dyes, The farmer often throws the caufe of
fcarcity upon Providence, that means to punifh
an ungratefull people, by ordering the fields
to mourn in weeds, and the corn to mock the
the threfhers toil with empty hufks; but it may
be with truth afferted, that this furmife is
often without foundation. He ought rather to
complain of his own imprudence, and accufe
himfelf that his granary is not better ftored.

We look up to the ftars", and without reafon fuppofe that the changes on earth will anfwer

---

" This looking up to the ftars for this purpofe, was tranf-
mitted down to us by the Greeks and Romans from Ægypt,
where the feafons being much more regular than in thefe northern parts, might be as fure a guide in that countrey, as any
they could follow. But an aftronomical calendar perhaps may

fwer to the heavenly bodies ; entirely negleǎ-
ing the things that grow round about us.

We

be not fo good a guide to us as the vegetation of certain plants ;
fuppofing we could once fix on the proper one for fowing
each kind of feed.   I have been told by a common hufbandman in Norfolk, that when the oak catkins begin to fhed
their feed, it is a proper time to fow barley ; and why might
not fome other tree ferve to direǎ the farmer as to other
feeds ? The prudent gardener never ventures to put his houfe
plants out, till the mulberry leaf is of a certain growth.

   It appears from Geminus in his elements of aftronomy,
that the coincidence of the feafons as to heat, cold, rain, &c.
with the rifings and fettings of the ftars, had caufed a notion
to prevail among the antients, that thefe celeftial phænomena
were not merely the figns, but the caufes of the different
feafons.   This notion, which he takes fome pains to overturn, would never have begun in fuch uncertain climates, as
are found in thefe parts of the world.   But in Ægypt, where
the Nile begins to rife regularly upon the appearance of Si-
rius, or the dog-ftar, where the Etefian winds begin, and
ceafe to blow conftantly about the fame time of the year ;
and in general the variation of the weather is nearly uniform, fuch a notion might eafily prevail in the minds of an
unenlightened, and fuperftitious people.   From them it was
propagated into Greece, where, tho' it muft have been frequently thwarted by a much lefs conftant uniformity, yet it
might ftill be upheld by that blind veneration, which generally
attends antiquity, efpecially amongft the ignorant, and unlearned.   As for the Romans, they went ftill farther, for
without even adapting an almanack to their own climate
and time, they fixed the feafons for hufbandry-work of all
kinds by the rifings and fettings of the ftars, fuch as they
found

We fee trees open their buds, and expand
their leaves; from hence we conclude that
spring

found them in the Greek calendars. To this cuftom Geminus
certainly alludes when he obferves, that an almanack, which
may pretty well foretell the weather in one countrey is good for
nothing in another, as one would think fhould be obvious at firft
fight. Yet this he thought neceffary to explain, and dilate
upon, in order to convince the Romans of their error; for
tho', as Petavius obferves, the later aftronomers went more
accurately to work, the prejudice ftill remained in the minds
of the countrey people, and the vulgar. Whether Geminus thought thofe predictions concerning heat, cold, rain,
drought, &c. which are found in the Alexandrian, Greek,
and Roman calendars, juft in fome of our modern ones, were
univerfally precarious, or whether he only thought they were
fo in fuch climates, as that of Rome, where he is fuppofed
to have lived, he commends Aratus for making ufe of the
natural figns, taken from the afpects of the fun, and fome of
the ftars, as alfo of the figns taken from brutes, inftead of
the rifing and fetting of the ftars, and gives this reafon of
his preference, that thofe predictions, which have fome natural caufe, have a neceffary effect; adding, by way of confirmation of his opinion, that Ariftotle, Eudoxus, and many
other aftronomers, made ufe of them. Thefe predictions
are copied by Virgil, but i do not recollect any place in his
Georgics, where the feafons for ploughing, fowing, &c. are
fixed by the appearance of birds of paffage, or of infects, or
by the flowering of plants, which method was begun by
Hefiod, but never afterwards attended to, that i know, till
Linnæus wrote. Hefiod fays, that if it fhould happen to
rain three days together when the *cuckow* fings, then late
fowing will be as good as early fowing. That when *fnails*

L 2   begin

ſpring approaches, and experience ſupports us
in this concluſion; but no body hitherto has
been

begin to creep out of their holes, and climb up the plants,
you muſt leave off digging about vines and take to pruning.
That when the *artichoak* begins to blow, and the *graſhop-
per* chirps upon trees, which, as Theophraſtus obſerves, was
about the ſummer ſolſtice, then goats are in full ſeaſon, &c.
That when the *fig leaf* is about as big as a crow's foot, the
time for ſailing comes on.   That when the voice of the
crane is heard overhead, then is the time for ploughing.   It
is true, the poet frequently marks the ſeaſons by the riſings
and ſettings of the ſtars, and as aſtronomy, beſides its many
important uſes, is connected with finer ſciences, has ſomething in it very ſtriking to the imagination, and has been
cultivated by men, who had leiſure to make calendars for general uſe, it was natural that it ſhould get the aſcendant over
rules ſurer perhaps in themſelves, and more adapted to the
purpoſe of the huſbandman, but which were deſtitute of the
advantages abovementioned, and were moſt probably looked
on only as poetical embelliſhments.
    It is wonderfull to obſerve the conformity between vege-
tation, and the arrival of certain birds of paſſage.   I will
give one inſtance as marked down in a diary kept by me in
Norfolk in the year 1755.   April the 16th *young figs* appear, the 17th of the ſame month the *cuckow* ſings.   Now
the word κακκυξ ſignifies a *cuckow*, and likewiſe the *young
fig*, and the reaſon given for it is that in Greece they appeared together.   I will juſt add that the ſame year i firſt
found the *cuckow flower* in blow the 19th of April.
    To the inſtance of coincidence of the appearance of the
cuckow, and the fruit of the *fig-tree* in Greece and England,
                                                    i will

been able to fhew what kind of tree Providence intended fhould be our calendar, fo that
we might know on what day the countreyman ought to fow his grain.

The fun acts on the earth by loofening,
warming, and preparing it, as the culinary fire
does on our meat, for which a certain degree
of heat is requifite. For the fun by its heat
drives the juices taken in by the roots thro' the
veffels of the tree, which do not return by circulation, but become more copious by the
daily addition of frefh heat. It. Scan. 23.

i will here add fome coincidences of the like nature, in
Sweden and England.

Linnæus fays, that the *wood-anemone* blows from the arrival of the *fwallow*. In my diary for the year 1755, i find
the *fwallow* appeared April the 6th, and the *wood-auemone*
was in blow the 10th of the fame month. He fays, that
the *marfh-marygold* blows when the *cuckow* fings. According to my diary the *marfh-marygold* was in blow April
the 7th, and the fame day the *cuckow* fung.

I have many other obfervations by me about the appear-
ances of birds and the flowering of plants, but as they were
made for one year only, and there are none of other authors
to compare them with, i fhall not trouble the reader with
them. I have been induced to publifh them for reafons that
i have mentioned in the preface. Vid. the Calendar of Flora,

§. 5.

Nature always takes the eafieft, and fhorteft way in all her works. He therefore who would imitate her muft do the fame. No one, i think, can deny but that the fame force, which brings forth the leaves of trees, will alfo make the grain vegetate ; and no one can juftly affert that a premature fowing will always, and every where accelerate a ripe harveft. Perhaps therefore we cannot promife ourfelves a happy fuccefs by any means fo likely, as by taking our rule for fowing from the leafing of trees. We muft for this end obferve in what order every tree according to its fpecies, heat of the atmofphere, and quality of the foil, puts forth its leaves. Afterwards comparing together the obfervations of many years, it will not be difficult from the leafing of trees to define the time, if not certainly, yet probably, when not only *barley*, but *vernal rye*, *oats*, and other annual plants ought to be fown.

§. 6.

To attain this end there were many, who by the exhortation of our prefident noted, not only

only the time of the foliation of trees, but the day alſo on which *barley* was ſown, and cut; and were ſo kind as to communicate to me their obſervations ʷ. I acknowledge myſelf much obliged to each of theſe worthy gentlemen for the benevolence ſhewn me on this occaſion, and more particularly to D. Torên, who for the ſpace of three years made his obſervations on a tree of the ſame ſpecies with care and diligence; as alſo to D. Eric Ekelund, who did the ſame with the like induſtry for two years. Some perhaps had not always time, or opportunity to make their experiments with the ſame attention; for thoſe, who are detained in cities, often want a number of trees to obſerve theſe things as they ought, and thoſe, who live in the countrey, are often drawn by domeſtic affairs from things of this nature. But if obſervations were made according to the following rules. 1ſt, That they ſhould be continued for *three years*, and thoſe ſpecified, as well as the *places* in every obſervation. 2d. That they ſhould be made on the

---

ʷ The author gives in a note a liſt of eighteen perſons who had communicated their obſervations made in Sweden, Norway, Finland, and Lapland, ſome for one, ſome for two, others for three years from 1750 to 1752 both incluſive.

ſame

fame *individuals*. And 3d. on trees which grow on the *fame foil*, and in the *fame expofition*, as the *field* that is to be fown. Were thefe circumftances, i fay, attended to, perhaps we might be able to form more certain rules for the ufe of the farmer; but fince thefe rules have been fometimes neglected, our bufinefs will not fucceed fo well; for who does not know that the *north wind*, *fhade*, and a *moift foil* hinder the leafing of trees as much as a *dry fituation* on the flope of a hill inclining to the fouth promotes it? Befides many errors have crept into thefe obfervations, e. g. fome trees between whofe leafing there ought not to intervene above two or three days, are often disjoyned from one another by the interval of a fortnight; not to mention the order of leafing § 3, which trees fcarcely, or rather never tranfgrefs, being tyed down to it by nature herfelf, but which often does not appear in thefe journals [x].

[x] In the original there follows a fection which i have not tranflated. The intent of it is to explain a table giving an account of the different days of the foliation of fome trees and fhrubs in Sweden, Norway, &c. which i have omitted, as thinking it would afford little, or no entertainment to the reader.

§. 7.

§. 7.

If we confider the year 1750, we may remember, that the winter was milder than ordinary, and the fpring very early. Whence
fome in Upland fowed their lands about the
end of February; which they fcarcely ever do
in other years before April. I am not ignorant, that the lands in fome of the northern
provinces, efpecially thofe which abound in
clay, require early fowing, that the ground
may be broken with lefs trouble, and that
the firft fhoots of the barley may make their
way through it before it grows ftiff. But the
people of Schonen, and others, that dwell near
the fea, fow late whether the fpring be early
or not; and that fometimes to their great lofs,
for no other reafon but that they received
this cuftom from their anceftors. The moft
northern inhabitants of Sweden find it neceffary to fow, as foon as the froft breaks
up; that the fhort fummer may perfectly ripen
the grain before the winter approaches. For
as eggs require a fixed time for the exclufion
of the young, fo the barley does in different
provinces, to ripen the feed. To prove this
i will produce fome examples.

Sowing

		Sowing.	Harveſt.	Days
Pithoa.	1740	June 4	Sept. 1	89
	1741	May 29	Aug. 31	94
	1742	27	29	94
	1743	27	26	91
	1744	31	26	87
	1745	24	27	95
	1746	26	25	91
	1747	28	23	87
	1748	June 4	22	79
	1749	May 21	22	93
	1750	19	14	87
	1751	21	11	92
			Medium	85

Upſal.	1747	April 28	Aug. 17	111
	1748	29	20	113
	1749	May 6	27	113
	1750	April 16	30	155
	1751	28	24	118
	1752	30	31	92
			Medium	105

Sowing

		Sowing.	Harveſt.	Days.
Naſinge	1750	April 20	Aug. 12	113
toward		May 4	7	95
Norway		19	12	85
		21	14	85
		26	15	81
		June 13	25	73
			Medium	93
Korn an	1731	May 28	Aug. 31	95
iſland of	1732	June 18	Sept. 14	88
Bahus.	1734	May 9	Aug. 18	101
	1735	25	15	82
	1736	29	27	90
	1738	June 3	Sept. 5	94
	1739	May 8	3	118
			Medium	100

From theſe obſervations, which i have produced, and many others, i can conclude nothing at preſent, unleſs that the *ſowing of barley* nearly coincides with the *foliation of the
birch*, at leaſt in Upland, and other places adjacent; and if this ſign is not to be depended
upon every where, yet it would be eaſy for us,
on a due examination, to find out ſome other
tree,

tree, more fuited to this purpofe; and which fome provinces might ufe as a calendar, while the greateft part might confult the *birch*.   It is a popular error, that lefs time paffes between the fowing, and ripening of wheat in our northern provinces, than here at Upfal, and that this happens becaufe the fummer days are longer in the north, and there is fcarcely any night to retard its growth.   But this error is made evident by the grain ripening in as fhort a time in Schonen as in Lapland.   For barley in the champain part of Schonen is fown about May the 29th, and reaped fooner than in Upland.   But why *barley* ripens later in Upland and Weffmania, than in the other provinces of Sweden, is to me abfolutely a fecret.

§. 8.

If a number of future obfervations fhall confirm the doctrine, which i have been delivering, i do not doubt but that we may reap many advantages from it. ´ For then we fhould not want a fure guide for the hufbandman to regulate himfelf by in fowing his grain, and for the gardener to fow his kitchen, and other feeds. What great benefit therefore would arife to the
public,

public, if one in every province would yearly make obfervations in this way, and at laft com-municate them in the fame manner, as aftro-nomers do their meteorological ones to the royal fociety, or academy of fciences?

It will befides be neceffary to remark what fowing, made on different days in the fpring, produces the beft crop; that comparing thefe with the foliation of different trees, it might appear which is the moft proper time for this purpofe. In like manner it will not be amifs to note at what time certain plants, efpecially the moft remarkable in every province, blow; that it might appear whether the year made a flower or a quicker progrefs. For we fee, although obfervations of this kind have yet not come into ufe, that the mower can guefs at the time proper for cutting grafs, either from the flow-ers of the *parnaffia*, the *devil's bit*, the *marfh gen-tian*, or the *baftard afphodel* burfting forth, or from the flowers of the *purple meadow trefoil* withering, or from the ripening of the feeds of the *yellow rattle*, or in higher places from the yellow hue of the leaves of the *leopard's bane*. Would botanifts like aftronomers note the time of foliation, and flowering of trees and herbs, and the days on which the feed is fown, flowers

and

and ripens; and continue thefe obfervations for many years, there can be no doubt, but that we might find fome rule, from which we might conclude at what time grains, and culinary plants, according to the nature of each foil, ought to be fown; nor fhould we be at a lofs to guefs at the approach of winter; nor be ignorant whether we ought to make our autumn-fowing later or earlier. Laftly, the gardener would have a more fure prophet to confult; whereas now he guides himfelf by nothing but very fallacious conjectures.

§. 9.

This is all which i think fit to produce upon this copious fubject, and i hope the candid reader will not be furprifed, that i am fo fhort upon it, as it has hitherto not been handled; and is far from being hitherto perfectly underftood. It is much above my power to go to the bottom of this affair, but by touching upon it in a fummary way i mean to excite men of greater ability, who may treat it in the manner it deferves.

O F

OF THE

USE of CURIOSITY.

✕✕✕✕✕✕✕✕✕✕✕✕✕✕✕✕✕✕✕✕✕✕

OF THE

USE of CURIOSITY.

BY

CHRISTOPHER GEDNER.

Upfal, 1752. October 21.

Amæn. Academ. vol. 3.

§. 1.

A S the three kingdoms of nature were created for the ufe of man, fince to him
alone is granted the prerogative of converting
their inhabitants to his own advantage, fo that
part of knowledge which is converfant about
the creatures throughout the terraqueous globe
is the firft, and chief by which men are enabled
to provide themfelves with what is neceffary,
both for the prefent, and future; and the
more fo becaufe, befides thefe three kingdoms, and the elements there is nothing in
M   nature

nature which can be of ufe to him. All thofe things by which man is fupported and grows, with which he is cloathed, and in which he prides himfelf, by which he is preferved, and becomes infolent; all the pomp, the fplendor, the richnefs, the luxury of drefs, as well as the neceffary covering from hence have their origin. Without thefe things man muft be as naked, as he was created, and came into the world. However obvious this truth may be, there is a common queftion propofed by the vulgar to men, who are bufied in examining the productions of nature, and that with fome fort of fneer; *To what end are all thefe inquiries?* By which they mean to infinuate, that thefe *vertuofi* are at the bottom but madmen, who fpend their time in a kind of knowledge, which promifes no advantage; and in this way of thinking they are the more convinced of being right, as they find natural hiftory no part of public inftitutions, not received into academies amongft the philofophical fciences, and as holding no rank either in church, or ftate. For this reafon they look on it as a *mere curiofity*, which only ferves as an amufement for the idle, and indolent. This objection has been made to myfelf, and almoft all others who give themfelves

felves up to the ftudy of nature, and by its frequent repetition has at laft quite worn out my patience. For which reafon i think it will not be amifs to confider the queftion, and prepare fuch an anfwer to thofe, who for the future fhall not be afhamed to urge over and over the fame objections, as may convince them, if they will take the pains to read the few following pages, and confider them thoroughly. All i defire of the reader is a candid hearing.

§. 2.

The kind of men, who moft frequently afk this queftion ; *To what end all thefe inquiries?* are of a heavy, dull, and phlegmatic difpofition, of weak judgment, and low education. Amongft ourfelves, in great cities, in large towns, and at academies, the fearching into nature ceafes now to be uncommon. Nor is this queftion ever heard among men of folid learning. It is chiefly, and frequently put in the more remote provinces by the inferior order of people ; who think of nothing but indulging their low appetites, and look on every thing as ufelefs, which does not ferve that purpofe.

When electrical experiments firft began to make a noife in the world, Samuel Klingenfti-

erna

erna was fent for by his majefty Frederic the
firft to fhew him fome of the electrical phænomena. When all was over, a man of great
rank, who happened to be one of the fpectators on this occafion, faid with a fneer, " Mr.
" Klingenftierna of what ufe is all this?" Klingenftierna replyed with fome acutenefs ; ' Sir,
' this very objection was made to me by J. C.'
(this J. C. was a very rich dry falter). Upon
which the king faid fmiling, to the nobleman,
i think he has given it you. Such men as thefe
refemble more the brute creation, than rational
creatures. They do not confider, that the all-
wife Creator made every thing for man's ufe.
They forget that every thing, which was created at the beginning, was declared to be good.
To thefe men whatever is curious is difguft-
full, and inquiries into nature are deemed
mere folly.

Ternftóm 'Chrift.) when he went with the
Oftend fleet to the Eaft Indies, was treated
with contempt by fome of the company for his
curiofity *. They thought nothing of confequence, but what belonged to the winds, and
waves.

* Bellonius in his Obfervations, p. 3. fays the fame hap-
pe ;ed to him.

Bart-

Bartfcius (John) when he arrived at Surinam, where he went in order to make obfervations in natural hiftory, was defpifed for looking after plants, and infects. The inhabitants there thought nothing worth minding, but what belonged to *fugar* and *coffi* plantations. Vid. his letters to Linnæus.

Profeffor Kalm dared not at the hazard of his life let the favages of Canada, amongft whom he refided, know that he defcribed any plant or other natural object, but was forced to carry on all his refearches in private.

When our prefident was gathering, and defcribing the *rhen-deer-fly* on the Lapland mountains, the inhabitants wondered, and laughed at him for troubling his head about catching infects. Vid. Act. Stockhol. vol. 1. p. 121, And we find that he, and his companions were ftared at as a fpectacle in his journey through Oeland. It. Oeland. p. 85. 109.

Dr. Haffelquift was forced to have a guard whenever he went out of Cairo in order to defcribe any natural object; and even then he was not quite fafe from the vulgar on account of his curiofity. Thefe examples may fuffice without producing any more.

§. 3.

We were created for the glory of the Creator, which cannot be brought about unlefs we
know him, either by revelation, or the works
of the creation. As to the latter i fufpect, that
many come into the world, and remain here
even to old age, who never faw the creation,
but from afar; juft like the brute beafts,
which cannot fail of feeing the verdure, and
various colors, that cloath the earth, but go
not one ftep farther. This feems to me as if
any one, who fhould be carried into a botanic
garden to fee the immenfe variety of plants
brought together from all parts with incredible
trouble, care and expence, fhould only obferve that the leaves were green, and the flowers of various colors, juft as they are every
where elfe. Could fuch an one be truly, and
juftly faid to have feen the garden ? Or if any
one fhould go into a mufeum, filled with natural objects of the rareft kind preferved in
fpirit of wine, and fhould only attend to the
clearnefs of the liquor, and, though he faw a
body hanging in it, fhould not inquire what
body it was; would not he, who took the
trouble of fhewing thefe fights to fo curious a
perfon,

perfon, think his time thrown away? Would
fuch a fpectator deferve to be let into fuch a
place?

I cannot help on this occafion calling to
mind the manner, in which our prefident ufed
fometimes to excite attention in his audience
by an apt fimilitude, when he was reading upon *infects* to his pupils. The fimilitude or rather fable was as follows. ' Once upon a time
' the feven wife men of Greece were met toge-
' ther at Athens, and it was propofed that every
' one of them fhould mention what he thought
' the greateft wonder in the creation. One of
' them, of higher conceptions than the reft,
' propofed the opinion of fome of the aftrono-
' mers about the fixed ftars, which they believed
' to be fo many funs, that had each their pla-
' nets rolling about them, and were ftored with
' plants and animals like this earth. Fired with
' this thought they agreed to fupplicate Jupiter,
' that he would at leaft permit them to take a
' journey to the moon, and ftay there three days
' in order to fee the wonders of that place, and
' give an account of them at their return. Ju-
' piter confented, and ordered them to affemble
' on a high mountain, where there fhould be a
' cloud ready to convey them to the place they

M 4   ' defired

' defired to fee. They picked out fome chofen
' companions, who might affift them in defcrib-
' ing, and painting the objects they fhould meet
' with. At length they arrived at the moon,
' and found a palace there well fitted up for
' their reception. The next day, being very
' much fatigued with their journey, they kept
' quiet at home till noon ; and being ftill faint
' they refrefhed themfelves with a moft delici-
' ous entertainment, which they relifhed fo well,
' that it overcame their curiofity. This day they
' only faw through the windows that delightfull
' fpot, adorned with the moft beautiful flowers,
' to which the beams of the fun gave an uncom-
' mon luftre, and heard the finging of moft me-
' lodious birds till evening came on. The next
' day they rofe very early in order to begin their
' obfervations ; but fome very beautifull young
' ladies of the countrey, coming to make them a
' vifit, advifed them fi:ft to recruit their ftrength
' before they expofed themfelves to the labori-
' ous tafk they were about to undertake.

  ' The delicate meats, the rich wines, the
' beauty of the damfels prevailed over the re-
' folution of the e ftranger. A fine concert of
' mufic is introduced, the young ones begin to
' dance, and all is turned to jollity ; fo that this

            I   ' whole

' whole day was fpent in gallantry, till fome of
' the neighbouring inhabitants, growing envi-
' ous at their mirth, rufhed in with drawn
' fwords. The elder part of the company tryed
' to appeafe the younger, promifing the very
' next day they would bring the rioters to
' juftice. This they performed, and the third
' day the caufe was heard, and what with accu-
' fations, pleadings, exceptions, and the judg-
' ment itfelf the whole day was taken up, on
' which the term fet by Jupiter expired. On
' their return to Greece all the countrey flocked
' in upon them to hear the wonders of the moon
' defcribed, but all they could tell was ; for
' that was all they knew; that the ground was
' covered with green, intermixed with flowers,
' and that the birds fung amongft the branches
' of the trees ; but what kinds of flowers they
' faw, or what kinds of birds they heard, they
' were totally ignorant. Upon which they were
' treated every where with contempt.' If we apply this fable to men of the prefent age, we
fhall perceive a very juft fimilitude. By thefe
three days the fable denotes the *three ages*
of man. Firft *youth*, in which we are too
feeble in every refpect to look into the works
of the Creator. All that feafon is given up to
                                    idle-

idlenefs, luxury and paftime. 2dly. *manhood*, in which men are employed in fettling, marrying, educating children, providing fortunes for them, and raifing a family. 3dly. *old age*, in which, after having made their fortunes, they are overwhelmed with lawfuits, and proceedings relating to their eftates. Thus it frequently happens that men never confider to what end they were deftined, and why they were brought into the world.

§. 4.

As to bodies, the vulgar are ready enough to admire them in the larger kinds of animals, plants, minerals and metals. But when they perceive any one examining into the minute parts of nature, fuch as *infeéts* and *fhells*, *graf-fes*, and *moffes*, *earthy particles*, and *petrifaéti-ons*, they look upon it as idle curiofity. And when they fee us fearching after fuch natural produétions of forreign countries, as are not found with us, their wonder increafes, and they think then they attack us with double advantage. Since we not only fpend our time in examining prefent objeéts, that are wholly ufelefs, but even fuch diftant ones, as we have fcarcely any means of coming at. They
have

have no notion that thefe can be of any manner of ufe but to thofe amongft whom they
are found.   To the end therefore that we may
gain a clearer conception of the harmony, and
ufe of thefe things, it will be neceffary to run
thro' fome of the moft obvious particulars, re-
lative to this fubject, that every one from
hence may better comprehend the advantage   `
of natural hiftory in general.

§. 5.

The antients were of opinion, that the bodies about us concerned us no farther than as
they were good for *food* or *phyfic*. Hence
their inquiries all tended to find out what were
fit to eat, and what would cure fome diftemper, and whatever plant or animal could not
be referred to one of thefe claffes was neglected [y]. It is true that the immediate ufe of
many

[y] J muft take the liberty to contradict the ingenious author on this occafion. For any one who has ever looked
into Ariftotle's hiftory of animals, and Theophraftus's of
plants, muft at once be convinced of the contrary. This
juftice i thought due to thofe two firft fketches of natural
hiftory, in which the fagacious, and extenfive genius of the
mafter, and the difciple fully fhine forth.   It is true this fpirit was not long kept up, nor is it to be wondered at, that
extravagant fpeculations, and fyftems concerning things out
of

many bodies is hitherto unknown to us, yet we
have great reafon to believe, that all the bodies in the univerfe, fome way or other, contribute to our advantage. *Hay*, which men
take fuch pains to collect in the fummer, is
of no ufe to man immediately, but it is a com-
modity of the utmoft confequence to him mediately, as being the food of cattle of all forts,
without which we could not well fubfift. Thofe
minute infects called *tree lice*, that live upon
the branches of trees, and plants, are looked
upon as of no ufe to us. Thefe are devoured
by *flies, cochineals, golden eyes*, &c. in their firft
ftate; which alfo feem to be of no ufe to us,
but then many of the *fmall birds* feed upon

of mens reach, which are purfued in the clofet with eafe,
and when ingenious are apt to ftrike the imaginations of
mankind, fhould take place of the fober, and painful refearches into nature, little minded by the generality of people, and therefore lying out of the paths of reputation.
Thus what was fo well begun by Ariftotle and Theophraftus dropped at once for want of encouragement, and never
raifed its head again, till after the reftoration of learning;
when Gefner, Bauhin, Cæfalpinus, &c. in imitation of
thofe firft mafters, began to revive this part of knowledge;
and kindled up a fpark, which has never been totally ex-
tinguifhed fince, and has been raifed into a diffufive light
by feveral naturalifts of the laft age, and particularly by the
excellent Linnæus.

- them,

them, and thefe not only delight us with their
fine fongs but afford us moft delicate food. '
The *nettle* is a plant which is fcarcely eat by any
domeftic animal (Iter. Scand. p. 15.) but the
Author of nature has allotted to it more feed-
ers than to almoft any other plant, v. gr. *butterflies, moths, wevils, chermes,* &c. which devour it almoft entirely, and thefe infects are a
prey to many birds, which could by no means
live on the plant immediately. *Minute aquatic
worms,* and thofe in no fmall number are eat
by the larger, and thefe are eat by the fifhes,
and aquatic birds, and thefe by us ; and befides
food thefe birds fupply us with moft delicate
foft down to warm and repofe ourfelves upon.
It would be tedious to enumerate all the mediate advantages, which we obtain from the
moft contemptible; as they are deemed; both
plants and animals.

§. 6.

Many look upon *fhells,* and *corals* of various
kinds, which are collected and ranged in mu-
feums by the diligent inquirers into nature, as
an idle curiofity; fince they neither ferve for
food or phyfic; but if thefe are neglected, how
many of the wonderfull works of the Creator
would

would be unknown ? What man of fenfe is not
ftruck with wonder, when he beholds the innumerable objects, which the Author of nature
has buried, as it were, in the great abyfs. Objects for color, fhape, and mechanifm fo admirable, that they furpafs the imagination of
man to conceive without feeing them. If we
vifit a royal palace, and there behold the walls
covered with tapeftry, pictures, fculpture, and
other ornaments, are we not delighted, and
even in rapture ? We ought therefore to feel the
fame pleafure, when we behold the beauties of
this our globe.   To defcribe every fhell on this
occafion would far exceed the bounds of my
defign. At prefent i will only mention one, viz.
the *knotted marginated Cypræa*. Rump. t. 39.
f. C. Argenvnill· t. 21. f. K. Petiv. Faz. 97. t.
8.   This is a fmall fhell, about the bignefs of
a hazel nut, and is gathered in the Maldivee
iflands by the women along the fea fhore in
fuch quantities, that 30 or 40 fhips are loaded with them yearly for Africa, Bengal and
Siam; fo that in thofe parts there are large
palaces filled with them, where they are preferved as treafures of the greateft value.

Thefe fhells ferve there as gold, and filver
with us, for all kinds of commerce.   In other
coun-

countries other shells are made use of for various purposes; some instead of horns to blow
with at their religious ceremonies; some for
vessels for washing; some for cups; some for
boxes; some for inlaying; all of them far exceeding the best artificial works.

Nor are those innumerable *petrifactions*, so
various in species, and structure, to be looked
upon as vain curiosities. We find in our mountains, and even in the middle of stones, as it
were embaumed, *animals, shells, corals,* which
are not to be found alive in any part of Europe. These alone, were there no other reason, might put us upon looking back into antiquity, and considering the primitive form of
the earth, its increase, and metamorphosis.
This is a subject, that would require a whole
volume to treat it amply as it deserves.

Wild beasts, and *ravenous birds,* though
they seem to disturb our private œconomy,
are not without their uses; which we should
be sensible of, if they were extirpated [z].
When

[z] Thus in Suffolk, and in some parts of Norfolk, the
farmers find it their interest to encourage the breed of rooks,
as the only means to free their grounds from the grub,
from which the tree or blind beetle comes, Vid. Lister's
Goedact. p. 265. pl. III. Scarabæus. Melolontha. S. N. 10.
p. 351. which in its grub state destroys the roots of corn
and

When the *little crow* was driven out of Virginia, and that at the expence of several tuns
of gold, the inhabitants would willingly have
brought them back again at double the price,
as we find by professor Kalm. The *vultures*
in Cairo are invited yearly, and daily to remain there, as doctor Hasselquist relates in
Act. Sac. reg. Scient. Stockhol. 1751. p. 196.
et sequ. These creatures of prey cleanse the
ground from carcases, and make it wholesome,
and pure, and besides they serve to keep up a
due proportion between animals, so that one
sort may not starve the rest.

The vulgar think, and those who think
themselves wiser than the vulgar, make no
scruple to say ; *let him who has nothing to do
employ himself in hunting after mosses and flies.*
By which they would insinuate, that search-
ing after the minute plants, and animals is
unbecoming, or at least unnecessary for a ra-

and grafs to such a degree, that i myself have seen a piece of
pasture land, where you might turn up the turf with your
foot.
  Mr. Matthews a very observing and excellent farmer, of
Wargrove in Berkshire, told me that the rooks one year,
while his men were houghing a turnep field, sat down in
part of it. where they were not at work, and that the crop
was very fine in that part; whereas in the other part there
were no turneps that year.

tional

tional creature.   As for *moſſes*, i grant we have
not authority on our fide; for till the end of
the laſt century, they were almoſt wholly neglected; but now within thefe fifty years their
hiſtory is very near compleat by the diligence
of Dillenius.   C. Bauhin knew very few *moſſes*;
Dillenius has defcribed near 600.   With unwea-
ried pains he went through this very difficult,
and extenſive branch of natural hiſtory.   But
to what end? it is afked.   I will not take upon
me to anfwer this queſtion by ſhewing the particular ufe of every *moſs*, that grows; although i am certain the Lord of nature has
made nothing in vain.   But i will venture to
aſſert, that poſterity will, one time or other,
find as many advantages ariſing from *moſſes*, as
from other vegetables.   I aſſert this with the
greater confidence, becaufe fince our acquaint-
ance with *moſſes*, we have many experiments,
which ſhew their ufefulnefs, a few inſtances of
which i ſhall fubjoyn.   The *bog moſs* covers
deep bogs with its ſpongy fubſtance, and thus
by degrees turns them into fertile meadows;
not to mention its repelling virtue in medicine;
at prefent alfo its turf is ufed inſtead of wood
in many provinces, and it is a cuſtom eſtabliſh-
ed among the workers in metals to burn it in-

N   to

to cinders in their forges. The Laplanders, who lay their children upon it in the cradle, find that it abates the acrimony of the urine. Act. Stock. 1740. p. 421.

The *fontinalis antipyretica*, a kind of *mofs*, contrary to the nature of all other *moffes*, guards the walls of houfes in cafe of fire. It. Scand. p. 20.

The *maiden-hair* furnifhes a very convenient bed to the Laplander, and the *bear* with this prepares his winter habitation. Moft of our *tumps* confift of this kind of *mofs*.

The *club-mofs* is ufed for making mats.

The *cyprefs-mofs* furnifhes a yellow dye.

The upright *fir-mofs* frees cattle from vermin, and purges ftrongly. It. Oel. p. 28.

The *fountain-mofs* points out cool fprings.

The *hypnum proliferum*, a kind of *mofs*, covers the ground in fhady places, where no other plant will grow. Iter. Oeland. p. 28.

The *hypnum parietinum* ferves for ftoppiag crevifes in walls.

All the kinds of *hypna* and *brya* [z] cover the earth with green, and keep it from being quite naked, as in beech groves and in the woods of both the Indies. They preferve the minute feeds of plants during the winter, fhelter their

---

[z] Names of *moffes*.

roots

roots and keep them from freezing; and gardeners gather *moffes* in the autumn, in order to preferve their plants from the froft; they are gathered by the birds to build their nefts; they grow in the moft barren foil; by degrees they rot towards the bottom, and thus lay a foundation for fertility.

The *bryum hypnoides* covers the rocks in the coldeft mountains.

The *mnium hygrometricum* fhews the drinefs, and moifture of the atmofphere.

Some kinds of *brya* cover the mountains, others the marfhes, fome are ufefull in moift meadow ground, fome fpread over the naked fields, fome are found upon ftones, and rocks, others on trunks of trees; and all of them bear the moft fevere winter, when the generality of other plants grow fickly.

§. 7.

As to the *lichens* or *liverworts*, they are not of lefs ufe; for many of them afford a beautifull dye. e. g. the *roccella* yields a moft valuable red color, Act. Soc. reg. Scien. 1742. p. 21. to which purpofe the *lichen tartareus* ferves as a fuccedaneum. The *lichenes ftygius, onuphalodes*, &c. afford alfo a red dye, and the

lichenes

lichenes croceus, vulpinus a good yellow. There is no doubt, but that many colors in procefs of time may be obtained from this kind of plants.

If we confider the vertues of the *lichenes* or *liverworts* upon animate bodies taken internally, they are not inconfiderable. The *lichen vulpinus* is a deadly poifon to wolves. It. Scan. p. 40. The *lichen pyxidatus*, or *cup-mofs*, is efficacious in the hooping cough. The *lichen jubatus*, or *rock-hair* in exulcerations of the fkin. The *lichen omphalodes* in ftopping hæmorrhages. The *lichen aphthofus* in thrufhes, and againft worms. The *lichen caninus* or *afh-colored ground liverwort*, in the hydrophia and madnefs. The *lichen pulmonarius*, or *lungwort*, is found to be good in confumptions. The œconomical ufe of the *lichens* is of no fmall confequence. e. g. the *lichen rangiferinus* affords the moft delicious pafture to the rhen-deer. Upon this the whole œconomy of the Laplander turns, and by the help of this many millions of men are fupported. This *lichen* is alfo given to other cattle by the people of Norland. Act. Soc. reg. 1742. p. 153. Some of the kinds of *lichens* are the delight of *goats*. The moft barren woods, where no other plants grow, afford us the

lichen

lichen iſlandicus, which in times of ſcarcity ſerves inſtead of bread. Act. Soc. reg. Sc. 1742. p. 154.

The *lichen prunaſtri*, or *plumb-liverwort*, is ground to powder for the hair.

The *lichen puſtulatus* may be converted into a very black pigment. The very *ſmall lichens* called *leproſus*, cover barren rocks, and makes them look pleaſant; it gives birth to black mould, and conſequently affords the firſt degree of vegetative power. After all this can any one juſtly ſay that the knowledge of theſe plants is uſeleſs?

The *muſhroom* kind alſo make a claſs of vegetables by no means to be deſpiſed. One ſpecies is uſed in amputations and hæmorrhages, and another is lately come into reputation for ſtopping the bleeding of arteries; inſomuch that the inventor of this uſe of it was amply rewarded for the diſcovery.

The *trufle* and *phalli* contribute to make our ſoups more delicate, and are commonly uſed at the tables of the great. Many *muſhrooms* are eat by the Muſcovites and the inhabitants of other countries, but ſome of them are a moſt deadly poiſon; ſo that it is of the utmoſt conſequence not to commit miſtakes in this part of knowledge.

N 3   There

There is a *mushroom* called *agaricus mufca-rius*, on account of its driving away flies, and the fame plant is the fafeft remedy hitherto difcovered to deftroy the *bug*. Thus the know-ledge of thefe plants is of great ufe to man.

§. 8.

* The *graffes* alfo are a kind of plants of great value, as affording food for cattle.

The *reed canary grafs* ferves for thatching houfes.

The *meadow fox-tail grafs* is an excellent *grafs*, which may be fown to advantage in low meadows. It. Oel. p. 156.

The *turfy-hair* caufes the meadows in the regio cuprimontana to be fo extremely fertile. Act. Soc. R.S. 1742. p. 30.

The *water meadow* is a large and very ufe-full *grafs*, which grows by the fides of moft ditches and rivers. It. W. Goth. p. 41.

The *narrow-leaved meadow* is the moft com-mon pafture in our parts.

The *feed of the flote* or *manna grafs*, affords a very pleafing and wholefome nourifhment to man.

---

* Who is curious to know more of thefe graffes may con-fult the laft piece in the book, intitled, *Obfervations on graffes*.

The

The *sheep's fescue* makes our sheep very fat.

The *perennial darnel* is the best *grass* for *hay* on chalky hills.

The *sea lyme-grass* and *sea mat-grass* keep the sands on barren maritime tracts from being blown away.

The most minute seeds of *grass* afford nourishment to small birds. The *grasses* besides give a most agreeable color to the earth, and fill up the intervals between plants of other kinds; so that they serve both for pleasure, and utility. The Creator has assigned certain species of *grass* to every different species of soil, which the husbandman is obliged to know in order to make the most advantage of his lands. Besides certain *grasses* are eat by some animals, and left untouched by others; so that without the knowledge of these he cannot avoid falling into error. It. Scand.

§. 9.

He that would exercise the art of husbandry with the greatest advantage, ought to endeavor to get acquainted with all kinds of vegetables, and find out what sort of soil suits each of them best. He ought to know, that some delight in open and exposed situations, others in shady; some in moist ground, others

in dry; that some plants thrive moſt in ſandy
ſoils, others in claiey, others in black mould,
others in ſpungy ground, others in watry;
ſome ought to be ſown in pools, others on
the tops of hills.

Thoſe barren deſarts called Alvacu on the
mountains of Oeland, It. Oel. p. 206. had long
ago been covered with the *crocus*, from whence
the inhabitants might have reaped great benefit, if the nature of that plant had been
known to them. Our alps, that are more
than a hundred miles long, had not remained
to this day a mere waſte, if our induſtrious
huſbandmen, who not long ſince began to
improve the œconomical arts, had known how
to cultivate ſuch plants as might have been
uſefull in food, or phyſic; and if they had
known what uſefull trees, and herbs grow
on the forreign alps, viz. the Swiſs, the Sibirian, the Pyrenean, the Valeſian, &c. from
whence they ought to have got ſeed.

The banks of our lakes produce ſcarcely
any thing but *ruſhes, horſetail, water lilly, pond-
weeds, reeds*, &c. where nevertheleſs a great
number of plants fit for food might be ſown,
ſuch as *zizany* of Canada, *water caltrops*, &c.

Every province has its plants, which choak
the

the grain, and render the fields foul, and poor. It. Scand. p. 421. Books of hufbandry are full of inventions how to break the earth by inftruments, and fit it to receive the feed; this kind of knowledge is infufficient, as long as the hufbandman is unacquainted with the nature of thofe various herbs, to which agriculture ought to be adapted. From hence the neceffity of natural hiftory appears.

§. 10.

It is alfo neceffary for the hufbandman to know the duration of every plant he fows in his fields, and meadows, viz. whether it be perennial, biennial, or annual. He who wants to know the ufe of our plants in œconomy, and how few there are, whofe ufe is hitherto difcovered, let him look over the *Flora œconomica.* Amæn. Academ. vol. 1 *.

We fee how many in a time of dearth fuffer for want, fall into difeafes, and even perifh,

---

* The piece here referred to is full of new obfervations on the ufes of plants hitherto not attended to. I wifh i could have made fuch a tranflation of it, as could have been inftructive or entertaining to the public; but a long lift of the names of plants, which could have conveyed no ideas to fuch readers, as this work is intended for, muft have been very tedious, and very ufelefs.

for

for no other reafon but becaufe they do not know what plants are eatable, and how great a plenty there is of them in our countrey, of which D. Hiorth in this volume has given an account, which the moſt illuſtrious fenator Baron Lowenheilm has tranflated into Swe- diſh. Many people wonder, why the curious enquirers into nature will give themfelves fo much trouble about exotic plants; but they do not fufficiently confider, that many kinds of *grain*, many *roots*, *legumes*, *fruits*, *fallads*, and *trees* in common ufe with us for nou- riſhment, houfehold utenfils, cloathing, and ornament are originally exotics. Here fol- lows a liſt of fome, which have lately been brought into our countrey from the farther- moſt parts of Sibiria, that contribute to adorn our gardens, and change our œconomy.

Larkfpur, monks-hood, adonis, vetch, cow parf- nep, French *honey-fuckle, aftragalus, othonna, baftard-faffron, greater centory, colombine, dra- cocephalon, fpeedwell, claytonica, flax, hyacinth, lilly, lychnis, poppy, cat-mint, yellow-flowered fage, hooded willow herb, hyffop, wild navew, St. John's wort, fow-thiftle, faw-wort,* &c. From that diſtant countrey we have the *robinia's* and a *honey-fuckle*, that make excellent quick-hedges; from

from thence we have the Sibirian *nettle*, that
ferves for making facks. If we had a more
compleat knowledge of plants, that grow in
the fouthern parts of Afia, and America, we
fhould be able to make more ample, and ufefull experiments.

To preferve our woods we want to be provided with quick-hedges, for which purpofe
many kinds of trees are ferviceable, fuch as the
goofeberry bufh, the *black-thorn*, the *white-thorn*,
the *berberry*, the *fea buck-thorn*, the *alder*, the
fallow, &c. provided each be planted in a proper foil.

§. I I.

We have fome of our moft efficacious medicines, and beft fpices from the fouthern parts
of the world ; and were it not for the curious
in botany they had been neglected ; as the *lignum colubrinum* was for a long time. What
end would it ferve to know, that the *feneca root*
was good againft the bite of ferpents, unlefs
botanifts had alfo known the plant ? And who
would ever have dreamed, that our *milk-wort*
would anfwer the fame intent ? What end
would it have ferved, that profeffor Kalm was
witnefs

witneſs to the efficacy of the Virginia *avens*
and the *monacda* in intermitting fevers, and
of the root of the *ceanothus*, and *diervilla* in
venereal caſes; if we had not learned how to
raiſe theſe plants? Or to what end would it
have ſerved to croſs the ocean, and attain the
American *water gladiole*, if we had not found
out that it was of the genus of our *water gladiole?* The Europeans at vaſt expence went
on buying the *moxa* from China, the *figwort*
from Brazil, and the *jachaſchapuch* from North
America, till it was known that they grew in
our own countrey.

§. 12.

There is, as it were, a certain chain of created beings, according to which they ſeem all
to have been formed, and one thing differs ſo
little from ſome other, that if we fall into the
right method we ſhall ſcarcely find any limits
between them.   This no one can ſo well obſerve, as he who is acquainted with the greateſt
number of ſpecies.   Does not every one perceive, that there is a vaſt difference between
a ſtone and a monkey? but if all the intermediate beings were ſet to view in order, it
would

would be difficult to find the limits between them. The *polypus* and the *mofs* joyn the vegetable, and the animal kingdom together, for the plants called *confervæ* and the animals called *coralline*, are not eafy to diftinguifh, and the *corals* connect the animal, vegetable and foffil world.

Hence the botanifts of this age have been bufied about fettling natural claffes, which is an affair of the greateft importance, and difficulty; but fince the vegetables hitherto difcovered are not fufficient for that purpofe, this part of knowledge is not compleat. It is therefore incumbent on botanifts to get acquainted with exotic plants, that they may arrive at the end defired. If all the *columniferous* plants except the *mufk-mallow* were known, the *turnera* never could be referred to this order, but that, as foon as it was examined, connected the *turnera* with the *columniferous* plants.

Where the natural claffes are fettled we find the vegetables fo near akin to one another, that we can fcarcely diftinguifh them, as in the *umbellated*, the *filiquofe*, the *leguminofe*, the *compofite*, &c. moft of thefe orders grow in

Europe,

Europe, and therefore could be eafily known, and ranged.

He that knows but a few plants gives cha-racters, which are eafy to find out, but are in-fufficient to fettle any thing; and therefore tend to confound, rather than to advance know-ledge; fo that the natural method is the ultimate end of our fyftematical inquiries. Without this all is a mere chaos, and if the knowledge of vegetables fails, all that ufe of them is gone, which the learned in this way might difcover to the great benefit of man-kind.

It is true indeed that vegetables act upon the human body by fmell, and tafte; but thefe marks are not fufficient unlefs we know the natural orders of plants.

Thefe being known, and the vertues of fome vegetables being difcovered, we may go on fafely in the practice of phyfic, otherwife not. It follows from hence, that he who defires to make any confiderable improvement in this branch of knowledge, muft endeavor to get acquainted with thofe plants, whofe ufe he does not know; and thus he is obliged not to ne-glect the moft contemptible. e. g. no body

was

2

was able to form a right judgment of the *caf-carilla*, who did not know its natural order..
No phyfician would have even fufpected, that
our *milkwort* would be ufefull in the bite of
ferpents, and inflammatory fevers, unlefs the
principles of botany had led him to it. No
one has even thought of trying the *mitreola
Americana* againft the bite of ferpents, which
yet without ever feeing it, we may certainly conclude to be efficacious in thofe cafes from the
ophicrrhiza Afiatica or *true lignum colubrinum* [b].
When botanifts knew the above-mentioned
turnera, but were ignorant to what natural
clafs it ought to be referred, no man could
guefs

[b] This root is known in the Eaft-Indies to be a fpecific
againft the poifon of that moft dreadful animal called the
hooded-ferpent. There is a treatife in Amæn. Acad. vol. 2.
upon this fubject, wherein the author Joh. And. Darelius
undertakes, from the defcription of fuch authors as had feen
it upon the fpot, to afcertain the plant from which the genuine root is taken. It appears in this account that it had
puzzled the European phyficians, and what had been fold in
the fhops for it is the root of a very different plant and of a
poifonous nature.

The true root is called *mungos* for the following reafon.
There is a kind of *weefel* in the Eaft-Indies called *mungutia*
by the natives, *mungo* by Portuguefe, and *muncas* by the
Dutch. This animal purfues the *hooded-ferpent*, as the *cat*
does

guefs its vertues. But now that we know, that it is of the *columniferous* order, we may without experience be affured that it is of the emollient kind.

Without this knowledge of the natural orders, the *materia medica* would be ftill as uncertain, as amongft the antients, which is of the utmoft importance to us if life and health be fo.

§. 1 3.

We are ready enough to put a due value on the larger animals, but many look on the minute tribe of infeÉts, rather created to torment, than to be ufefull to mankind. We

does the *moufe* with us. As foon as this *ferpent* appears the *weefel* attacks him, and if fhe chances to be bit by him, fhe immediately runs to find a certain vegetable; upon eating which fhe returns, and renews the fight. The Indians are of opinion, that this plant is the *mungos*.

That celebrated traveller Kæmpfer, who kept one of thefe *weefels* tame, that eat with him, lived with him, and was his companion, wherever he went, fays he faw one of thefe battles between her and the *ferpent*, but could not certainly find out what root the *weefel* looked out for. But whether the *weefel* firft difcovered this antidote, or not, yet it is certain, adds Darelius, that there is a root, which is an infallible remedy againft the bite of the *hooded ferpent*. And this he undertakes to afcertain.

grant

grant that they are very troublefome to us.
But is therefore all care about them to be
given up? by no means. On the contrary
we ought to contrive means to get rid of
them, that they may not deftroy both us
and our poffeffions. This cannot be brought
about unlefs we know their nature; when
that is known we fhall more eafily find out
remedies againft them[c]. The ufe of infects
has been fufficiently explained by the noble
Carolus de Geer, lord of the bed-chamber to
his majefty, in an oration which he made in
the academy of fciences at Stockholm. Another of my fellow-ftudents has undertaken
to explain what damages infects of various
kinds do us, and another now is actually employed in fhewing what kind of infects live

[c] We have lately had a proof that the knowledge of the
nature of infects may fometimes be ferviceable to us. The
fagacious Dr Wall of Worcefter, upon feeing the cafe of the
Norfolk boy, who was cured of worms, by taking down a
large quantity of white lead, and oyl, gueffed that the cure
was performed by the oyl, knowing that oyl is fatal to worms
and other infects. Upon this he has fince tryed oyl in worm-
cafes with a great appearance of fuccefs, an account of which
i faw in a letter from him to be communicated to the Royal
Society. That oyl is deftructive to worms was known to the
antients, as appears by Arift. Vid. Hift. Anim. lib. 8. c. 27.

O

upon every plant [d]. This makes it unneceſ-
ſary for me to enlarge at preſent upon the
almoſt incredible miſchief inſects do us. I
will only in a very few words mention, that
we ſhall never be able to guard ourſelves
againſt them, but by their means. For as
we make uſe of *dogs*, and other beaſts, in hunting down *ſtags*, *boars*, *hares* and other animals, which do us much damage in our fields
and meadows; or as *hawks* may be bred up
to as ſo aſſiſt us in taking *herons*, *larks* and
other birds, ſo alſo we might make uſe of
the fiercer kinds of inſects, in order to get
the better of the reſt of theſe troubleſome
animals.

We ſhall never be able to drive *bugs* out
of our houſes, before we introduce other inſects that will devour them, v. g. the wild
bugs, &c.

We have no eaſier method of deſtroying
knats and *flies* which cauſe us ſo much diſturb-

---

[d] The two laſt-mentioned perſons hinted at are, i imagine
J. G. Forſkahl, and M. Backner, the firſt of whom has written
a treatiſe ſhewing the plants which different inſects live upon,
the laſt a treatiſe on the miſchiefs done by inſects. Both
theſe are publiſhed in Amœn. Acad. v. 3.

ance,

ance, than by providing ourfelves with the *libellula*, which devours them, as the *kite* does poultry. We oftentimes find our largeft trees entirely ftripped of their leaves by the *cater-pillars* of the *moth* kind, &c. but when we fearch after them we find they are all eat up by the larger kind of *carabi* called *fycophantæ*; from whence we may learn, that there is no remedy more efficacious in our gardens, where leaves, flowers, and fruits are almoft every year deftroyed by thofe *caterpillars*, than ga-thering and preferving the above-mentioned *carabi* till they lay their eggs, and then placing them at the roots of trees in rotten wood, till they are hatched. And thus we fhould effectually guard our trees from thefe inhof-pitable guefts.

§. 14.

But if we do not think it worth our while for any other reafon to turn our attention to the works of nature, yet furely for the glory of the great Creator we ought to do it, fince in every plant, in every infect we may obferve fome fingular artifice, which is not to be found in any other bodies; and upon comparing

thefe

thefe together, we may be convinced, that
this does not happen by chance, but was
contrived for fome certain end, viz. either
the propagation, or prefervation of the plant
or animal with refpect to thofe other bodies.
We find how many plants are fenced againft
the inclemencies of the elements, and the de-
vaftations of animals; and how every animal
is furnifhed with fome means, by which it
may defend itfelf againft the depredations of
the reft; fo that no fpecies can ever totally
perifh, which has been created.

Laftly, from the contemplation of nature
we may fee, that all created things fome way
or other ferve for ufe; if not immediately, yet
by fecond or third means. Nay we may fee,
that what we imagine, to be moft noxious to
us is not feldom highly ufefull. Without
fome of thefe things our œconomy would fuffer extremely. Thus were there no *thiftles*
or *briars*, the earth would be more barren.
We ought not to overlook the minuteft objects, but examine them with the glafs; for
we fhall then perceive how much art the Creator has beftowed upon them.

He who beholds one of the *jungermannia*, a
kind of *wrack* with a microfcope, muft be
forced

forced to confefs, that he beholds a moft ftupendous, and wonderful phænomenon. Many
thoufands of people are fupported by rye-
bread, not one of them perhaps ever faw, in
how furprifing a manner its hufks are armed;
which any one, who is defirous, may fee by
the help of a glafs.

The day would fooner fail me than matter,
were i to take notice of every thing, which this
fubject affords. Let this then be looked upon
as the end of created beings; that fome may
be ufefull to man as phyfic, others as aliment;
fome in œconomy immediately, others mediately; fome vegetables prepare the ground,
fome protect thofe which are more tender,
others cover the earth with a green, and moft
beautifull tapeftry, and that perennial; fome
form thofe groves to which we fly for cool-
nefs, others adorn our globe with their moft
elegant flowers, and regale our noftrils with
their moft delicious odors. Laftly, all things
demonftrate abundantly the omnifcience of the
wife Creator, who created nothing in vain, but
contrived every thing with fo much artifice,
that human art, however great it may be,
cannot imitate the leaft of his productions.
If we neglect therefore to confider thefe ob-

O 3   jects,

jects, they would be like pearl thrown before swine. I befeech you then, who afk me with a fneer to what end this or that ftone, plant or animal ferves, i befeech you to awake, and open your eyes while you live in this world. All thefe things are not the work of man, but of wifdom itfelf, which created both thee and me. He has fettled an œconomy in this globe, that is truly admirable by means of an infinite number of bodies, and all neceffary, which bear fome refemblance to one another; fo that they are linked together like a chain. For as in our œconomy neither the plough, nor the hedges, nor the dunghill are fit for food, or phyfic, yet are abfolutely neceffary, fo in the œconomy of nature there are many things, that are as neceffary, but not immediately. Men reckon their œconomy amongft the chief of human inventions, confider then the fublimity of the divine œconomy. You fee therefore that it muft at laft be granted me according to the opinion of divines and philofophers, that every thing was created for the ufe of man, and man for the glory of the Creator. Can you then believe, that any thing can be ufelefs that ferves not for food, or phyfic? The Creator has fo framed

the

the world, that man fhould every where behold the miraculous work of his hands, and
that the earth fhould afford an endlefs variety,
feemingly with intent that the novelty of the
objects fhould excite his curiofity, and hinder
him from being difgufted by too much uniformity, as it has happened to fome wretches,
whofe ftation in life placed them above labor,
and who wanted curiofity to look into thefe
things. Some objects were made to pleafe the
fmell, the tafte, the fight, the hearing, or other
fenfes, fo that nothing can be faid to be without its ufe. That branch of knowledge which
ferves to difcover the characters of natural
things and teaches us to call them by their
names, feems perhaps by no means neceffary.
But let it be confidered that the firft degree
of wifdom is to know things when we fee
them, i. e. to know them by their names; and
without this knowledge fcarce any progrefs
can be made. To know the letters of the
alphabet, to joyn them into fyllables, to underftand words is not folid erudition; yet it
is abfolutely neceffary for him, who would
become learned. Thus the characters, and
names of things muft be thoroughly learned
in order to obtain any ufe from natural hiftory.

We

We find in the journals of travellers, many
things mentioned, partly curious, partly ufefull concerning animals, plants, and ftones;
but thofe obfervations can be of no ufe to us,
till we are able to refer each to its genus;
that we may make them a part of the fyftem,
and know that this curiofity, or ufe belongs to
this, or that object, when it happens to come
in our way.

§. 15.

If man was created to give praife to his Creator; if the Creator has made himfelf known
to man by creation, and revelation; if all created things are formed with wonderfull mechanifm; laftly, if all things were created
for the ufe of man, and nothing but natural
things, and the elements can be of ufe to
him; then it may be inquired with the fame
reafon, to what end any other thing was created, as well as man; the fupreme Being
having created nothing but for a certain end,
and for fome valuable purpofe. We are often
ignorant what that purpofe is, but it would
therefore be impious to fay, that any thing was
created in vain, fince he declared that *every thing
which he had created was good.* Gen. i. 31.

O B-

OBSTACLES

TO THE

Improvement of PHYSIC.

✳✳✳✳✳✳✳✳✳✳✳✳✳✳✳✳✳✳✳✳✳

OBSTACLES

TO THE

Improvement of PHYSIC.

BY

JOH. GEORG. BEYERSTEIN.

Amæn. Acad. vol. iii.

PREFACE.

ALthough phyſic in its whole extent has received great improvements in this age, as moſt of its parts have been diligently looked into and reformed; yet its chief ſtrength ſeems to conſiſt in accurate knowledge of diſeaſes, and medicines, and when we turn our eyes on the preſent times, we find that many ſimple medicines have been neglected; which ſo little deſerve it, that they rather ought to be re-
vived,

vived, and brought into practise. Which being the cafe i have frequently endeavored to
find out the caufe of this common ignorance.
The refult of my inquiries i fubmit to the
judgment of the candid reader in this aca-
demical exercife, which, though far from
compleat, is the beft i could produce, and i
hope it may prove of fome ufe, and meet with
a favorable reception.

Various caufes have concurred to bring
many medicines into neglect.

I.

Fafhion which prevails in phyfic, as it does in
every other earthly thing. Hence phyficians prefcribe according to certain received forms, not
fufficiently confidering, whether the fuccefs an-
fwers. To this muft be referred the frequent
change of remedies.

Brooklime, borrage, buglofs, plantain, faxi-
frage, are properly only kitchen plants.
Larkfpur is fcarcely of any ufe, but to
adulterate fyrup of violets, for which purpofe it ought not to be ufed. *Bugle, mo-*
therwort, eye-bright, poley-mountain of
Crete, are kept in fhops more from
cuftom, than for any good, and fufficient
reafons. The *knot-grafs* is retained; while

on

on the other hand the *bear-berry* has been neglected, though an efficacious aftringent. The *grafs of Parnaffus*, and *fun-dew*, have crept into the fhop by chance. The *carline thiftle*, an excellent remedy in hyfteric complaints, is neglected. Thofe poor wretched plants the *vervains* increafe the number of officinals without any merit of their own, and only fupported by the teftimony of antiquity.

2.

The many theories and hypothefes of phyficians that vary in every age. For men have been vain enough to imagine that they knew the immediate caufes of difeafes, the manner in which medicines operate, and from their principles have undertaken to deduce the vertues of medicines.

Formerly *hot* and *volatile* medicines were ufed in acute diftempers. At prefent the *acid, cooling,* and *diluting* with *bleeding* are recommended. *Mufk, ambergris, civet* were looked upon as moft efficacious in *eruptive fevers,* now juft the contrary. And thus *meadow-fweet, woodruff, mufk cranes bill,* may in their turn come into credit, which now are feldom ufed for

driv-

driving out thefe eruptions; though we may be affured of their vertues by undoubted experiments long fince made.

3.

The negleɛɛ of fpecifying diftempers. Hence remedies, which are excellent for fome difeafes in one man ; nay even thofe very remedies that get the name of fpecifics on account of fome very remarkable vertue, when adminiftered to another, are either of no fervice, or even do mifchief; whereas they would perhaps never fail of a good effeɛt, if the fpecies of the diftemper were the fame. Therefore till phyficians regulate the doɛtrine of difeafes in the fame manner, that botanifts have done that of plants, medicines muft be neceffarily precarious *.

Were any one to fet about curing the *hæmorrhoidal colic* in a *plethoritic conftitution* by *fpirituous and hot carminatives*, which are proper for the *flatulent colic* in a *cold*, and *phlegmatic conftitution*, he would foon find moft fatal proofs of his error. Of this a very remarkable inftance may be feen in

* As well as i remember this obfervation is taken from Sydenham. But whoever is author of it, moft certainly phyfic muft ever be very imperfeɛt, till this grand defideratum be performed.

diff.

diff. med. dni. Arch. Bæck. de medicam.'
domeft.

4.

An hafty and imprudent judgment about poi-
fons, and their difference from medicines which in
reality differ only in degrees of ftrength. Hence
our anceftors fcarcely ever dared to prefcribe
the ufe of plants, which they imagined to be
poifonous.

The *laurel* is neither ufed in confumptions,
nor venereal complaints, though an excellent remedy ; becaufe it is fufpected to be
poifonous. The *pafque flower*, whofe root
is very efficacious in hyfteric complaints,
is gone out of vogue ; becaufe Helvigius
knew a perfon who dyed upon ufing a fyrup made of it ; as if all inebriating drinks
were to be difcarded, becaufe fome have
ᴜ loft their fenfes, and lives by an inordi-
dinate ufe of them. The *lignum colu-*
brinum ᵉ, that is famous in venomous
bites, and the quartan ague, is neglected
for the fame reafon. Scarce any one dares

ᵉ In vol. 2. Amæn. acadcm. there is a treatife on the *lig-*
num colubrinum, in which the author undertakes to determine from what plant this root is taken, and obferves that
druggifts, for want of a proper defcription, have confound-
ed it with two other plants, one of which, and that generally in the fhops, is of a poifonous nature.

recom-

recommend the ufe of the *mandragora*, al-though Schopperus has fhewn its vertues in the gout. The *deadly night-fhade* is not yet brought into practife, though we have great reafon to expect much from it in difperfing tumours of the breaft [f].

5.

The abufes of quacks, and their bold, and dan-

[f] I cannot omit faying a word or two on the fubject of the *deadly night-fhade* on this occafion, as the trial of it caufed fo much noife in this town fome time ago. I know the generality of people look on its fate as decided; and that it is deftined never to revive again; but that is not clear to me. Some of the faculty ftill entertain a good opinion of it, and have feen fome benefit done by it. *Antimony* was once en-tirely difcarded out of phyfic, yet we have feen it fince be-come one of the moft fafhionable remedies in many difeafes. New medicines, and particularly of fo ftrong a nature as the *night-fhade*, do not come at once into vogue. The not be-ing able to afcertain the proper manner of giving it, the uncertainty in what cafes it ought to be ufed, and how to obviate the inconvenience attending its ufe, not to mention many other reafons; thefe, i fay, joined together, are fully fufficient to overturn a medicine of the moft promifing ap-pearance for a time. But whatever may be the fate of the *night-fhade* itfelf, the difinterefted zeal of my worthy friend Mr. Gataker to find out fome remedy for the moft dreadfull and defperate of all difeafes; and the candid manner, in which every circumftance, relating to that affair was com-municated to the public, muft entitle him to the efteem of every humane perfon.

gerous

gerous experiments. Thefe have made many patients averfe to fome of the moft celebrated medicines, infomuch that a phyfician dares not prefcribe them. For fome timid injudicious friend is always at hand to impofe upon their weaknefs, and let them know, that they are going to take a remedy, which had proved fatal to others; not confidering that it was owing to the wrong application, and not to the nature of the remedy.

The *hellebore* formerly cured many deplorable diftempers, but by the errors of quacks, and their immoderate dofes, it has fo happened, that it is fallen into difufe; but the *wild cucumber* and *bitter apple* are beginning to revive again. The bark of the *berry-bearing alder* is a very excellent purge, yet phyficians have been almoft afraid to prefcribe it, perhaps terrifyed by the ill fuccefs of thofe daring men above-mentioned, who gave too large dofes of it. Many of the moderns for a long while dared not make ufe of opium even externally.

6.

The timidity, and caution of phyficians left they fhould hurt their patients by violent remedies.

P   For

For which reafon they give rather mild, than efficacious ones, and act the part of fpectators, rather than phyficians.

For this reafon perhaps the difciples of Stahl reject the *bark*; though from ignorance of botany they ufe the *cafcarilla*, which is certainly a very good medicine in fhiverings, but not totally void of malignity. Phyficians did not for a long while prefume to prefcribe the *wild cucumber*; which is indeed pretty violent, but by no means fo terrible, that it ought not to be ufed even in the dropfy. For the fame reafon they did not venture to ufe the *fquill*, whofe vertue is very great in thining vifcidities; viz. becaufe they did not know the proper dofe of either of them. The *gamboge* is neglected, though the Turks have taught us its efficacy in a quartan; and the experiments of our prefident in the hofpital at Stockholm have confirmed their practice.

7.

Small dofes of phyfic. For while phyficians have been over-cautious in their prefcriptions, they have fallen into the inconvenience of doing the patient no fervice; and to confefs

the

the truth, i fufpect they more generally err this way at prefent; while they order drachms of plants for an infufion, where ounces would be more proper. On the other hand mounte-banks, and quacks, men of an intrepid mind, and invincible impudence, oftentimes make a cure, when the phyfician of probity fails.

If any one were to prefcribe only two grains of *rhubarb* for a purge, he might as well do nothing at all. The *honey-fuckle* is ufed in decoctions, but not in the quan-tity neceffary; for which reafon its ver-tue in purifying the blood is known but to few. The dofe of the *china root* ought to be large, or no good can be expected from it in venereal cafes. Thofe reme-dies which are fought for amongft ve-getables for curing the venereal difeafe are perhaps given more fparingly, than they ought.

8.

The ignorance of apothecaries in botany, who often fell one plant for another; by which means, when the defired effect is not obtained, the phyfician is deterred from the ufe of them for the future.

For *rad. hermodact*, which is recommended

in the rheumatifm, the apothecary fometimes gives the root of the *meadow faffron*; fometimes of one of the *irifes*, which
differ from it in vertue.   Hence the
effect of the phyfician's prefcription being
uncertain, he is at laft obliged to give
it up entirely.   For the *fcabious* they give
the *centaury*, Fl. Suec. 708. For the *bran-
kurfine*, the *cow-parfnep*, 231; the root
of the *toothwort*, which is excellent in
the tooth-ach, is neglected, becaufe the
apothecary does not know, whether it
ought to be taken from the *toothwort*
565, or 518, or fome other plant.   Inftead of the root of the *burnet faxifrage*,
which is a good aftringent in the hæmor-
rhage, the root of the *burnet* is wrongly
fubftituted.   To this may be referred the
miftake of felling the *St. John's wort* 624
for the *St. John's-wort* 625, which is vulnerary and good in worm cafes.

9.

*The ignorance of phyficians in botany, or their
want of care to reject ufelefs, fpurious and improper fuccedaneums.*

We fufpect that this formerly was the cafe;
but now, that the knowledge of botany is
carried

carried fo far, we have reafon to hope, that things will go better. The *acmella* which is very ferviceable in the ftone, fince it is extremely rare, and dear, is to be fupplyed out of thofe plants which are really akin to it. This choice belongs to the botanift: for which reafon our prefident has obliged the world by informing it, that the *fieges beckia*, as neareft allyed to the *acmella*, may be rightly fubftituted in its room [g]; which Dr. Haffelquift has confirmed by an experiment made here at Upfal upon a young man afflicted with the ftone. The fkilfull in botany will eafily judge that the *German leopard's bane*, as well as the *common*, carries fufpicion of poifon; yet the former has been looked on as harmlefs by thofe, who were ignorant of botany, and the latter dangerous. The *daify* is cried up in vain on account of the excellent vertue it is fuppofed to poffefs. Practitioners, unlefs they be fkilfull in botany, will fcarcely allow the *wild rofemary*

[g] Vid. Amœnit. Academ. vol. 2. p. 151. where fome fuccedancums to the Senega root are mentioned, founded on the fame principles.

to

to be a moſt efficacious remedy againſt the hooping cough ; which yet is commonly uſed in this diſeaſe by the Weſtrogoths. The *Turkey baum* is kept in our ſhops, altho' much weaker than the *Canarian*, which is excluded. The *white ſaxifrage* and *dropwort*, tho' neither of them has any extraordinary quality, yet hold a place amongſt our officinals. The *mechoacana* is ſeldom uſed, as being of no great ſtrength, yet it is a very proper purge for infants. The *oak of Jeruſalem* is gathered from the *European* plant, whereas both taſte and ſmell inſtruct us, that we ought to get it from the *American*, as a moſt powerful remedy in conſumptions. The plant, and ſtalk of *black currants*, no contemptible medicine in the *hydrophobia*, in *feveriſh dyſenteries*, and other contagious diſtempers, are now neglected, as the antients have ſaid nothing about their vertues ; which yet are diſcoverable by the ſmell, tho' not by the taſte.

10.

The uſe of compound medicines. Simples are

ſo

fo very rarely ufed, that the vertues of plants
are not known for want of experience.

It is fcarcely neceffary to produce inftances
of this affertion. Whoever turns over
the writings of the antients will be afto-
niſhed at the prefcriptions, or rather in-
dexes, in which numberlefs things are
mingled together. This affair ought to
be looked into, and regulated ; that we
might not fall under the laſh of fome
future Serenus Sammonicus, who might
addrefs himfelf thus to fome phyficians :

Ye jumble in one mafs fuch coftly juices,
So various in their natures, in their ufes ;
That the poor patient, who relies upon you,
At once is cheated of his health, and money.

II.

*The mixing things together of a different na-
ture.* For oftentimes many things are con-
founded together, which feparately adminiftered might affift the patient, and give credit to the phyfician ; whereas mixed they
become ufelefs, one deftroying the effect of
the other.

Thus *watery* mixed with *dry, vifcous* with
faline, glutinous with *ſtiptical, fweet* with

P 4

acrid,

acrid, acid with *bitter, fapid* with *naufeous,*
mutually weaken each other [h].

12.

The ignorance of the natural claffes. From
hence it happens that we cannot form any
judgment, conformable to botanic principles,
of one plant from the knowledge of another.
And thus we are afraid of propofing any uncommon plant, being doubtful what we ought
to expect from it.

Dogs mercury has been given internally, for
want of knowing the natural claffes ;
whereas he, who is qualifyed to reafon
about the vertues of plants, will allow
only the external ufe of this plant, and
in glyfters. The *cow parfnep* has been

h I cannot help applying to this and the foregoing fection
two verfes of that fenfible old poet, œconomift, and hufbandman Hefiod, tho' in a different fenfe from what he ufes
them.

Νηπιοι ȣκ ισασιν οσω πλεον ημισυ παντος,

Ουδ' οσον εν μαλαχη τε κ̣ ασφοδελω μεγ' ονειαρ.

Which i fhall tranflate for the fake of the unlearned reader.
The meaning is as follows. " Foolifh man does not know
" how much the half is more than the whole, and what
" great benefit may be found from the plants, that grow
" every where about us.

ranked

ranked amongft the *emollients*, although not one among all the *umbilliferous kind* that i know of, is famous for this quality. The people of America ought to give the *mitreola*, Hort. Cliff. for the bite of ferpents inftead of the *ophiorrhiza*; which if they were to do, they would hardly ever fail of fuccefs, if botanifts be not greatly miftaken.

13.

The neglect of vulgar medicines eafily to be procured. For we owe the very beft of our medicines to the vulgar, who have been taught the ufe of them by neceffity, and conceal them as fecrets.

We learned the ufe of the *mezereon* in the cancer from the countrey people. The *noble liverwort* is reckoned a fpecific in hypochondriac affections by the Gothlanders. The *linnæg* is commonly ufed by the Oftrobothnians in gouty pains. The common people ufe *pepper* oftentimes very injudicioufly in acute diftempers; in eruptive fevers under certain circumftances very rightly. The countrey people taught us the vertues of the *thrufh-mofs* for fore throats; of the *hop*

in

in diflocations; and of the *tremella*, Flor.
Suec. 1017. for fixed pains in the joynts.
They alfo chew, and blow the fumes of
garlic into infants to aflwage their gripes;
or bruife, and apply it to the navel by
way of poultice [i].

14.

The neglect of travelling out of Europe. Which
would afford us an opportunity of knowing
plants, familiar to forreign nations. And I
fee not why we fhould be afhamed of learning
any thing ufeful from Barbarians.

It is not long ago that fome botanifts, who
went to America, difcovered to us thofe
excellent medicines, the *great water-dock*
in the worft fcorbutic cafes; the *monarda*
in intermittents; the *collinfonia* in the
colics of lying-in women; the *lobelia*, the
ceanothus, the *diervilla* in venereal cafes;
the *fenega root* and *ophiorrhiza* againft the
bite of ferpents and burning fevers. The
celebrated Kalm very lately let us know,

---

[i] Ulluoa obferves that fome difeafes at Carthagena are
become fatal, which formerly were not fo. Which he attributes to the neglect of the Indian remedies. For he fays the
old women even now fometimes cure the *chapetonade*, which
is one of the diftempers he mentions, and formerly never fail-
ed to cure it.

that

that the *water avens* is looked on as a
fuccedaneum to the *bark* by the people
of Canada. The *water figwort* that cor-
rects *fenna*; the *bark*, &c. were communicated by the Barbarians.

15.

The neglect of reading botanical writers, efpecially thofe, who in thefe latter times have
faithfully fet forth what they knew, by certain experiments concerning the vertues of
plants.

Of this kind are Rheede, Sloane, Feuilleè,
&c. The ufe of the *coris* is unknown
to moft people, who have not feen what
Shaw fays on that fubject. The vertues
of the ftalks of the *bitter-fweet* purifying
the blood were a fecret, till our prefident brought them to light. Before him
the apothecaries gave only the *garden
night-fhade*, or the leaves of the *bitter-
fweet*, yet few here have found any good
effect from them; as we have rarely given
this remedy hitherto in fufficient dofes.
The *reft-harrow* is feldom prefcribed, becaufe phyficians have not learned its vertues in the Hungarian fever from Scyl-
ler. The antients recommended the *cot-
ton-*

ion-thiſtle in cancerous caſes; but from neglect of reading the antients, this ſpecific is almoſt forgot.

16.

Neglect of a method in exhibiting medicines. For inſtance, phyſicians expect thoſe vertues from a dryed plant, or in a decoction, which is not to be found but in the freſh plant, or from its expreſſed juice. Hence it may juſtly be expected from apothecaries, that they ſet about cultivating plants; that ſuch, as ought to be uſed freſh, may be had daily from their gardens.

The *hedge hyſſop*, when freſh, purges very ſmartly and vomits; when old it produces no effect at all. The diuretic vertue of our *water flag*, which is very conſiderable, when the plant is freſh, intirely goes off, when it is kept long. Therefore we ought to expect this vertue from the expreſſed juice, and not from a decoction of it. The *ſtone crop*, when dry, has none of that efficacy in the ſcurvy, which is found in it, when freſh. The ſame may be ſaid of the *houſe-leek*, the juice of which is celebrated by the Hottentots. The *radiſh*, the *ſcurvy-graſs*, the *horſe radiſh*, the *garden, water*, and

and *Indian crefs*, and the *all-fawce*, ought to be fold in the fhops frefh, and not dryed; in order to be of any fervice in the fcurvy. The *recent* root of the *rofe-wort* is vaftly fuperior to the *dry* in head-achs. Befides it ought carefully to be confidered in what part of a plant its vertue refides. Thus it is the *juice* of the *poppy*, that fpreads over the brain, as it were, a Lethean drowfinefs; and not the *feeds*, for thefe are eatable. The fagacity of the moderns has reduced the immenfe number of diftilled waters to a very fmall lift.

17.

Neglect in cultivating plants. Hence apothecaries are neceffitated to fell plants which they have had by them many years, and which have loft all their vertues.

The *fpikenard* is more durable, perhaps than any other plant; for it will keep its fragrance above an age, as appears by Burferus's Herbary. But other plants are very different in this refpect. e. g. the root of *ginfeng*, tho' a great reftorative, being fo very coftly, is feldom prefcribed; and when it is, it generally has loft its properties thro' age. For which reafon we ought to
con-

contrive methods of cultivating it ourfelves. Inſtead of the leaves of the true
marum, which has not its equal in art, or
nature, the mouldy ſtalks of it are generally found in apothecaries ſhops. But we
would not be underſtood as if in all caſes
we prefer the cultivated plants to the wild
ones. On the contrary the *vipers graſs*, the
goats beard, the *ſuccory* from the fields are
ſuperior to thoſe which the induſtry of the
gardener has rendered more delicate ; on
account of the medicinal bitter, which is
wanting in their cultivated ſtate. See a
catalogue of ſuch plants as may be raiſed
with us in Linn. Mat. Med. p. 212.

18.

*The ignorance of phyſicians and apothecaries in
relation to our own plants.* From whence it happens that they are obliged to procure plants
from abroad, which may be had at home.

Thus our people buy the root of the *roſewort*
and root and ſeeds of the *garden angelica*
collected by the Norwegians on our alps,
and ſold by them to forreigners. For the
reſt ſee a catalogue of ſuch plants, as are
natives of our countrey, in Mat. Med.
above cited, p. 210. If a purge or any
other

other flight medicine is prefcribed to a poor countrey fellow, it muft be the produce of the • Indies, fo that they cannot afford to purchafe it. Hence people abhor the thoughts of employing a phyfician or an apothecary.

19.

The ignorance of many forreign plants. Hence we are uncertain whether thofe which are brought to us be genuine or fpurious; and hence alfo their genera being unknown, we are uncertain about their vertues.

To this head may be referred the *fea lavender*, the *myrobalan*, the *ftarry annifeed*, the *balfam* of *Copaiva*, the *balfam* of *Peru*, the *gum animæ*, *caraunæ*, *elemi*, the *gum rofins* of *myrrh*, *bdellium*, *fagapenum*, the *aloes wood*, *calambac* [k].

20.

The ufual cuftom in apothecaries fhops of providing only drugs of quick fale. Thus they will not procure fome whofe vertues are now-a-days well known, for fear they fhould lye up-

[k] Hence appears one of the advantages amongft many others that may arife from the voyages of the difciples of Linnæus into the remoteft parts of America, and Afia, from whence many of our drugs come.

on

on their hands. It is the bufinefs therefore of the phyfician who has any regard for his own reputation, and the patient's welfare, to require the apothecary to procure fuch plants, as he thinks may be ufefull.

Simorouba an excellent remedy in the dyfentery, the *fenega root* in venomous bites, the *profluvii cortex* in the diarrhæa, the *camphorata* in the green ficknefs, the *auricularia* in deafnefs, the *Peragua* in the diabetes, the *fouth-fea tea* in the fmall-pox, the *ferpentum radix* againft venomous bites, the *wild flax*, a very ufefull purge, are neglected. The juice of the *hypociftis*, and *fungus melitenfis*, altho' powerful medicines in hæmorrhages, and the *herba dyfenterica* [1], which is named fo from its peculiar vertues, have not yet got a place amongft our officinals.

21.

Want of care in gathering fimples at a proper time, and keeping them, when gathered, in a proper manner.

[1] I fuppofe the Inula diffenterica L. Conyza Media. R. 174. is here meant; as i find this note upon it in Fl. Suec. edit. 2. 'General Keith told me that the Ruffians, when 'extremely reduced by the bloody flux, in their expedition 'into Perfia, were reftored to health by this plant.'

The

The root of the *avens*, unlefs gathered in the beginning of the fpring, before the fap by nourifhing, and pufhing out the leaves has wafted its aromatic vertue, will by no means anfwer what may be juftly expected from it. *Rhubarb* ought not to be brought into an apothecary's fhop under ten years from the time of its gathering. The flowers of the St. *John's wort* ought to be gathered before they are full blown, that their balfamic vertue may be preferved. The root of the *angelica* is good for nothing unlefs it be gathered in the winter. *Sloes* ought to be gathered before they are ripe, and the juice preffed out of them in this ftate, i. e. before the harfhnefs is foftened by the froft, if it be defigned for an aftringent. *Marum* ought to be kept in veffels well clofed, left the volatile part, in which its vertue refides, fhould evaporate.

―― Still an ample field remains,
But not for me, to others i give way,
Who choofe a longer courfe.

Q   As

AS i do not pretend to underſtand the ſubject of this piece, and therefore cannot
ſay how far the obſtacles to the advancement
of phyſic charged upon the Swedes ſubſiſt in
this countrey, or whether all thoſe obſtacles,
which the author has mentioned, be real or not,
my ſole motive for tranſlating it was to draw it
out of that obſcurity in which it was buried
amongſt many other pieces, relating to curioſities of natural hiſtory. I think i may be allowed to ſay a piece is buried in obſcurity,
which is only known to a few, who happen to
be in the way where ſuch curioſities are talked
of; and an attempt to ſpread it over the nation cannot but be right, if the doctrine be ſo-
lid, and affects our practitioners.

Tho' as i ſaid i do not pretend to underſtand
the ſubject of this piece; yet i hope the learned reader will excuſe me, if i add one obſtacle
more to the foregoing liſt : it is *the notion
which has and i believe ſtill does prevail a-
mongſt ſome phyſicians, that the doctrine of
ſpecifics is groundleſs, and took its riſe merely
from ignorance in natural philoſophy.* I will
not undertake to treat this ſubject, as the importance of it deſerves; and therefore ſhall

refer

refer thofe who choofe to look farther into this affair, to a very curious and ingenious book publifhed not many years ago by doctor Martyn, entitled, *Eſſaies Philoſophical and Medical.* The reader may perhaps find there fufficient reaſons to incline him to lay fome ftrefs on the old-fafhioned doctrine concerning the peculiar vertues of fome medicines preferably to others, feemingly of the fame intention. I will add that the phænomena of chemiftry give continual proofs of the reality of this doctrine, and afford fo many inftances of it, that we i fo inclined, i could eafily fill fome pages with them out of Mr. Boyle and other authors of credit. Ray in his hiftory of plants, p. 49. cites fome very curious obfervations of this tendency from Grew, which are well worth the confideration of phyficians. Upon the whole i cannot help thinking that the want of true and genuine philoſophy ought rather to be imputed to thofe who deny, than to thofe who maintain the doctrine of fpecifics; and that we might as well undertake to open all locks with one key, as purge all humors with one medicine.

Q 2   THE

THE
CALENDAR
OF
FLORA,

SWEDISH and ENGLISH.

Made in the YEAR 1755.

Φραζειθς δ'ευτ'αν φωνην γερανε επακεσης, &c.
Ημος κοκκυξ κοκκυζει, &c.
Ημος δε σκολυμος τ'ανθει κ̀ ηχετα τετλιξ, &c.
Ημος δη το πρωτον, οσοντ' επιβασα κορωνη.

Hefiod.

Absolvent Posteri.

Q 3

PREFACE.

IN my notes on thofe treatifes felected out of the Amœnitates Academicæ, which i publifhed not long ago, i marked the day of the month on which certain trees leafed in the year 1755; and likewife mentioned fome co-incidences of the coming of birds, and the flowering of plants in this and other countries. The inftances i there gave were but few, as i could then find no more parallel obfervations made in other countries to compare mine with. Since that time another volume of the Amæn. Academ. is come out, in which is a fmall treatife entitled, the Calendar of Flora. This treatife contains an account of the leafing, flowering, &c. of a great number of plants, as alfo of the departure and return of birds. As thefe obfervations happen to be made the very fame year in which mine were, and as they are the firft of the kind perhaps that ever were made, i was induced to look over my papers again, which i had thrown by as of no confequence; thinking that in thefe circumftances fome ufe ought to be made of them, as they might prove entertaining at leaft, if not inftructive to thofe whofe genius leads them to curiofities of this kind. I am very fenfible how fmall the number of fuch perfons is, but i am contented to write for thofe few, nay, indeed i write becaufe they are fo few, being willing as far as lies in my power to increafe their number.

But it may be afked perhaps by fome, even after they have confidered all that is faid on this fubject in the introduction to the following Swedifh Calendar, and in the piece De Vernatione Arbo-

Arborum, why endeavor to increaſe their number ? Are there not idle people enough already ?
What ſignifies whether ſuch a plant be in blow or
in leaf at the ſame time with ſome others ; or
when ſuch a bird comes or goes; ſings or is
ſilent ? If we hear the bird ſing, and know for
what purpoſes the plant is uſeful, we know all
that is neceſſary ; every thing beyond that is but
the wiſh, or rather dream of enthuſiaſm, which
wants to give an air of importance to its favorite ſubject.   This perhaps may be ſaid by ſome ;
but the ſame way of reaſoning applied to other
things will ſhew, that it may poſſibly be wrong.
For inſtance, the ſea ſwells twice in 24 hours,
and the moon paſſes thro' the meridian circle as
often in the ſame time.   Now ſhould it be ſaid,
that if we know each of theſe truths ſeparately
it is enough ; and that to know farther what relation in point of time one of theſe phænomena
has to the other, is nothing to the purpoſe ; i
believe ſuch an aſſertion would at this time appear abſurd, however it might have paſſed in ignorant ages.   I think we may aſſert univerſally,
that whenever two things, however diſparate in
their nature, conſtantly accompany one another,
they are both actuated and influenced by the
ſame cauſe.   Now that cauſe may probably operate on other things that lye within the reach of
our powers, and depend on our determination.
Thus that conſtitution of the air, which cauſes
the cuckow to appear about the time, when the
fig-tree puts forth its fruit, may indicate the pro-
pereſt ſeaſon to ſow ſome of our moſt uſeful ſeeds,
or do ſome other work which it imports us to do
at a right time ; and that time may not be according

cording to certain calendar days, but according
to a hitherto unobserved calendar, which varies
several weeks in different years. I do not absolutely assert, that we can come to make use of
such a calendar, but i desire that others will not
assert the contrary at present, but leave this affair to be decided by the only proper way, which
certainly must be experience.

We know from Hesiod, that husbandry was in
part regulated by the blowing of plants, and the
coming or going of birds ; and most probably it
had been in use long before his time, as astronomy was then in its infancy * ; but when artificial
calendars came into vogue the natural calendar
seems to have been totally neglected, for i find
no traces of it after his time, whether for good
and sufficient reasons i pretend not to determine.
That it was laid aside before the time of Aristophanes we have a positive proof in his *Aves,* where
he makes Pisthetairus say, ' Formerly the kite
' governed the Græcians, which according to the
' explication of the scholiast means, that formerly
' the appearance of the kite was looked on as a sign
' of spring. He says afterwards, that the cuckow
' formerly governed all Ægyt. and Phœnicia, be-
' cause when that bird appeared they judged it
' was time for wheat and barley harvest.'

I shall make no farther mention at present of
the use of plants in directing the husbandman,
but take this opportunity of making a digression

* Hesiod himself was one of the earliest of the Greek astro-
nomers. He lived, according to Sir Isaac Newton, about 70
years after Chiron, who formed the constellations for the use
of the Argonauts ; and from Hesiod the gross and coarse method of astronomy was called the Hesiodean method.

about

about birds in relation to their prognoftic nature. Henceforward then, i. e. from the time
of Hefiod, they feem to have been looked upon
as no longer capable of directing the hufbandman in his rural affairs, but they did not however lofe their influence and dignity ; nay, on
the contrary, they feem to have gained daily a
more than ordinary, and even wonderful authority, till at laft no affair of confequence, either
of private or public concern, was undertaken
without confulting them. They were looked upon
as the interpreters of the gods, and thofe who
were qualified to underftand their oracles were
held among the chief men in the Greek and Roman ftates, and became the affeffors of kings, and
even of Jupiter himfelf *.   However abfurd fuch
an inftitution as a college of augurs may appear
in our eyes, yet like all other extravagant inftitutions, it had in part its origin from nature.
When men confidered the wonderful migration
of birds, how they difappeared at once, and appeared again at ftated times, and could give no
guefs where they went, it was almoft natural to
fuppofe, that they retired fomewhere out of the
fphere of this earth, and perhaps approached the
ætherial regions, where they might converfe with
the gods, and thence be enabled to predict
events.   This i fay was almoft natural for a fuperftitious people to imagine, at leaft to believe,

---

* Jovi optimo maximo fe confiliarum atque adminiftrum da-
tum meminerit augur.   Cicero.
Lacedæmonii reges augurem affefforem habuerunt. Id.
Aves internunciæ Jovis.   Id.
Sacerdotum collegium vel nomine folenne. Plin. Nat. Hift.
fpeaking of the augurs.

as

as foon as fome impoftor was impudent enough
to affert it. Add to this, that the difpofition in
fome birds to imitate the human voice muft contribute much to the confirmation of fuch a doctrine. This inftitution of augury feems to have
been much more antient than that of arufpicy; for
we find many inftances of the former in Homer,
but not a fingle one of the latter that i know of;
though' frequent mention is made of facrifices in
that author. From the whole of what i have obferved, i fhould be apt to think that natural augury gave rife to religious augury, and this to
arufpicy, as the mind of man makes a very eafy
tranfition from a little truth to a great deal of
error.

A paffage in Ariftophanes gave me the hint for
what i have been faying. In the comedy of the
Birds he makes one of them fay thus : ' The
' greateft bleffings which can happen to you
' mortals are derived from us; firft we fhew you
' the feafons, viz. fpring, winter, autumn. The
' *crane* points out the time for fowing, when fhe
' flies with her warning notes into Ægypt; fhe
' bids the failer hang up his rudder and take his
' reft, and every prudent man provide himfelf
' with winter garments. Next the *kite* appear-
' ing, proclaims another feafon, viz. when it is
' time to fhear your fheep. After that the *fwal-*
' *low* informs you when it is time to put on fum-
' mer cloaths. We are to you, adds the chorus,
' Ammon, Dodona, Apollo; for after confult-
' ing us you undertake every thing; merchandize,
' purchafes, marriages, &c. Are we not then to
' you on the footing of Apollo, &c.' Now it
feems not improbable, that the fame tranfition

was made in the speculations of men, which appears in the poet's words, and that they were easily induced to think, that the surprising foresight of birds, as to the time of migration, indicated something of a divine nature in them; which opinion Virgil, as an Epicurean, thinks fit to enter his protest against; when he says,

Haud equidem credo quia fit divinitus illis
Ingenium.

But to return to Aristophanes. The first part of the chorus from whence the afore-cited passage is taken, seems with all its wildness to contain the fabulous cant, which the augurs made use of in order to account for their impudent impositions on mankind. It sets out with a cosmogony, and says, that in the begining were Chaos, and Night, and Erebus, and Tartarus. That there was neither water, nor air, nor sky; that Night laid an egg, from whence, after a time, Love arose. That Love, in conjunction with Erebus, produced the bird kind, and that they were the first of the immortal race, &c.

With this passage in Aristophanes, the account of the oracle of Dodona seems to agree. This oracle was the oldest in Greece, and there a *dove* prophesied, according to the concurrent testimony of history; but according to the explication of Herodotus, this strange opinion arose from hence, that the Theban priestess, who was stolen by the Phœnicians, and carried into Greece, was called a *dove*, because being a barbarian, she seemed to the Dodoneans to chatter like a bird, till she had learned the Greek language, and then she was said to speak with a human voice. This
expli-

explication feems to me extremely forced, and
every thing is much better accounted for by fuppofing, that at Dodona natural augury was firft
changed into religious augury; for there the oaks
alfo prophefied; which plainly fhews the firft
ftate of religious augury, when it had not wholly
put off its antient form, but like the monfters in
Ovid's Metamorphofes, ftill retained enough of it
to convince us what it had once been. That
Dodona was one of the firft places where augury
was practifed, is highly probable; for it is
mentioned by Homer as an oracle of eftablifhed
reputation at the time of the Trojan war: now
Pliny tells us, that Tirefias invented augury and
arufpicy; and that he was reputed an augur appears by Sophocles in the Œdipus Tyrannus,
where he is introduced faying thus to Tirefias,
' If you have received any information concern-
' ing the death of Laius from the birds, or by
' other means, do not envy it us.' Tirefias therefore, according to Sophocles, lived in the time of
Laius; and Laius, according to Sir Ifaac Newton, lived not 80 years before the taking of
Troy.

I will here fubjoin an account of what has
been obferved about the difappearance of birds,
which will ferve to confirm what i faid above concerning the effect, which that phænomenon might
not improbably have on the minds of men; and
give room for the fuperftitious impoftures that
arofe from thence. Ariftotle has a chapter on
that fubject; wherein he fays, ' that many birds,
' and not a few, as fome imagine, hide themfelves
' in holes;' he then enumerates the *fwallow*, the
kite, the *thrufh*, the *ftarling*, the *owl*, the *crane*,

the

the *turtle*, the *blackbird*, and the *lark*, as certainly hiding themselves; which shews how little was known of their real state in his days; nay, so much was he puzzled about this subject, that in another place he suppofes some of the birds to be changed in their form and voice at different seasons. Thus he says, that the *redstart* changes into the *robin redbreast*; and Gesner gives this reason for Aristotle's falling into this opinion, that during the summer the *robin redbreast* lives in desert places, and comes towards towns and houses in the autumn, when the *redstart* disappears. Again Aristotle says, that the *black cap* changes into a *beccafigo*, which last appears, as Gesner observes, about autumn, when the figs are ripe, and the former after the autumn. It is true Aristotle mentions some kinds of birds which go to warmer climates when they disappear, which is a proof that their migrations were not wholly unknown in those days; and indeed the poems of Homer prove that they were in part known much earlier. Nor could it happen otherwise, when the inquisitive genius of Greece began to work, and carry men into Phœnicia and Ægypt, with a view of improving themselves in all parts of learning; where they could not avoid observing, that some birds which left Greece in the winter were found at that time in those warmer climates. But the superstition was already confirmed before this happened. Dodona was established on a foundation not to be shaken by the weak attempt of reason and experience. The birds had given good advice time out of mind, and brought many a general and a magistrate, as well as private men without number,

out

out of difficulties ; and therefore, whether they wintered in Ægypt or not, fignified little ; and indeed it was only fuppofing them to go a little further, viz. into Æthiopia, and there they might meet Jupiter at his annual vifit, μεθ' αυυμοιας Αιθιοπιας, and have the gift of prophecy conferred upon them, or confirmed. Agreeably to thefe notions we find feveral birds were looked upon as facred to particular gods ; thus the owl to Minerva, the peacock to Juno, the eagle to Jupiter, the crow to Apollo whofe meffenger he was called as appears by Hefiod.

Some will be apt to think that i have dwelt much longer upon this fubject that it deferved ; but i cannot help thinking, that even the infirmities of the human mind, efpecially fuch as have like this prevailed amongft the moft ingenious and fagacious people we read of, and for a long courfe of time influenced their moft ferious concerns, ought to be looked upon as not below our notice.

It may feem wonderful to fome, that naturalifts have been fo long without being able to determine any thing certain about the ftate of feveral birds when they difappear. The beft writers have given it as their opinion, that *fwallows* lye under water all winter ; one of the lateft ornithologifts, a writer of great character, falls into this opinion, and the author of the following Calendar adopts it ; and indeed till Monf. Adanfon cleared up this point, it muft appear a problematical point to any man. But though the migration of this bird is at laft determined, yet what becomes of the *nightingale*, the *cuckow*, the *goat-fucker*, and feveral others, is ftill undecided.

Nor is this wonderful, though it may feem fo; for the generality of mankind, and efpecially thofe who travel merely for the fake of a livelihood, or a fortune, are fo little folicitous about things of this kind, that the air might be filled with *fwallows* in winter without their obferving it, as was plainly the cafe at Senegal.

The number of birds that difappear in this kingdom is much greater than is generally imagined; efpecially if we reckon amongft them the birds which fhift quarters at different feafons, but do not crofs the feas. I fhall not attempt to give a lift of them, but recommend it to the curious, who live in the countrey the year round to watch them more narrowly, than they have hitherto been. Linnæus fays, that moft of that genus of birds, which he calls *motacillæ*, i. e. *thofe fmall birds, which . have a beak fubulated aud ftrait, with chaps nearly equal, noftrils of a pointed oval form, and tongue jaggedly indented,* live upon infects and not grain; and therefore migrate from the northern to the fouthern parts towards winter; but it appears, that many birds migrate not only in Sweden, but in Greece and other climates, that live with us all the year round.

It is poffible, that after all i have faid, tending to revive natural augury, and after all the neceffary obfervations fhall have been regiftred, that no ufe can be made of it; but i am certain, that as long as men have ears and eyes, they muft think that one of the greateft delights of the countrey, efpecially during the fpring months, is owing to the lively motions, beautiful fhapes and colours, and melodious notes of birds, which
will

will afford more pleafure, as they are more obferved; and therefore, i am not furprifed, that
Peter the Great of Mufcovy did not think it beneath his attention to endeavor to enliven his
new feat of empire, by fending for colonies of
them from other parts, as they were fcarce where
he refided.

I will finifh this digreffion with a reflection that
occurs to me on the different fates of natural and
religious augury. The firft was fimple, unattend-
ed with any of thofe circumftances that are apt
to roufe the paffions of man; and therefore, tho'
likely to prove ufeful, if purfued with proper diligence, fell into neglect. The latter was com-
plicated, applying itfelf to fome of the ftrongeft
paffions in man, and therefore, though unlikely
to a ferious mind, to have the leaft foundation in
truth, or ever to be ufeful, was encouraged and
adorned with all the pomp that a fuperftitious
people could invent in honor of a flattering, and
therefore favorite art.

I fhall now come to fome points that more
immediately relate to the following Calendars.

1. I have retained the Linnæan names of every
plant, and animal in the Swedifh Calendar; and
have added the Englifh names to the plants taken
from Ray's Synopfis, and his hiftory, with no
fmall trouble, as any one will eafily believe who
has done the like *. The numbers which follow
the Englifh names refer to the above-mentioned
books with an H. to diftinguifh the hiftory. The

---

* This trouble we fhall for the future be relieved from,
when that accurate and fkilful botanift, Mr. Hudfon, has publifhed his Flora Anglica, which is now in the prefs.

num-

numbers after the Englifh names of animals refer either to his Hiftoria Avium, or Pifcium, according to the fubject †. I chofe to refer to Ray,
as well as barely give the Englifh names, for the
eafe and fatisfaction of fuch as put a due value
on that ineftimable writer, whofe works do honor
to our nation, as a late difciple of the great Swedifh naturalift juftly obferves. I cannot help faying farther upon this occafion, that no writer till
his time ever advanced all the branches of natural hiftory fo much as that fagacious, accurate,
and diligent Englifh obferver, whofe fyftematical
fpirit threw a light on every thing he undertook,
and contributed not a little to thofe great and
wonderful improvements, which have been fince
introduced.

2. I have omitted moft of the plants which are
not natives of England; both becaufe it is not
eafy to find Englifh names for them which have
any authority, and becaufe i had fcarcely any obfervations in my own Calendar, but on fuch plants
as are native. Some foreign ones however i have
retained, particularly fuch as are common in almoft every garden; and fuch as are marked in
the Calendar, as more than ordinary prognoftic.
Thefe laft are printed in large characters.

3. I have retained the divifion of months according to budding, leafing, flowering, &c. tho'
i could not imitate this method in my own Calendar for want of more•experience; but i am

---

† Some perhaps may think that i need not have referred to
Ray for birds fo well known as feveral mentioned in the Calendars; but the want of this caution in many authors, has
produced great confufion and doubt about the things meant in
every branch of natural hiftory.

convinced

convinced that this method marks more precifely when we may expect the flowering of any plant, or the return of any bird, &c. than the bare mention of the day of a common calendar month, and at the fame time marks it more univerfally. Thus, when Ariftotle fays *, That the nightingale fings continually day and night for fifteen days about the time when the young leaves begin to expand and thicken the woods, he not only marks a time, when they might expect to hear the nightingale in Greece, but in every other countrey; for thus it happens in Sweden and England, as may be feen in the following Calendars; whereas if he had faid, it appeared in fuch a day of the month, it would bear true perhaps for that year only; and in fact we find in the old almanacks the fame author marking days very diftant from one another, for the appearance of the fame birds, and thus it muft be likewife in relation to plants.

Thus far for the Swedifh Calendar. As to my own, ift. i have marked every circumftance down as i found it in my journal, and hope the learned reader will pardon any miftakes which might happen, either from want of judgment or attention. It is poffible, that i might put down fome plants as firft being in bud, or flower, or

---

* His words are ὅταν τὸ ὄρος ἤδη δασύνηται. i. e. when the mountain is thickening, where it is certain the word *mountain* is ufed for the trees which generally grow upon it. Thus Homer applies the word σκιόεντα to κρεα for that reafon, Iliad. A. 157. and Euftathius upon the place fays, ἰσέον δὲ ὅτι, σκιόεντα μέν, ἀπὸ τῦ παραχολυθεντος, λεγει. τα δασέα χ) σκιας αποτελεσικα δια το της υλης λασιον.

Pliny tranflates this paffage, *denfante fe frondium germine.*

R 3 eaf

leaf, becaufe i happened then firft to obferve
them, or they might be in thofe ftates fome time
before in fome place where i happened not to
go.

2. I wanted fuch a guide as the ingenious author
of the Swedifh Calendar. My obfervations then
perhaps might have been lefs unworthy of the
public, as they would have been better directed
to a particular purpofe; but now the reader muft
expect to find in it all the imperfections that generally accompany firft attempts of any kind.

3. I have caufed all the prognoftic plants,
which are mentioned in my Calendar, to be
printed in large letters as in the Swedifh. The
other marks i fhall explain in a page by itfelf,
for the more eafy recurring to it.

4. Thefe two Calendars would perhaps upon
comparifon have furnifhed me with fome obfervations, had i been able to find time fufficient
for that purpofe; but a ftrong defire to communicate them to the public early in the year, that
others might be induced to keep journals of the
fame kind, determined me to fend them out
in this naked condition; and the more fo, as i
am affured on very good authority, that fuch
journals will be kept in Sweden, Germany, Italy,
and France, the next year; and i think it would
be pity, that an opportunity fhould be loft of
making fo curious a comparifon between thefe
different climates, and which perhaps may not
occur again, or at leaft not for many years.

5. The obfervations on heat and cold were
made with a thermometer, marked in a way peculiar to myfelf. The degrees are thofe of Farenheit, which i chofe as being in common ufe,
but

but inftead of 32 i have made o the freezing
point. This method is more fimple, natural, and
uniform, and conveys a more diftinct idea to the
mind. To this fcale i have reduced the Swedifh
author's obfervations, as well as thofe of Dr.
Hales, taken from his Vegetable Statics; who i
am pleafed to find has made ufe of the method
above-mentioned, in his late works, and i wonder it is not univerfally adopted. The degrees
below o i have marked thus,—1.—2.—3, &c.

6. My botanical obfervations were made on
plants growing in the fields chiefly; the Swedifh
plants growing in the Upfal garden; which method is beft, where either is in our power, i cannot determine. There are conveniences and inconveniences attending each; but there is one great
convenience vifibly on the fide of the garden;
which is, that the plants lye within a fmall compafs, and therefore may be looked over more furely and regularly every day.

7. I once defigned to place the two Calendars
over-againft one another, in oppofite pages, part
by part, according to the days of the month, but
upon confideration i found, the climates being
fo different, that there would be great vacancies
in many of the pages; at the fame time that the
fame plants would be in different pages, and the
bulk of the book would be increafed without any
advantage to the reader; i therefore thought it
would be better to make an index, which will
furnifh an eafy method to the curious of comparing the two climates.

8. If ever any ufe be made of Calendars of
this kind, it muft be by finding out, after a long
feries of obfervations, and publifhing by itfelf a

lift

lift of a few regularly prognoftic plants, either
common in every field, if native; or, if not native, common in every garden.   For it muft be
noted, that many plants will blow even in the
depth of winter, if the weather be mild.   This
is the cafe of *dandelion, chickweed, fhepherd's purfe,
daify,* &c.   As for other precautions, I will refer
the reader to the piece concerning the leafing of
trees in the Amæn. Academ.

   This Calendar was made at the hofpitable feat
of my very worthy and ingenious friend Mr.
Marfham, who has likewife made obfervations
of this kind, and lately communicated to the
world his curious obfervations on the growth of
trees.   All the countrey about is a dead flat; on
one fide is a barren black heath, on the other a
light fandy loam; partly tilled, partly pafture land
fheltered with very fine groves.

T H E

THE

CALENDAR of FLORA.

By ALEXAND. MAL. BERGER,

Upſal 1755.   Latitude 59. 51.$\frac{1}{2}$

Poma dat autumnus, formoſa eſt meſſibus æſtas,
Ver præbet flores.   OVID.

INTRODUCTION.

BEFORE i fet forth the Calendar of Flora, or the delights of the year, arifing from mere fublunary things according to its progrefs, and that from obfervations made in the climate of Upfal, ann. 1755. i think it neceffary to fay fomething by way of introduction. Time moves on flowly; every thing is in progreffion and motion, and has its allotted time, as the wifeft of men Solomon obferves; to which purpofe Virgil fays, *Stat fua cuique dies.*

Aftronomers have exerted all their power to meafure time. To them we owe the accurate divifions of it; for they by obferving the courfe and motion of the celeftial bodies, have been at laft enabled to reduce it to ftated periods, and to divide it in fuch a manner into years, months, weeks and days, that we have calendars conftructed for common ufe, as a rule by which to obferve and number its equal parts.

As the ftars radiate, fhine, and adorn the celeftial regions of the fummer months, fo flowers beautify and illuminate the earth with a wonderful variety of bright and delightful colors. Thus, according to the ftile of the chymifts, that which is above is as that which is below.

How much time foever and labor botanifts have beftowed for many ages back, in order to know the names, nature and vertues of plants, they have not hitherto arrived at that degree of perfection, as to be able to equal the fuccefs of aftronomers, in noting the properties and phænomena of each of them.

Every

Every flower has its appointed feafon. It would therefore be in vain for us to feek the fpring plants in autumn, and the autumn plants in the fpring. We fee them at ftated times emerging, ftalking, flowering, fruiting, decaying. Again in another feafon we fee others rifing in their room, and that in fo fhort a time, by fo regular and conftant a law, according to the direction of their natures, that it feems impoffible for any one to behold this feries and variety, without the higheft admiration.

The fun at the fame time that it raifes, as it were, to life thefe beings, that are deftitute of animal functions, brings them forth alfo fooner, or later, according to the nature and difpofition of each, i. e. as this or that plant requires a leffer or a greater degree of heat, before it can obtain its juft maturity. For as eggs, differing in fpecies, when fit on by a hen, will not all be hatched the fame day, but fome fooner, fome later, fo neither do flowers come forth together, but at ftated times, as they fhall have received the degree of heat proper to their natures.

Altho' the year was formed by the Creator in fuch a manner, as to be divided into diftinct parts, by the fun fending forth its rays equally on the furface of the earth, yet we are not therefore from thence to define and meafure the fummer, the quantity of ice and fnow and Northern colds hindering the air from being equally foon warmed in different years; and according to the heat of the air, the feafons are advanced or retarded, and this is beft known and meafured by the various kinds of flowers.

Since therefore the fummer feafon depends

upon

upon the greater or leffer degree of heat, fo that flowers come forth proportionably to thofe different degrees, but yet in fuch a manner, that one fpecies follows another in a regular order; fince this is the cafe, i fay, the feafons of the year, and particularly the fummer, may eafily from thence be meafured; which hitherto has been a defideratum, on account of œconomical ufes, in fpite of all the affiftance from aftronomers.

Hence plants in different years often flower a month fooner or later, although, as i obferved before, they ftill follow one another in their natural order, as far as the fummer folftice; at which time they hardly ever differ in any year; and in the fame manner they proceed, haften on, or are retarded, the nearer they approach towards autumn, and the winter is farther off or nearer at hand. Now in order to determine accurately the acceleration or retardation of the winter, we muft obferve all the different kinds of flowers in every place, at what time they firft appear, and this daily, that the order which they obferve may be better afcertained.

By way of fpecimen i have exhibited the flowers in the fame order in which they appeared the laft year, 1755, in the Upfal garden. I muft obferve, that almoft all the plants mentioned in the following calendar grew in the open air, and in the fame kind of foil, which is rather low and loamy, excepting about half a fcore, which were gathered in the woods not far diftant, and which are with difficulty raifed in the garden.

I have marked the month and day all along

on

on the fide of the page, not meaning that any one fhould thence imagine that the flowers will return every year on the fame day and month, but with intent to fet forth the calendar of that individual year, and that it might appear with what diligence and circumfpection it was made.

In order to diftinguifh the cultivated plants from the wild, i have ufed italics for the firft, and have marked the plants which appear to be moft prognoftic by an afterifk *.

I have befides thought fit to difpofe them all into months, according to a divifion the apteft i could contrive; but i did not think it neceffary to form equal months, as my defign was not to determine days, but chiefly and indeed only the greater or leffer acceleration of fummer.

Having fo accurately obferved the flowers, i thought fit to add the times at which the animal kingdom undergoes certain alterations, fuch as when birds of paffage come and go, when birds of every kind lay, or hatch, or moult, when feveral kinds of fifhes celebrate their nuptials near the fea fhore, when it is fowing time, when grain flowers, ripens, &c.

By the help of fuch obfervations we may at laft come to know what is to be done, or obferved, every day, by the flowering of plants. But much time is required to bring this to perfection; and he who obferves, muft, if he means to do any thing to the purpofe, live in the countrey, where it is much eafier to fee every thing that prefents itfelf.

---

* Inftead of an afterifk i have ufed great letters.

If

If the gentlemen of our own, or other countries, took delight in fuch obfervations, they might amufe themfelves very agreeably, by giving up fome of their time to things of this kind; and i am moft certainly perfuaded, that this fo flight a fketch, gaining continually new additions, would at laft produce a work of great ufe; as it might furnifh materials for directing private œconomy, and the more fo as the times for fowing of feeds, for reaping, and mowing, and for gathering fruits of various kinds, might from thence be beft fettled.

Gardeners might thence learn at what time of the fpring, they ought to lay the roots of plants bare, when to fow their feeds, when to expofe to the open air, and when to put under fhelter their tender plants, and how to furnifh the garden with flowering plants; fo that there might be a perpetual blow all poffible months of the year; thus the *lilac* follows the *cherry*, the *mock orange* follows the *lilac*, and the *late rofes* follow the *mock orange*.

THE ORDER OF BLOWING OF THE BULBOUS PLANTS IN BORDERS, AND THEIR DURATION. N. B. The plants are numbered from the firft day of budding, by the figures bered on the left hand, the other figures on the right hand fhew the duration of their blow*.

* The meaning is this, as explained to me by Mr. Solander; fuppofe the *fnow-drop* buds on any given day, then the *crocus* will bud the fecond day after it, the *hyacinth* the 12th day after it, &c.

3   I. Snow-

1. Snow-drops, 1144. H. Galanthus *nivalis*, 26.
Violet, *bulbous* 1144. H. Leucoium *vernale*, 26.

2. Crocus, *spring*, 1174. H. Crocus *vernus*, 17.

12. Hyacinth, *oriental*, 1159. H. Hyacinthus *orientalis*, 18.

20. Fumitory, *bulbous*, 975. H. 4. Fumaria *bulbosa solida*, 20.

23. Hollow-root, 975. H. 5. Fumaria *bulbosa cava*, 20.

28. Hyacinth, *grape*, 1161.28. H. Hyacinthus *botryoides*, 19.

34. Daffodil, *English*, 371. 2. Narcissus *pseudo-narcissus*, 19.

Daffodil, *sweet*, Narcissus *odorus*, S. N. 19.

37. Crown, imperial, 1105. H. Fritillaria *imperialis*, 10.

Fritillary, *Pyrenean*, 1107. H. Fritillaria *Pyrenaica*, 14.

38. Lilly, *chequer'd*, 1106. H. Fritillaria *meleagris*, 10.

44. Tulip, 1146. H. Tulipa *Gesneriana*, 13.

47. Primrose, *peerless*, 1133. H. Narcissus *poeticus*.

50. Hyacinth, *summer*, 1160. H. Hyacinthus *amethystinus*.

15. Hyacinth, *Spanish*, 1160. 21. H. Hyacinthus *cernuus*.

59. Star of Bethlehem, 1153.9. H. Ornithogalum *umbellatum*.

68. Lilly, *fiery*, 1110. 3, 4, 5, 7. H. Lilium *viviparum*.

69. Moly, *yellow*, 1123. 4. H. Allium *moly*.

76. Martagon *of Pompony*, 1114.7. H. Lilium *Pomponium*.

79. Star of Bethlehem, *spiked*, 1151.1.H.Ornithogalum *Pyrenaicum*.   69. Moly,

80. Corn flag, 1168. H. Gladiolus *communis*.
81. Martagon, *common*, 1112. H. Martagon *vulgare*, 15.
86. Martagon, *white*, 1112. Martagon *album*, 13.
100. Lilly, *white*, 1109. H. Lilium *album*.
111. Hyacinth, *dun-coloured*, 1160. 22. H. Hyacinthus *ferotinus*.
113. Saffron, *meadow*, 373. Colchicum *autumnale*.

When many calendars of this kind fhall be made in different places and nations in the fame year, it will be eafy to collect from the blowing of thefe forts of flowers, and from the leafing of trees, how one climate differs from another, and why plants brought from the Southern parts feldom produce fruit with us, whereas the Northern plants fucceed very well. Thus at Montpelier the fpring is forwarder than at Upfal by 31 days, at London by 28, at Falconia by 6; and the winter comes on as much later in thofe places.

Botanifts and apothecaries, whofe bufinefs it is to gather plants juft when they are in blow, may by this means learn at what time that may be done, and need not feek in vain at an improper feafon, and may farther know by their garden plants, what wild ones are to be found in the fields precifely at the fame time; and on the contrary.

The night frofts which fo often deftroy our plants, and which i imagine come to us from Lapland, may be known in the fame way.

Thus the LEAD cold arifing from the thaws in Lapmarck, happens at the end of the leafing feafon.

S   The

The BRASS cold from the snow melting in Lapland in the beginning of the fruiting season.

The IRON cold from the freezing on the Lapland alps in the middle of the sowing season.

These colds do not happen with us the same night as in Lapland, but arrive in about 8 days.

On these and such like calendars vulgar practical husbandry ought to be established; but the foundation hitherto not having been sufficiently well laid, this method is become so much out of use, that it is even looked upon as absurd and chimerical; nevertheless it may and ought to be carried so far, that no prudent œconomist will choose to be without such a guide, and the husbandman shall find it the surest way to regulate his affairs by, not to mention other particulars.

THE

CALENDAR

OF

FLORA,

SWEDISH and ENGLISH.

Made in the YEAR 1755.

S 2

THE MONTHS.

I.   Reviving winter month from Dec. 22.
to March 19.

II.   Thawing month from Mar. 19. to Apr. 12.

1.   S P R I N G.

III.   Budding month from April 12 to May 9.
IV.   Leafing month from May 9 to May 25.
V.   Flowering month from May 25 to June 20.

2.   S U M M E R.

VI.   Fruiting month from June 20 to July 12.
VII.   Ripening month from July 12 to Aug. 4.
VIII. Reaping month from Aug. 4 to Aug. 28.

3.   A U T U M N.

IX.   Sowing month from Aug. 28 to Sept. 22.
X.   Shedding month from Sept. 22 to Oct. 28.
XI.   Freezing month from Oct. 28 to Nov. 5.

4.   W I N T E R.

XII.   Dead winter month from Nov. 5 to Dec. 22.

THE

CALENDAR of FLORA.

I. REVIVING WINTER MONTH.
From the winter folftice to the vernal æquinox.

Dec. XII.
    xxii. *Butter fbrinks and feparates from the fides*
        of the tub.
    xxiii. Afp flower buds begin to open.
Jan. I. i. *Ice on lakes begins to crack.*
    ii. *Wooden walls fnap in the night.*
        Cold frequently extreme at this time, the
        greateft obferved was 55.7.
    iv. **Horfe dung fpirts.*
    viii. *Epiphany rains.*
    xxvi. St. *Paul's rains.*
Feb. II.
    xxii. *Very cold nights often between Feb.* 20 *and*
        28, *called* STEEL NIGHTS.

---

* Note. This was explained to me by Mr. Solander, an ingenious and learned difciple of Linnæus, now in England, who fays, that horfe dung, in very fevere frofts, throws out particles near a foot high, and that no other dung does the like.

      II. THAW-

II. THAWING MONTH.

From the first melting of the snow to the floating of ice down the rivers.

Vere novo gelidus canis cum montibus humor
Liquitur, et zephyro putris se gleba resolvit.

VIRG.

Mar. III.

 xix. *Eves drop towards the noontide sun.*
  Sallow, *round leaved*, flower-buds, 449,
   15. Salix *caprea*, open,

 xx. *Snow melts against walls.*
  LARK *begins to sing.*

 xxii. *Water flows by the walls.*

 xxv. *Roads very dirty and full of water.*

April IV.

 i. *Horse dung melts the ice.*
  Moss, *upright fir.* Lycopodium *selago*,
   106. sheds its dust.

 iii. STONES *are loosened from the ice.*

 vi. *Hills begin to appear, the snow being melted.*
  Serpents come out of their holes.
  SPIDER, *water, frisks about. The* FLY *creeps forth.*
  GAME, *black*, 53. *Tetrao tetrix.*
  LAPWING, 110.*Tringa vanellus, returns.*

 vii. BUTTERFLY, *nettle, Papilio urticæ, appears in abundance.*

Some people, says Pliny, think the appearance of the butterfly the surest sign of spring, on account of the delicacy of the animal.

DUCK,

THE CALENDAR OF FLORA. 263

April IV.
    vii. DUCK, *tame*, 145. *Anas bofchas, fits.*
    Wild DUCK *returrs.*
    x. *An inundation of fnow water.*
        SWAN, 37. *Anas cygnus, and* DAKER-
        HEN, 58. 8. *Rallus crex, by their ap-*
        pearance proclaim the fpring.
    RIVERS *are unbound, and ice floats down.*
N. B. *The river at Upfal, for* 70 *years, has never*
been frozen beyond the 19th *of April, according to*
the obfervation of O. Celfius, fen.
        PIKE, 112. *Efox lucius, fpawns. This*
        fifh gives over fpawning when the frog
        begins.
    xi. *Snow water foaks into the earth.*
    Subterraneous places are inundated.
    FROG *comes forth.*
    Winter fhelters ought to be removed from
    garden plants, that they may not be too
    much drawn up.
    Hot-beds for melons fhould be fown,

Solvitur acris hyems grata vice veris et Favonii.
               HOR.

III. BUDDING MONTH.
From the return of the WHITE-WAGTAIL,
Motacilla alba, 75. 1. *to the coming of the fwal-*
low; or from the firft flower to the leafing of the
firft tree, during the whole time of the flowering of
the bulbous violet.

A Favonio veris initium notant. CICERO.

April IV.
    xii. Hafel-nut tree, 439. Corylus *avellana.*
      S 4   COLTS-

264 THE CALENDAR OF FLORA.

April IV.
- xii. COLTSFOOT, 173. Tuffilago *farfara.*
- xiii. Saffron, 374. Crocus *fativus.*
  VIOLET, *bulbous,* 1144. H. Lcucoium *vernale,* 26.
  Snow drops, 1144. H. Galanthus *nivalis,* 26.
  WAGTAIL, *white,* 75. 1. *Motacilla alba,* returns.
  KESTREL, 16. 16. *Falco tinunculus,* returns.
  FROG, 247. *Rana temporaria,* croaks.
  Saffron, 374. Crocus *fativus,* 17.
- xv. Pilewort, 246. Ranunculus *ficaria.*
  Star of Bethlehem, *yellow,* 372. Ornithogalum *luteum.*
  Grafs, *whitlow,* 292. Draba *verna.*
  Mezereon, 1587. H. Daphne *mezereon.*
  TURKEY *hen,* 51. 3. *Meleagris gallopavo,* fits.
  Honeyfuckle, *double,* 1490. H. Lonicera *perfoliata.*
- xvi. Liverwort, *noble,* 580. H. Anemone *hepatica,* 34.
  The time for fowing barley at Upfal.
- xvii. Lilly, *yellow water,* 368.1. Nymphæa *lutea,* leaves emerge.
- xix. Afp, or *trembling* poplar, 446.3. Populus *tremula,* 13.
  Abele, 446.2. Populus *alba,* 13.
  Hot-beds to be fown from the budding of the poplar to the leafing month.
- xxi. SMELT, 66.14. *Salmo eperlanus,* fpawns, *at which time generally tempeft, and fnowy weather at* Upfal, *and intermitting fevers very common.*

April IV.

  xxi. Hellebore, *black*, 271.1. Helleborus *viridis*.

  Willow, *round leaved*, 449. 15. Salix *caprea*.

  xxx. Crake *berries*, 444. Empetrum *nigrum*.

  Poplar, *black*, 446. Populus *nigra*.

  Bur *butter*, 179. Tuſſilago *petaſitis*, 25.

May V.

  i. Mercury *dogs*, 138. 1. Mercurialis *perennis*.

  Polyanthus, 1083. Primula veris *hortenſis*.

  iii. ANEMONE, *wood*, 259.1. Anemone *nemoroſa*, 21.

  Saxifrage, *golden*, 158. 2. Chryſoſplenium *alternifolium*.

  Violet *with throat-wort leaves*, 365. 8. Viola *hirta*.

  Aſſarabacca, 158.1. Aſarum *Europæum*.

  Violet, *ſweet*, 364.8. Viola *odorata*, 24.

  Pepperwort, 304. Lepidium *petræum*.

  Fields are covered with verdure.

After the return of the WHEAT EAR*, 75.1. *Motacilla Oenanthe, there is ſeldom any ſevere froſt, and therefore the peaſants in Upland have this proverb; When you ſee the* WHITE WAGTAIL *you may turn your ſheep into the* † *fields ; and when you ſee the* WHEAT EAR, *you may ſow your grain.*

---

* If this bird does not quit England, it certainly ſhifts places. For i have obſerved, that about harveſt time they were not to be found where there were before great plenty of them.

† The ſheep are houſed all winter in Sweden, as Mr. Solander informs me, who gave me the tranſlation of the Swediſh proverb in the very words here printed.

Oſier,

May V.

vii. Ofier, 450.21. Salix *viminalis*.
Bramble, 467.1. Rubus *fruticofus*, leafs.
STARLING, 67.1. *Sturnus vulgaris,
returns.*

viii. Mofcatel, *tuberous*, 267. Adoxa *mofca-
tellina.*
*Seeds of kitchen plants to be fown. Ten-
der plants to be taken out of the green
houfe.*
ELM TREE, 469. Ulmus *campeftris.*
Snow melts even in the fhade.

Diffugere nives, redeunt jam gramina campis.
Arboribufque comæ. HOR.

IV. LEAFING MONTH.

---

*The compleat leafing of trees from the bird cherry to
the afh; from the coming of the fwallow to the
tulip.*

Nunc herbæ rupta tellure cacumina tollunt;
Nunc tumido gemmas cortice palmes agit. OVID.

May V.

ix. SWALLOW *and* STORK *return.*
CHERRY, BIRD, 463. Prunus *padus**. L.
Filberd, 439. Corylus *avellana*. L.

xi. Afp, 446.3. Populus *tremula, out of blow.*

xii. CUCKOW, 23. *Cuculus canorus, fings.*

---

* The letter L. at the end of the lines fignifies that thofe plants
came into leaf on the days marked. All the plants befides throughout this Calendar are fuppofed to have flowered on the days marked,
unlefs the contrary is exprefled.

I   Sorrel

May V.

xiii. Sorrel *wood*, *281. Oxalis *acetofella*.
BIRCH TREE, 443. Betula *alba*. L.
Barberry bulh, 465. Berberis *vulgaris*.L.
The beft time for fowing barley, and the
feeds of of garden plants.
Ofier, 450.21. Salix *viminalis*. L.

xiv. Spindle tree, 468.Euonymus*Europæus*.L.
Bear's ear, 1083. H.Primula *auricula*, 12.
Goule, or Dutch myrtle, 443.Myrica*gale*.
Orange, *mock*, 1763. H. Philadelphus
coronarius. L.
Elder, *water*, 460. Viburnum *opulus*. L.
Lilac, 1763. H. Syringa *vulgaris*. L.
Privet, 463. Liguftrum *vulgare*. L.
Buckthorn, *fea*, 445. Hippophae *rham-*
noid. L.
Alder tree, 442. Betula *alnus*. L.

xv. Daffodil, *wild Englifh*, 371.1. Narciffus
pfeudonarciffus, 19.
Rofes *garden*.
Elm tree, 469. Ulmus *campeftris*. L.
NIGHTINGALE, 78. *Motacilla lufci-*
nia, returns.
Thorn, *white*, 453.3. Cratægus *oxya-*
cantha. L.
Apple tree, 451. Pyrus *malus*. L.
Primrofe, 284. Primula *veris*, 16.
Cherry tree, 463. Prunus *cerafus*. L.
Thorn *buck*, 466. Rhamnus *catharti-*
cus. L.
Cinquefoil, *fmall rough*, 323. Potentilla
verna, 16.

xvi. Sallow, *round leaved*, 449.15.Salix *caprea*.
L.

Beam

May V.

xvi. Beam tree, *white*, 453. Cratægus *aria*.L.
Chefnut tree, *horfe*, 1683. Æfculus *hippocaftanum*. L.
Beech tree, 439. Fagus *fylvatica*. L.
Hornbeam, 451. Carpinus *betulus*. L.
Poplar, *black*, 446. Populus *nigra*. L.

xx. Afp, 446. Populus *tremula*. L.

xxi. Marygold, *marfh*, 272. Caltha *paluftris*.
Lime tree, 473. Tilia *Europæa*. L.
Alder, *berry bearing*, 465. Rhamnus *frangula*. L.
*Fly, dragon, Moufet, p.*67. Libellula.
Salmon, 63.2. *Salmo, falar.*
Oak tree, 440. Quercus, *robur*. L.
ASH TREE, 469. Fraxinus *excelficr*. L.

xxiv. *While the afh is leafing there is fcarcely any more froft : therefore green houfe plants ought to be brought into the open air.*

THE LEADEN NIGHTS *happen before the leafing of the afh ; from that time the fummer is fettled.*

There are very few flowers in this month ; for nature being intent on the young offspring of the bird kind, prepares abundance of flowers, againft the hatching feafon.

V. FLOWERING MONTH.

From the firft ear of rye to its blow.
From the tulip, 1146. *Tulipa Gefneriana, to the wall pepper*, 270. 5. *Sedum acre.*

It ver, et Venus, et Veneris prænuncius ante
Pinnatus graditur zephyrus veftigia propter.
LUCRET.

* CHERRY,

May V.

xxv. * CHERRY, BIRD, 463. Prunus *padus*.
Currants, *black*, 456. Ribes *nigrum*.
Jack by the hedge, 293. Erysimum *alliaria*.
Cicely, *wild*, 207. Chærophyllum *sylvestre*.
TULIP, 1146. 11. Tulipa *Gesneriana*, 13.
Milkwort, *287. Polygala *vulgaris*.
Lady's mantle, 158. Alchemilla *vulgaris*.
ROCHE, 122. Cyprinus *rutilus*, *spawns*.
First ear of rye.

xxvi. Saxifrage, *white*, 364. 6. Saxifraga *gra-
nulata.*
Ivy, *ground*, 243. Glechoma *hederacea*.
Goldilocks, 248. Ranunculus *auricomus*.
Pear tree, 452. Pyrus *communis*, 14.

xxvii. Celandine, *greater*, 309. Chelidonium
majus.
Cloud berries, 260. Rubus *chamæmorum*.
Cat's foot, 181. Gnaphalium *dioicum*.
CRANE'S BILL, 361. 18. Geranium *syl-
vaticum.*
Globe flower, 272. Trollius *Europæus*.

xxviii. Cuckow flower, 299. Cardamine *pratensis.*
*While the cuckow flower blows, the salmon goes up
the rivers, and dragon fly comes forth.*
Thorn, *black*, 462. Prunus *spinosa*, 10.
Cherry tree 463. Prunus *cerasus*, 10.
Plumb tree, 462. 2,3. Prunus *domestica*.
Pease, *wood*, 124.2. Orobus *tuberosus*.
Plantain, *hoary*, 314.3. Plantago *media.*

---

* While the bird cherry flowers, happens what is called the grey
weather, between the old and new moon. I am indebted to Mr. Solander for the interpretation of this passage: it is in the original called the plenilunium cornicu n, but ought to be read interlunium.

Butter-

May V.

xxx. Butterwort, *281. Pinguicola *vulgaris*.

Lilly in the valley, 264. Convallaria *Maialis*, 21.

Bugle, *mountain*, 245.2. Ajuga *pyramidalis*.

Rush, *hare's tail*, 436. Eriphorum *vaginatum*.

Grafs, *cotton*, 435. Eriophorum *polyſtachyon*.

Honeyfuckle, *dwarf*, 261. Cornus *Suecica*.

Whorts, *red*, 457. Vaccinium *vitis idæa*.

CROWFOOT, CRANE'S BILL, 361.18. Geranium *ſylvaticum*, 120.

Catchfly, *red German*, 340.14. Lychnis *viſcaria*.

Germander, *wild*, 282. 11. Veronica *chamædrys*.

BREAM, 116.5. *Cyprinus brama, ſpawns.*
The bream ſports while the bird cherry fades, and the juniper begins to blow, and when this fades the dragon fly comes out.

Nunc frondent fylvæ, nunc formofiffimus annus.

June VI.

i. Fir, *ſpruce*, 441. Pinus *abies*, drops its male flower.

ii. PEIONY, 694. H. Pæonia fl. *ſimplici*, 10.

AVENS, PURPLE MOUNTAIN, 253. Geum *rivale*.

Tormentil *ſeptfoil*, 257.1. Tormentilla *erecta*.

APPLE TREE, 451. Pyrus *malus*.

Rye in ear.

iii. Juniper tree, 444. Juniperus *communis*.

Quicken tree, 452. Sorbus *aucuparia*.

Buck-

June VI.
  iii. Buckbean, 285. Menyanthes *trifoliat.* 18.
  iv. Grafs, *foxtail*, 396.1. Alopecurus *pratenfis*.
  v. Plantain, *ribwort*, 314.5. Plantago *lanceolata*.
   Crane's bill, *dufky*, 361. 21. Geranium *phæum*.
  vii. Orchis, *male handed*, 310.19. Orchis *latifolia*.
   Goofeberry bufh, 1484. H. Ribes *groffularia*.
   Paris, *herb*, 264. Paris *quadrifolia*.
   Trefoil, *bird's foot*, 334. 1. Lotus *corniculata*.
   Bilberry bufh, *great*, 457. Vaccinium *uliginofum*.
   Comfrey, 230. Symphytum *officinale*.
   Flax, *purging*, 362.6. Linum *catharticum*.
   Columbines, 273. Aquilegia *vulgaris*.
   Violet, *dame's*, 790. H. Hefperis *matronalis*.
   Flora unrobed. The pear, plumb, Scotch fir and fpruce out of blow.
The fummer is then in its higheft beauty, when Pomona, dreffed as it were in her fnow-white garment, celebrates her nuptials ; while the tulip, narciffus and peiony adorn the garden, the frefh fhoots of the fir illuminate the woods, and the juniper fheds its impregnating vapour.
   Chriftopher, *herb*, 661. Actæa *fpicata*.
   Grafs, *melic*, 403.6. Melica *nutans*.
   Bramble, *ftone*, 261. Rubus *faxatilis*.
   Crowfoot, *bulbous*, 247.2. Ranunculus *bulbofus*.
                                          Hawk-

June VI.

vii. Hawkweed; *dandelion*, 245. Leontodon *hifpidum*.

viii. Barberry, 465. Berberis *vulgaris*.
LILAC; 176. H. Syringa *vulgaris*.
The meadows glow with crowfoots.

ix. Crane's bill, *dovefoot*, 359.11. Geranium *molle*.

x. Flower de luce; *yellow water*, 374. Iris *pfeud-acorus*.

xi. Crane's bill, *crowfcot*, 360.17. Geranium *pratenfe*.
Bell flower, *leffer round-leaved*; 277. 5. Campanula *rotundifolia*.
Camomile, *Roman*, 189. Matricaria *chamomilla*.
Cinquefoil, *fhrubby*; 256. 4. Potentilla *fruticofa*.

xii. Beam tree, *white*; 453. Cratægus *aria*.
Vetch, *kidney*, 325. 1. Anthyllis *vulneraria*.
Henbane, 274. Hyofcyamus *niger*.

xiii. Catchfly, *white*; 340.11. Silene *nutans*.
Avens; 253.1,2. Geum.*urbanum*.
Adonis, *flower*, 251. Adonis *annua rubra*.
The fingle peiony fades before the double blows, as is the cafe of rhubarb and rhapontic.

xiv. Lilly, *yellow water*, 368.1. Nymphæa *lutea*.
Orchis, *female handed*, 381. 20. Orchis *maculata*.
Robert, *herb*, 358.6. Geranium *robertianum*.
Cinquefoil, *upright baftard*, 255. Potentilla *rupeftris*.
Campion, *white*, 339. 8. Lychnis *dioica*.
Elder,

June VI.

xiv. Elder, *water*, 460. Viburnum *opulus*.

xv. Rofe, *pimpernel*, 454.3. Rofa *fpinofiſſima*.
Briar, *ſweet*, 454.2. Rofa *eglanteria*.
Thorn, *buck*, 466. Rhamnus *catharticus*.
Orchis, *leſſer butterfly*, 380.18. Orchis *bifolia*.

xvi. Grafs of Parnaſſus, 355.1. Parnaſſia *paluſtris*.
Grafs, *marſh goofe*, 255.3. Galium *uliginoſum*.
Lilly, *white water*, 368.3. Nymphæa *alba*.
Tanſey, *wild*, 256.5. Potentilla *anferina*.
Alder, *berry bearing*, 465.1. Rhamnus *frangula*.
PEIONY, DOUBLE, 693. H. Pæonia *plena*, 13.
Rampions, 274.4. Campanula *patula*.
Rhapontic, 170. H. Rheum *rhaphonticum*.

xvii. Pink, *meadow*, 338. Lychnis *flos cuculi*.
Valerian, *great wild*, 200.1. Valeriana *officinalis*.
Vetch, *chichling*, 320.5. Lathyrus *paluſtris*.
Daify, *great, or ox eye*, 184. Chryfanthemum *leucanthem*.

xvii. Eyebright, *284. Euphrafia *officinalis*.
Spear wort, *leſſer*, 250.7. Ranunculus *flammula*.
Groundfel, 178.1. Senecio *vulgaris*.
Thorn, *white*, 453. Crætagus *oxyacantha*.

xviii. Lilly, *bulbous*, 1110. H. Lilium *bulbiferum* to VII. 4.
Saxifrage, *burnet*, 213.1,2. Pimpinella *faxifraga*.

T   Tor-

June VI.
  xviii. Tormentil *cinquefoil*, 255.2. Potentilla *argentea*. `
  Grafs, *quaking*, 412. Briza *media*.
  Nightfhade, *deadly*, 265. Atropa *belladonna*.
  RYE, *winter*, 388.1. Secale *hybernum*.
Winter rye flowers generally from the firft blow of wall pepper, 270.5. Sedum acre, to the firft blow of the rofe bay willow herb, 310.1. Epilobium anguftifolium, with the bulbous lilly, beginning oftentimes four days before the folftice.

VI. FRUITING MONTH.

During the whole blow of the wall pepper. From the yellow to the red day lilly.

―――Revoluta ruebat,
Matura jam luce dies.   VIRG.

  xx. PEPPER, WALL, 207.5. Sedum *acre*.
  Orchis, *frog*, 381.22. Satyrium *viride*.
  Ciftus, *dwarf*, 341. Ciftus *helianthem*.
  LILLY, YELLOW DAY, 1191. H. Hemerocallis *flava*.
  Cinquefoil, *marfh*, 256.2. Comarum *palujtre*.
  xxi. *After the folftice trees fcarcely grow, and therefore hedges fhould then be clipped. The higheft degree of heat with us is hardly above 54.8. within the tropics the heat is not much above 57.6, nor below 40.8. the heat of a hatching hen between 63 and 68.4. a heat above 72 deftroys the embryo.*

                              BRASS

June VI.

 xxi. BRASS NIGHTS *from the thaw of the high-est mountains.*

 xxii. Orchis, *fly*, 379.13. Ophrys *infeɛtifera myodes.*

  Blue bottle, 198. Centaurea *cyanus.*

  Vetch, *great tufted wood,* 322.4. Vicia *sylvatica.*

  Dropwort, 259. Spiræa *filipendula.*

  Thiſtle, *gentle,* 193.2. Carduus *heleniodes.*

  Looſe ſtrife, *yellow,* 283.3. Lyſimachia *thyrſiflora.*

  Self heal, 283. Prunella *vulgaris.*

  Gentian, *vernal dwarf,* 275.4. Gentiana *campeſtris.*

 xxiii. Mayweed, *ſtinking,* 185.4. Anthemis *cotula.*

  Yarrow, 183.1. Achillea *millefolium.*

  WILLOW HERB, *roſe bay,* 310. Epilobium *anguſtifolium.*

  Moonwort, 128.1. Oſmunda *lunaria.*

  Liquorice, *wild,* 326.1. Aſtragalus *alpinus.*

  Knapweed, *great,* 198.1. Centaurea *ſcabioſa.*

  Vetch, *tufted,* 322.3. Vicia *cracca.*

  Nightſhade, *woody,* 265.1,2. Solanum *dulcamara.*

  Golden rod, 176.1. Solidago *virgaurea.*

  ORANGE, MOCK, 1763. H. Philadelphus *coronarius,* 14.

  Sweet-william, 991.2. H. Dianthus *barbatus.*

  POPPY, *Turkey,* Papaver *orientale,* 13.

  Flax, *perennial blue,* 362.3. Linum *perenne.*   T 2   Dewberry

June VI.

xxiii. Dewberry bush, 467.3. Rubus *cæsius*.

xxv. Nettle, *hedge*, 237. Stachys *sylvatica*.
Spiked willow of Theophrastus, 1699.
H. Spiræa *salicifolia*.
Lilac out of blow.

xxvi. Willow herb, *hooded*, 244.1. Scutellaria
galericulata.
Willow herb, *great smooth leaved*, 311.4.
Epilobium *montanum*.
Twayblade, 385.1. Ophrys *ovata*.
Strawberries ripening.

xxvii. Hawkweed, *Hungarian*, 167.17. Hypo-
chæris *maculata*.
Medic, *yellow*, 333.1. Medicago *falcata*.
Parsley, *great bastard*, 219.2. Tordylium
. *latifolium*.

xxviii. Toad flax, *yellow*, *281.1. Antirrhinum
·*linaria*.
Grass, *sea dog*, 390.1. Elymus *arenaria*.
Bryony, *white*, 261.1,2. Bryonia *alba*.
Campion, *wild purple*, 341.17. Silene
armeria.

xxix. Marygold, *corn*, 182.1. Chrysanthemum
segetum.
Heath, *Dutch or besom*, 471.4. Erica
tetralix.
Bilberry bush, 457.2. Vaccinium *myrtill*.
Berries ripe.
Pease, *everlasting*, 319.1. Lathyrus *lati-
folius*.
Throatwort, *little*, 277.3. Campanula
glomerata.
Feverfew, 187.1. Matricaria *parthenium*.
PEACOCK *moults*.

Ox-eye,

June VI.

xxix. Ox-eye, 183.1. Anthemis *tinctoria*.
Sneezewort, 183. Achillea *ptarmica*.
Rupturewort, 160.1. Herniaria *glabra*.
Hawkweed, *fuccory-leaved*, 166.12. Crepis *biennis*.
PINK, MAIDEN, 335.1. Dianthus *deltoides*.
SCABIOUS, FIELD, 191.1. Scabiofa *arvenfis*.
St. John's wort, *large flowered*, 1017.1.
H. Hypericum *afcyron*.
Elder tree, 461.1. Sambucus *nigra*.
Woad, 367.1. Ifatis *tinctoria*, out of blow.

July VII.

i. Willow herb, *purple fpiked*, 367.1. Lythrum *falicaria*.
Parfnep, *cow*, 205.1,2. Heracleum *fphondylium*.
Bindweed, *fmall*, 275.1. Convolvulus *arvenfis*.
Knapweed, 198.2. Centaurca *nigra*.
Mullein, *white flowered*, 287.2. Verbafcum *lychnit. alba*.
Rampions, 277.4. Campanula *ranunculus*.

ii. Throatwort, *giant*, 276. Campanula *latifolia*.
Afphodel, *Lancafhire*, 375.1. Anthericum *offifragum*.
Mullein, *black*, 288.4. Verbafcum *nigrum*.
Rue, *meadow*, 203.1. Thalictrum *flavum*.
Hellebore, *baftard*, 383.1. Serapias *hellebor. paluftr*.
The hotteft days.
Bindweed, *great*, 275. Convolvulus *fepium*.
Willow herb, *yellow*, 282.1. Lyfimachia *vulgaris*.

Moneywort,

July VII.

iv. Moneywort, 283.1, Lyſimachia *nummularia.*

Foxglove, purple, 283.1. Digitalis *rubra.*

Meadow fwèet, 259.1. Spiræa *ulmaria.*

Cockle, 338. 5. Agroſtema *githago.*

Speedwell, *ſpiked male,* 279.2. Veronica *ſpicata.*

Graſs, *ſoft tufted meadow,* 404.14. Holcus *lanatus.*

Primroſe, *evening or tree,* 862. Oenothera *biennis.*

vi. Yarrow, 183.1. Achillea *millefolium.*

Bedstraw, yellow lady's, 224.1. Galium *verum.*

Agrimony, 202.1. Agrimonia *eupatoria.*

Throatwort, *great,* 276. Campanula *trachelium,* 25.

St. John's wort, 342.1. Hypericum *perforatum.*

St. John's wort, *tutſan,* 343.4,5. Hypericum *hirſutum.*

Spearwort, *great,* 250.8. Ranunculus *lingua.*

Carrot, 218. Daucus *carota.*

Stone crop, *yellow* 269.1. Sedum *rupeſtre.*

Gladdon, *ſtinking,* 375.3. Iris *fætidiſſima.*

Knapweed, 198.2. Centaurea *jacea.*

Hops, 137.1. Humulus *lupulus.*

Reſt harrow, 332.1. Ononis *ſpinoſa.*

Parſley, *Scotch ſea,* 214. Liguſticum *Scoticum.*

vii. Briar, or dog rose, 454.1. Roſa *canina.*

Roſe, *white,* 1373.23. H. Roſa *alba.*

Roſe, *French,* Roſa *Gallica.*

July VII.

vii. *The late rofes now begin to blow.*

Hay harveſt begins with the lime tree, clover being out of blow, and yellow rattle or coxccmb, *284. *ſhedding its ſeeds.*

Burnet, 203.2. Sanguiforba *officinalis.*

Poppy, *wild,* 308.1. Papav.. *ſomniferum.*

Sneezewort, 183.1. Achillea *ptarmica.*

Lilly, *yellow day, out of blow.*

Chervil, *wild,* 207.1. Chærophyllum *ſylveſtre, out of blow.*

Barley every where in ear.

Peaſe ripe.

Cherries ripe.

Beginning of hay harveſt.

Motherwort, 239.1. Leonurus *cardiaca.*

viii. Pink, *Deptford,* 337.1. Dianthus *armerius.*

Orange, *mock, out of blow.*

Bilberries ripe,

ix. Thiſtle, *muſk,* 193.1. Carduus *nutans.*

Burdock, 196. Arctium *lappa.*

Horehound, *baſe,* 339.1. Stachys *Germanica.*

Hemp, 138. Cannabis *ſativa.*

351.13. Frankenia *pulverulenta.*

Red currants ripe.

x. Mugwort, 190.1. Artemiſia *vulgaris.*

Thiſtle, *ivy leaved ſow,* 162.5. Prenanthes *muralis.*

Marjoram, *wild,* 236.1. Origanum *vulgare.*

Horehound, *ſtinking,* 244.1. Ballota *nigra.*

Baſil, *great wild,* 239. Clinopodium *vulgare.*

Pine, *ground,* 244. Teucrium *chamæpitys.*

T 4   Betony,

July VII.

   x. Betony, *water*, *283.1. Scrophularia a-
quatica.
Nightſhade, *enchanters*, 289. Circæa ca-
nadenſis.
Clover, 328.4. Trifolium *pratenſe*, *out of
blow*.

   xi. Thiſtle, *tree ſow*, 163.7. Sonchus *arvenſis*.
LIME TREE, 473.1,2,3. Tilia *Europea*,
out of blow.
Marjoram, *wild*, 236. Origanum *vulgare*.

Feſtinat decurrere velox floſculus æſtatis.

VII. RIPENING MONTH.

From the white ſtonecrop, 271.7. *Sedum album*, *or
the red day lilly*, *to the devil's bit*, 191.3. *Sca-
bioſa ſucciſa*.

---

   xii. SUCCORY, WILD, 172. Cichorium *intybus*.
Willow herb, *great hairy*, 311.2. Epi-
lobium *hirſutum*.
Langue de bœuf. 166.13. Picris *echi-
oides*.
Woodbind, 456. Lonicera *periclymenum*.
Mallow, *vervain*, 252. Malva *alcæa*.
St. John's wort, *large flowered*, 1017. H.
Hypericum *aſcyron*, *out of blow*.

   xiii. Fleabane, *ſmall*, 174.2. Inula pulicaria.
Pepperwort, 304.1. Lepidium *latifolium*.

   xiv. STONECROP, WHITE, 271.7. Sedum *album*,
out of blow.

   xv. Agrimony, *hemp*, 179. Eupatorium *can-
nabinum*.

Tanſey,

July VII.
 xv. Tanfey, 188. Tanacetum *vulgare*.
  Golden rod, *white*, 175.1 Erigeron *ca-nadenfe*.
  Saw-wort, 196.1. Secratula *tinct. prealt*.
  Mint, *red*, 232.5. Mentha *gentilis*.
  Mint, *long leaved horfe*, 234.5. Mentha *fpicata*.
  Pepper, *wall*, 270.5. Sedum *acre*, *out of blow*.
  CUCKOW *is filent*.
 xvi. Hawkweed, *bufhy*, 168.3. Hieracium *umbell*.
  LILLY, RED DAY, 1191.2. H. Heme-rocallis *fulva*.
  All the marvels of Peru, 398. H. Mira-biles.
  The height of hay harveft.
 xvii. Thiftle, *fpear*, 194.8. Carduus *lanceolatus*.
  ELDER, DWARF, 461.4. Sambucus *ebulus*.
 xviii. Touch me not, 316.1. Impatiens *noli tangere*.
  Saffron, *meadow*, 373.1. Colchicum *autumnale*. *Leaves fall*.
  Teafel, *wild and manured*, 192.3. Dipfa-cus *fullonum*.
 x. LILLY, WHITE, 1109. H. Lilium *candidum*.
  Teafel, *fmall wild*, 192.3. Dipfacus *pilofus*.
 xxi. Thiftle, *marfh tree fow*, 163.8. Sonchus *paluftris*.
 xxii. Soapwort, 339.6,7. Saponaria *officinalis*.
  Grafs, *Effex cocks foot*, 393.4. Dactylis *cynofuroides*.
  Knapweed, great, 198.1. Centaurea *fca-biofa*.   Spikenard,

July VII.

xxiii. Spikenard, *plowman's*, 179.1. Conyza
. *squarrofa.*
xxiv. Elecampane, 176.1. Inula *helenium.*
xxv. Fleabane, *middle*, 174.1. Inula *dyfenter.*
xxvi. Violet, *Calathian*, 274.1. Gentiana *pneu-
monanthe.*
Baum, 570. H. Meliffa *officinalis.*
xxvii. Thiftle, *great foft cr gentle*, 193.3. Ser-
ratula *alpin. lat.*

Aug. VIII.

i. Chickweed, *berry bearing*, 267.1. Cucu-
balus *baccifer.*
· Orpine, 269.1. Sedum *telephium.*

Mirabar celerem fugitiva æftate rapinam,
Et dum nafcuntur confenuiffe rofas.

VIII. REAPING MONTH.

*From the devil's bit to the blow of the meadow
faffron.*

iv. DEVIL'S BIT, 191.3. Scabiofa *fuccifa.*
Rye harveft.
*Winter rye has for many years ripened with
the firft blow of the devil's bit, in the
garden at Upfal.*
BIRDS OF PASSAGE, *after having celebrated their nuptials in the vernal
months, and feafted on the fummer fruits,
now prepare for departing.*
vii. Rofe, *French*, Rofa *Gallica, out of blow.*
xiv. Wormwood, 188.1. Artemifia *campeftris.*
xvi. *Barley harveft.*
xxvi. Lilly, *red, out of blow.*

*IX. SOWING MONTH.

From the firſt blow of the meadow ſaffron to the departure of the ſwallow.

Pomifer autumnus fruges effudit et mox
Bruma, recurrit iners.

Aug. VIII.
xxviii. SAFFRON, MEADOW, 373.1. Colchicum *autumn.*

This plant ought to admoniſh gardeners to put Indian plants under ſhelter, as the iron nights are near. The IRON NIGHTS, *as they are called with us, generally happen between Auguſt 17 and 29, and deſtroy tender plants.*

After the blow of the meadow ſaffron, we have ſtorms that ſhake off ripe ſeeds.

Fern, female, 124.1. Pteris *aquilina, grows yellow in the woods after the firſt cold nights.*

xxxi. *A gentle froſt that ſcarcely did any damage.*
Sept. IX.
i. Adonis flower, 251.1. Adonis *annua ſer.*
Mulberry tree, 1429. H. Morus *nigra, grows pale.*
iv. Fig tree, 1431. H. Ficus *carica, grows pale.*
vi. Wormwood, *ſea,* 188.2. Artemiſia *maritima.*
Travellers joy, 258.1. Clematis *vitalba.*
xi. *The froſt has deſtroyed ſouthern plants.*
xii. *The froſt milder.*
xiv. *Seeds to be gathered.*

* By ſowing, in this place, is meant not man's but nature's.

I   Sampire

Sept. IX.
>xvii. Sampire, *golden flowered*, 174.1. Inula
>crithmoid.
>>*SWALLOW *goes under water.*
>>WAGTAIL, *white, departs.*

Nos quoque floruimus, fed flos fuit ille caducus.

X. SHEDDING MONTH.

From the firſt fall of the leaves of trees to the laſt.

>xxii. Orach, *fca*, 152.8. Artiplex *maritima.*
Leaves *of trees are changed, of the oak, maple, robinia caragana, elm, lime, to a yellow ; of the ſpin-
tree to a brown ; of the quicken tree and ſumach,
to a red colour.*
>>*Leaves of the oak dry and yellow.*
>xxiv. ‖*Leaves of the maple begin to fall in the night.*
>xxv. *Hoar froſt.*
>xxvi. *Leaves of the robinia caragana fall.*
>>*Sycamore ſtripped of its leaves.*
Oct. X.
>iv. Cherry, *bird, ſtripped of its leaves.*
>v. *A ſtorm.*

* Adamſon in the account of his voyage to S negal, p. 121. ſays, that October 1749, European ſwallows lodged on the veſſel in which he went from Goree to Senegal, and that they are never ſeen there but at this time of the year, along with quails, wagtails, kites, and ſome other birds of paſſage, and do not build neſts there. This teſtimony ſeems to take away all doubts about this long conteſted point.

‖Geminus, either from himſelf or Democritus, which is much the ſame, as Rome and Abdera were nearly in the ſame latitude, ſays that the leaves of trees began to drop the fourth of Scorpio, which anſwers to October 28.

Green

Oct. X.
vi. *Green leaves of the afh fall. When they fall fouthern plants ought to be put under fhelter.*
vii. Elm *is ftripped.*
A ftorm.
Froft.
xii. *The leaves of the lime tree fall.*
Green houfes ought to be fhut.
xiii. *The afp tree ftill in leaf.*
xiv. *Ice.*
xvii. *Hafel nut tree ftripped.*
xxv. Abele, 446.2. Populus *alba, ftripped.*
xxvi. Saffron, *meadow, juft out of blow.*
Poplar, *black, ftripped.*
xxvii. *Summer ended.*
xxviii. *Sallows only in leaf.*

Vernantefque comas triftis ademit hyems.
PETRON.

XI. FREEZING MONTH.
From the laft fhedding of leaves to the laft green plant.

Iva *annua.*
Nov. XI.
ii. *Alternate fnow and froft.*
v. Milleria *quinqueflora.*
Thaw with rain.
The earth covered with fnow.
Rivers are frozen.
Snow with a thaw.
Firm fnow.
Thaws again.
Ditches

Ditches filled with water.
Winter thoroughly settled.

Heu quam cuncta abeunt celeri mortalia curfu.

XII. DECLINING WINTER MONTH.

From the laft green plant to the winter folftice.

Nov. XI.
    v. *Moffes and lichens only flourifh.*
       Thermometer, gr. 34.2.
   vi. *Thaws.*
   xx. *Cold changeable weather.*

Quælibet orta cadunt, et finem cæpta videbunt.

THE

CALENDAR of FLORA.

By BENJAMIN STILLINGFLEET.

Made at STRATTON in NORFOLK,
Anno 1755. Latitude 52° 45'.

MARKS EXPLAINED.

b fignifies buds fwelled.

B - - - - buds beginning to open.

f - -- - - flowers beginning to open

F - - - - - flowers full blown.

l - - - - - leaves beginning to open.

L - - - - leaves quite out.

r. p. - - - fruit nearly ripe.

R. P. - - fruit quite ripe.

E - - - - emerging out of the ground.

D - - - - flowers decayed.

THE
CALENDAR of FLORA.

I. MONTH.

Reviving nature feems again to breath,
As loofen'd from the cold embrace of death.

Jan. 5. Rofemary, 515. H. Rofmarinus *officinal.* f.
   11. Honeyfuckle, 458. Lonicera *periclymenum*, l.
   23. Archangel, *red*, 240.2. Lamium *purpu-
reum*, F.
      Hafel nut tree, 439. Corylus *avellana*, f.
      Honeyfuckle, 458. Lonicera *pericly-
menum*, L.
      Lauruftinus. 1690. H. Viburnum *tinus*, F.
      Holly, 466. Ilex *aquifolium*, f.
   26. Snow drops, 1144. H. Galanthus *nivalis*,
F.
      Chickweed, 347.6. Alfine *media*, F.
      Spurry, 351.7. Spergula *arvenfis*, F.
      Daify, 184. Bellis *perennis*, F.

II. MONTH.

Love's pleafing ferment gently now begins
To warm the flowing blood.
     U'   WOOD

Feb. 4. WOOD LARK, 69.2. *Alauda arborea,*
fings.
Elder tree, 461. Sambucus *nigra,* f.

12. ROOKS, 39.3. *Corvus frugilegus, begin to*
pair.
GEESE, 136.1. *Anas, anfer, begin to lay.*
*WAGTAIL WHITE, 75.1. *Motacilla*
alba, appears.

16. THRUSH, 64.2. *Turdus muficus, fings.*
†CHAFFINCH, 88. *Fringilla cælebs.*
fings.

20. *Thermometer,* 11. *Higheft this month.*
Thermometer, -2. *Loweft this month.*

22. PARTRIDGES, 57. *Tetrao perdix, begin*
to pair.
Hafel tree, 439. Corylus *avellana,* F.

25. Goofeberry bufh, 1484. H. ⎫
Ribes *groffularia,* l. ⎬ both young
Currant, *red,* 456.1. Ribes ⎭ plants.
rubrum, l.
Thermometer from the 19th *to the* 25th, *be-*
tween 0 *and* -1 *with fnow.*
Wind during the latter half of the month be-
tween E. and N.

---

* The wagtail is faid by Willughby to remain with us all the year
in the fevereft weather. It feems to me to fhift its quarters at leaft, if
it does not go out of England. However, it is certainly a bird of
paffage in fome countries, if we can believe Aldrovandus, the author
of the Swedifh Calendar, and the author of the treatife De Migrationibus Avium. Linnæus obferves, S. N. Art. Motacilla, that moft
birds which live upon infects, and not grains, migrate.
† Linnæus fays, that the female chaffinch goes to Italy alone, thro'
Holland; and that the male in the fpring, changing its note, foretells
the fummer: and Gefner, ornithol. p. 388. fays that the female
chaffinch difappears in Switzerland in the winter, but not the male.

III.

III. M O N T H.

Winter ftill ling'ring on the verge of fpring,
Retires reluctant, and from time to time
Looks back, while at his keen and chilling breath
Fair Flora fickens.

March

2. ROOKS, 39.3. *Corvus frugilegus, begin to build.*
   Thermometer, 10.
4. THRUSH, 64.2. *Turdus muficus, fings.*
   Thermometer, 11.
5. DOVE, RING, 62.9. *Columba palumbus, cooes.*
7. *Thermometer,* o. *Loweft this month.*
11. Sallow,   Salix,   F.
   Lauruftinus, 1690. H. Viburnum *tinus,* l.
   *BEES, *Apis mellifera, out of the hive.*
   Laurel, 1549. H. Prunus *laurocerafus,* l.
   Bay, 1688. H. Laurus *nobilis,* l.
20. *Vernal equinox.*
21. Grafs, *fcurvy,* 302.1. Cochlearia *officinalis,* F.
   Afp, 446.3. Populus *tremula,* F.
26. Speedwell, *germander,* 279.4. Veronica *agreftis,* F.
   Alder, 442. Alnus *betula,* F.
28. Violet, *fweet,* 364.2. Viola *odorata,* F.
   Parfnep, *cow,* 205. Heracleum *fphondylium,* E.
   Pilewort, 296. Ranunculus *ficaria,* F.

---

* Pliny, nat. hift. lib. 11. §. 5. fays, that bees do not come out of their hives before May 11. and feems to blame Ariftotle for faying that they come out in the beginning of fpring, i. e. March 12.

Thermometer,

March

28. *Thermometer*, 25.50. *Higheſt this month.*
29. Cherry tree, 463. Prunus *ceraſus*, B.
    Currant buſh, 456.1.Ribes *rubrum*, B.
    Primroſe, 284.1. Primula *veris*, F.
    Yew tree, 445. Taxus *baccata*, F.
    Elder, *water*, 460. Viburnum *opulus*, B.
    Thorn, haw, 453.3. Cratægus *oxyacantha*, B.
    Larch tree, 1405. H. Pinus *larix*, B.
    Hornbeam, 451. Carpinus *oſtrya*, B.
    Tanſy, 188. Tanacetum *vulgare*, E.

IV. M O N T H.

- - - - - - - - Airs, vernal airs,
Breathing the ſmell of grove and field, attune
The trembling leaves.   MILTON.

April 1. Cheſnut, *horſe*, 1683. Æſculus *hippocaſ-tanum*, B.
    BIRCH, 443. Betula *alba*, L.
    Willow, *weeping*,   Salix *Babylo-nica*, L.
    ELM TREE, 468. Ulmus *campeſtris*, F.
    Quicken tree, 452.2. Sorbus *aucuparia*, f.
    Apricot, 1533. H. Prunus *Armeniaca*, F.
    Narciſſus, *pale*, 371.2. Narciſſus *pſeuda-nar.*
3. Holly, 466.1. Ilex *aquifolium*, f.
    Bramble, 467.1. Rubus *fruticoſus*, L.
    Raſberry buſh, 467.4. Rubus *idæus*, L.
    Currants, *red*, 456. Ribes *rubrum*, F.
    Dandelion, 170.1. Leontodon *taraxicum*, E.

Cleavers,

April 3. Cleavers, 225. Galium *aparine*, E.
  4. Lauruftinus, 1690. H. Viburnum *tinus*, F.
     APPLE TREE, 451.1,2. Pyrus *malus*, B.
     Orpine, 269.1. Sedum *telephium*, B.
     Briar, 454.1. Rofa *canina*, L.
  6. Goofeberry, 1489. H. Ribes *groffularia*, f.
     Maple, 470.2. Acer *campeftre*, B.
     Peach, 1515. H. Amygdalus *Perfica*, L.
     et F.
     Apricot, 1533. H. Malus *Armeniaca*, L.
     Plumb tree, 462. Prunus *præcox*, L.
     Pear tree, 452. Pyrus *communis*, B.
     *SWALLOW, 71.2. Hirundo *urbica*,
     returns.
  7. Filberd, 439. Corylus *avellana*, L.
     Sallow,   Salix, L.
     Alder, 442.1. Betula *alnus*, l.
     Lilac, 1763. Syringa *vulgaris*, l.
     Oak, 440.1. Quercus, *robur*, f.
     Willow, *weeping*,   Salix *Babylonica*, b.
  8. Juniper, 444. Juniperus *communis*, b.
  9. Lilac, 1763. Syringa *vulgaris*, b.
     Sycamore, 470. Acer *pfeudoplatanus*, L.
     Wormwood, 188.1. Artemifia *abfinthium*,
     E.
     †NIGHTINGALE, 78. *Motacilla lu-*
     . fcinia, fings.

                                 U 3   Auricula,

---

* According to Ptolemy, Swallows return to Ægypt about the latter end of January.

† From morn 'till eve, 'tis mufic all around;
  Nor doft thou, Philomel, difdain to join,
  Even in the mid-day glare, and aid the quire,
  But thy fweet fong calls for an hour apait,
  When folemn Night beneath his canopy,
  Enrich'd with ftars, by Silence and by Sleep
                                        Attended,

April

9. Auricula, 1082. H. Primula *auricula*, b.
10. Bay, 1688. H. Laurus *nobilis*, L.
    Hornbeam, 451. Carpinus *betulus*, b.
    Willow, *white*, 447.1. Salix *alba*, b.
    BEES *about the male fallows.*
    Feverfew, 187.1. Matricaria *Parthenium*, E.
    Dandelion, 170.1. Leontodon *taraxicum*, E.
    Hound's tongue, 226.1. Cynogloffum *officinale*, E.
    Elm, 468. Ulmus *campeftris*, l.
    ANEMONE, *wood*, 259. Anemone *nemorofa*, F.
    Jack in the hedge, 291. Eryfimum *alliaria*, E.
    Quince tree, 1452. H. Pyrus *cydonia*, L.
11. Elder, *water*, 460. Viburnum *opulus*, L.
    Alder, *berry bearing*, 465. Rhamnus *frangula*, L.
12. Acacia, 1719. H. Robinia *acacia*, l.
    Mulberry tree, 1429. H. Morus *nigra*, l.
    Lime tree, 473.1,2,3. Tilia *Europæa*, l.
    Mercury, *dogs*, 138.1 Mercurialis *perennis*, F.
    *Elm, *wych*, 469.4. L.
    Ragweed, 177. Senecio *jacobæa*, E.

Attended, fits and nods, in awful ftate ;
Or when the Moon in her refulgent car,
Triumphant rides amidft the filver clouds,
Turning them as fhe paffes, and with rays
Of mildeft luftre gilds the fcene below ;
While zephyrs bland breath thro' the thickening fhade,
With breath fo gentle, and fo foft, that e'en
The poplar's trembling leaf forgets to move,
And mimic with it found the vernal fhower ;
Then let me fit, and liften to thy ftrains, &c.

Linnæus does not feem to know this fpecies of elm.

April

13. Laburnum, 1721. Cytifus *laburnum*, f.
    Strawberry, 254. Fragaria *vefca*, F.
    Quicken tree, 452.2. Sorbus *aucuparia*, L.
    Sycomore, 470. Acer *pfeudoplat.* L.
    Laurel, 1549. H. Prunus *laurocerafus*, L.
    Goofeberry bufh, 1484. H. Ribes *grof-fularia*, F.
    Currant bufh, 456.1. Ribes *rubrum*, F.
    Mallow, 251.1. Malva *fylveftris*, E.
    Hornbeam, 451. Carpinus *betulus*, L.
14. Flixweed, 298.3. Sifymbrium *fophia*, E.
    Apple tree, 451. Pyrus *malus*, L.
    Hops, 137.1. Humulus *lupinus*, E.
    Plane tree, 1706. H. Platanus *orientalis*, b.
    Walnut tree, 438. Juglans *regia*, f. '
    BITTERN, 100.11. Ardea *ftellaris*, *makes a noife.*
15. Vine, 1613. Vitis *vinifera*, B.
    Turneps, 204.1. Braffica *rapa*, F.
16. Abele, 446.2. Populus *alba*, B.
    Chefnut, 138.2. H. Fagus *caftanea*, B.
    Ivy, *ground*, 243. Glechoma *hederacea*, F.
    Fig tree, 1431. Ficus *carica*, b.
    Apricots and peaches out of blow.
    RED START, 78.5. Motacilla *Phæni-curus*, *returns.*
    Tulip tree, 1690. H. Liriodendron *tuli-pifera*, B.
    Plumb tree, 462. Prunus *domeftica*, F.
    Sorrel, *wood*, *281.1,2. Oxalis *acetofella*, F.
    Marygold, *marfh*, 272. Caltha *paluftris*, F.
    Laurel, *fpurge*, 465. Daphne *laureola*, F.
17. Jack in the hedge, 291.2. Eryfimum *alliaria*, F.

Willow,

April

17. Willow, *white*, 447.1. Salix *alba*, L. et F.
Cedar, 1404. H. Pinus *cedrus*, l.
Elder, *water*, 460.1. Viburnum *opulus*, f.
Abele, 446.2. Populus *alba*, L.
*CUCKOW, 23. Cuculus *canorus*, *fings*.

18. Oak, 440.1. Quercus, *robur*, l. F.
Thorn, *black*, 462.1. Prunus *fpinofus*, B.
Pear tree, 452. Pyrus *communis*, f.
Mulberry tree, 1429. H. Morus *nigra*. B.
Violet, *dog*, 364.3. Viola *canina*, F.
Lime tree, 413.1,2,3. Tilia *Europæa*, L.
Nightfhade, 265. Atropa *belladonna*, E.
Cherry tree, 463.1. Prunus *cerafus*, F.
Afh tree, 469. Fraxinus *excelfior*, f.
Maple, 470. Acer *campeftre*, L,
Broom, 474. Spartium *fcoparium*, b.
Chefnut, 138.2. Fagus *caftanea*, L.
Fir, *Scotch*, 442. Pinus *fylveftris*, b.
Cuckow flower, 299. Cardamine *pratenfis*,

20. *Thermometer*, 42. *the higheft this month*.

21. Walnut-tree, 438. Juglans *regia*, L.
Plane tree, 1706. H. Platanus *orientalis*, L.
Fir, *Weymouth*, 8. dend. Pinus *tæda*, B.
Acacia, 1719. H. Robinia *pfeudo-acacia*,
L.
Fig tree, 1431. H. Ficus *carica*, L.
Wall flower, 291. Cheiranthus *cheiri*, F.
Poplar, *black*, 446.1. Populus nigra, L.
Beech tree, 439.1. Fagus *fylvatica*, L.

22. Fir, *balm of Gilead*,   Pinus *balfamea*,
l. et f.

---

* Ariftophanes fays, that when the cuckow fung the Phœnicians
eaped wheat and barley. Vid. Aves.

Young

April

22. *Young Apricots.*

Fir, *Scotch*, 442. Pinus *fylveftris*, f.

Ash, 469. Fraxinus *excelfior*, F. et L.

Broom, 474. Spartium *fcoparium*, L.

Poplar, *Carolina.* L.

Meadow fweet, 259. Spiræa *ulmaria*, E.

Fig tree, 1431. H. Ficus *carica*, *fruit formed.*

Tormentil, 257.1. Tormentilla *erecta*, E.

Phyllerea, 1585. H. Phyllerea *latifolia*, F.

Thorn, *evergreen*, 1459. H. Mefpilus *pyracantha*, F.

Rofemary, 515. H. Rofmarinus *officinalis*, F.

Campion, *white*, 339.8. Lychnis *dioica*, F.

Buckbean, 285.1. Menyanthes *trifol.* F.

Furze, *needle*, 476.1. Genifta *Anglica*, F.

Stitchwort, 346.1. Stellaria *holoftea*, F.

23. Crab tree, 451.2. Pyrus *malus fylv.* F.

Apple tree, 451.1. Pyrus *malus*, f.

Robert, *herb*, 358. Geranium *Robertian.* F.

Fieldfares, 64:3. *Turdus pilaris, ftill here.*

24. Broom, 474. Spartium *fcoparium*, F.

Mercury, 156.15. Chenopodium *bonus henr.* F.

Yew tree, 445. Taxus *baccifera*, L.

Holly, 466.1. Ilex *aquifolium*, B.

Furze, 475. Ulex *Europæus*, l.

Agrimony, 202. Agrimonia *eupator.* E.

25. Sycomore, 470. Acer *pfeudoplat.* F.

Hornbeam, 451. Carpinus *betulus*, F.

Afp, 446. Populus *tremula*, l.

Spurge, *fun*, 313.8. Euphorbia *peplus*, F.

Elder tree, 461.1. Sambucus *nigra*, f.

Nettle, 139. Urtica *dioica*, F.

April

25. Bindweed, *small*, 275.2. Convolvulus *ar-venf*. E.

Fir, *balm of Gilead*, Pinus *balfamea*, L.

Cicely, *wild*, 207.1. Chærophyllum *fyl-vefre*, F.

Young currants and goofeberries.

26. Plantain *ribwort*, 314.5. Plantago *lanceol*. F.

Germander, *wild*, 281.11. Veronica *chamæd*. F.

Cuckow pint, 266. Arum *maculatum*, *fpatha* out.

Holly, 466. Ilex *aquifolium*, F.

Harebells, 373.3. Hyacinthus *nonfcript*. F.

27. LILAC, 1763. H. Syringa *vulgaris*, F.

Crane's bill, *field*, 357.2. Geranium *ci-cutar*. F.

St. John's wort, 342.1. Hypericum *per-forat*. E.

Betony *water*, 283.1. Scrophularia *aquat*. E.

Bryony, *white*, 261. Bryonia *alba*, E.

Birch tree, 443.1. Betula *alba*, F.

28. Jeffamine, 1599.1. H. Jafminum *officinale*, l.

Thorn, *white*, 453.3. Cratægus *oxyacantha*, f.

*BLACK CAP, 79.12. *Motacilla atra-capilla*, *fings*.

---

* The black cap is a very fine finging bird, and is by fome in Norfolk called the mock nightingale. Whether it be a bird of paffage i cannot fay.

WHITE

April

28, *WHITE THROAT, 77. Motacilla
fylvia.
Juniper, 444.1. Juniperus *communis*, f.
Rafberry bufh, 467.4. Rubus *idæus*, f.
Quince tree, 1452. H. Malus *Cydon.* f.
Crowfoot, *fweet wood*, 248.1. Ranunculus
auric. F.

29. Bugle, 245. Ajuga, *reptans*, F.
Bay, 1688. H. Laurus *nobilis*, f.
Peas and beans, f.
Snow.
Chervil, *wild*, 207.1. Chærophyllum *te-
mulent*, f.
Parfnep, *cow*, 205.1. Heracleum *fphon-
dyl.* f.
Pine, *manured*, 1398.1. H. Pinus *pinea*, f.

30. *Snow.*
† *Thermom.* 5. *The lowest this month.*

---

* I have fome doubt whether this bird be the Sylvia of Linnæus,
though the defcription feems to anfwer to Ray's, and to one of my
own, which I find among my papers.

† Vernal heat, according to Dr. Hales, at a medium, is 18.25. ¶

V. MONTH.

All that is fweet to fmell, all that can charm
Or eye or ear, burfts forth on every fide,
And crouds upon the fenfes.

May 1. Crofswort, 223.1. Valantia *cruciata*, F.
Avens, 253.1. Geum *urbanum*, F.
Mugwort, 191.1. Artemifia *campeftris*, E.
Bay, 1688. H. Laurus *nobilis*, L.

Lilly

May 3. Lilly of the valley, 264. Convallaria *Mai-alis*, f.

Violet *water*, 285. Hottonia *paluſtris*, F.

4. Lettuce *lambs*, 201. Valeriana *locuſta*, F,
Tulip tree, Liriodendron *tulipifera*, L,
Hound's tongue, 226.1. Cynogloſſum *officinale*.

Cowſlips, 284.3. Primula *veris*, F.

Valerian, *great wild*, 200.1. Valerian *officinalis*, F.

Rattle, *yellow*, 284.1. Rhinanthus *criſta galli*, F.

Ice.

Thermom. 8. *The loweſt this month.*

Fir, *ſilver, buds hurt by the froſt.*

5. Twayblade, 385. Ophrys *ovata*, f.
Tormentil, 257. Tormentilla *erecta*, F.
Celandine, 309. Chelidonium *majus*, E.
Betony, 238.1. Betonica *officinalis*, E.

6. Oak, 440. Quercus, *robur*, F. et L.
Time for ſowing barley.
Saxifrage, *white*, 354.6. Saxifraga *granulata*, F.

Aſh, 469. Fraxinus *exelſior*, f.
Ramſons, 370.5. Allium *urſinum*, F.
Nettle, *white*, 240.1. Lamium *album*, F.
Quicken tree, 452.2. Sorbus *aucuparia*, F.

7. Fir, *Scotch*, 442. Pinus *ſylveſtris*, F,

8. Woodruffe, 224. Aſperula *odorata*, F.

9. Cheſnut tree, 1382. H. Fagus *caſtanea*, f.

10. Celandine, 309. Chelidonium *majus*, F.
Solomon's ſeal, 664. Convallaria *polygonat.* F.
Thorn, *white*, 453.3. Cratægus *oxyacantha*, F.

3   Maple,

May
11. Maple, 470.2. Acer *campeſtre*, F.
Roſes, *garden*, f.
12. Barberry buſh, 465. Berberis *vulgaris*, F.
Cheſnut, *horſe*, 1683. H. Æſculus *hip-
pocas*. F.
Bugloſs, *ſmall wild*, 227.1. Lycopſis *ar-
venſis*, F.
13. Grafs, *water ſcorpion*, 229.4. Myoſotis
ſcorpⁱoid. F.
Quince tree, 1452. H. Pyrus *Cydonia*, F.
Cleavers, 225. Galium *aparine*, F.
14. Mulberry tree, 1429. H. Morus *nigra*, L.
Aſp, 446.3. Populus *tremula*, l.
Crowfoot, *bulbous*, 247.2. Ranunculus
bulbos. F.
Butter cups, 247. Ranunculus *repens*, F.
15. *Young turkies*.
Lime tree, 473. Tilia *Europæa*, f.
Milkwort, *287.1,2. Polygala *vulgaris*, F.
Crane's bill, 359.10. Geranium *molle*, F.
Walnut, 1376. H. Juglans *regia*, F.
16. Muſtard, *hedge*, 298.4. Eryſimum *offici-
nale*, F.
20. Bryony, *black*, 262.1. Tamus *communis*, F.
*Many oaks, and more aſhes and beeches,
ſtill without leaf.*
Violet, *ſweet*, 364.1. Viola *odora*, D.
Stitchwort, 346. Stellaria *holoſtea*, D.
Anemone, *wood*, 259.1. Anemone *ne-
moroſa*, D.
Cuckow flower, 299.20. Cardamine *pra-
tenſis*, D.
Earth nut, 209. Bunium, bulbocaſt. F.
Mulberry tree, 1429. H. Morus *nigra*, f.
Night-

May

21. Nightfhade, 265. Atropa *belladonna*, f.
RYE, 288. Secale *hybernum*, *in ear*.

23. Pellitory *of the wall*, 158.1. Parietaria
officin. F.

24. Bramble, 467. Rubus *fruticofus*, f.

25. Moneywort, 283.1. Lyfimachia *nummul*.
F.

Columbines, 173.1. Aquilegia *vulgar*.
F. *in the woods*.

26. Tanfy, *wild*, 256.5. Potentilla *anferina*, F.
Henbane, 274. Hyofcyamus *niger*, F.

27. Campion, *white*, 339.8. Lychnis *dioica*, F.
Clover, 328.6 Trifolium *pratenfe*, F.

28. Avens, 262.1. Geum *urbanum*, F.
Chervil, *wild*, 207. Chærophyllum *te-
mulent*. F.

30. Bryony, *black*, 262.1. Tamus *communis*, F.
Brooklime, 280.8. Veronica *beccabunga*, F.
Cuckow flower, 338. Lychnis *flos cuculi*, F.
Creffes, *water*, 300.1. Sifymbrium *nafturt*.
F.

Thermom. 32. Higheft this month.

31. Spurrey, 351.7. Spergula *arvenfis*, F.
Alder, *berry bearing*, 465. Rhamnus *frangula*, F.

VI. MONTH.

Now the mower whets his fcythe,
And every fhepherd tells his tale
Under the hawthorn in the dale.   · MILTON.

June 2. Elder, *water*, 460.1. Viburnum *opulus*, F.
Lilly, *yellow water*, 368.1. Nymphæa
lutea, F.   Flower

June 2. Flower de luce, *yellow water*, 374. Iris *pfeudo-acor*. F.

Mayweed, *ftinking*, 185.3. Anthemis *cotula*, F.

Pimpernel, 282.1. Anagallis arvenfis, F.

3. Arfmart, 145.4. Polygonum *perficaria*, F.

* Thyme, 430.1. Thymus *ferpyllum*, F.

Parfnep, *cow*, 205. Heracleum *fphon-dylium*, F.

Quicken tree, 452. Sorbus *aucuparia*, D.

5. Radifh, *horfe*, 301.1. Cochlearia *armo-rac*. F.

Thorn, *evergreen*, 1459.3. H. Mefpilus *pyracantha*, F.

Bramble, 467. Rubus *fruticofus*, F.

† GOAT SUCKER, or FERN OWL, 27. Caprimulgus *Europæus*, *is heard in the evening*.

6. Vine, 1613. H. Vitis *vinifera*, b.

Flix weed, 298.3. Sifymbrium *fophia*, F.

Rafberry bufh, 467.4. Rubus *idæus*, F.

Mallow, *dwarf*, 251.2. Malva *rotundi-folia*, F.

Elder, 461.1. Sambucus *nigra*, F.

Stitchwort, *leffer*, 346. Stellaria *graminea*, F.

Tare, *everlafting*, 320.3. Lathyrus *praten-fis*, F.

---

* Pliny, lib. 11. §. 14. fays, the chief time for bees to make honey is about the folftice, when the vine and thyme are in blow. According to his account then thefe plants are as forward in England as in Italy.

† This bird is faid by Catefby, as quoted by the author of the treatife De Migrationibus Avium, to be a bird of paffage.

Gout

June 6. Gout *weed*, 208.3. Ægopodium *podagrar*. F.

Bryony, *white*, 261.1,2. Bryonia *alba*, F.
ROSE, DOG, 454.1. Rofa *canina*, F.
Buglofs *vipers*, 227.1. Echium *vulgare*, F.

7. Grafs, *vernal*, 398.1. Anthoxanthum *odorat.* F.
Darnel, *red*, 395. Lolium *perenne*, F.
Poppy, *wild*, 308.1. Papaver *fomnifer*, F.
Buckwheat, 181. H. Polygonu'm *fago-pyrum*, F.

8. Pondweed, *narrow leaved*, 145.9. Polygonum *amphib.* F.
Sanicle, 221.1. Sanicula *Europæa.* F.

9. Eyebright, *284.1. Euphrafia *officinalis*, F.
Heath, *fine leaved*, 471.3. Erica *cinerea*, F.
Saxifrage, *bugle, hyacinth*, D.
Broom, 474.1. Spartium *fcoparium, podded.*
Nettle, *hedge*, 237. Stachys *fylvatica*, F.

12. Wheat, 386.1. Triticum *hybernum, in ear.*
Meadow fweet, 259.1. Spiræa *ulmaria*, f.
SCABIOUS, FIELD, 191.1. Scabiofa *arven-fis*, F.
Valerian, *great water*, 200.1. Valeriana *officinal.* f.
Cinquefoil, *marfh*, 256.1. Comarum *pa-luftre*, F.
Orchis, *leffer butterfly*, 380.18. Orchis *bifolia*, F.

13. Willow herb, *great hairy*, 311.2. Epilobium *hirfutum*, F.
Parfnep, *cow*, 205. Heracleum *fphondyl.* F.
Betony, *water*, 283.1. Scrophularia *aquat.* F.

Cockle,

June

13. Cockle, 338.3. Agroftemma *githago*, F.
    Sage, 510.7. H. Salvia *officinalis*, F.
15. Mallow, 251.1. Malva *fylveftris*, F.
    Nipplewort, 173.1. Lapfana *communis*, F.
    Woodbind, 458.1,2. Lonicera *pericly-men*. f.
    NIGHTINGALE, *fings*.
16. Fir, *Weymouth*, 8. dend. Pinus *tæda*, F.
    Hemlock, 215.1. Conium *maculatum*, F.
  - Nightfhade, *woody*, 265. Solanum *dulca-mara*, F.
    Archangel, *white*, 240. Lamium *album*, F.
17. Vervain, 236. Verbena *officinalis*, F.
    Agrimony, 202. Agrimonia *eupator*, F.
    Hemlock, *water*, 215. Phellandrium *aquatic*. F.
    Acacia, 1719. H. Robinia *pfeudo-acacia*, F.
18. Yarrow, 183. Achillea *millefolium*, F.
19. *Thermom*. 44.25. *Higheft this month*.
21. Orache, *wild*, 154.1. Chenopodium *album*, F.
    Solftice. About this time ROOKS *come not to their neft trees at night*.
    Wheat, 386.1. Triticum *hybernum*, F.
    RYE, 388.1. Secale *hybernum*, F.
    Self-heal, 238. Prunella *vulgaris*, f.
    Parfley, *hedge*, 219.4. Tordylium *anthrif-cus*, f.
    Graffes of many kinds, as feftuca, aira, agrof-tis, phleum cynofurus, in ear.
22. Horehound, *bafe*, 239. Stachys *Germa-nica*, F.

X   St.

June

22. St. John's wort, 342. Hypericum *perfo-ratum*, F.
Parfnep, 206.1. Paftinaca *fativa*, F.
Mullein, *white*, 287. Verbafcum *thapfus*, F.
Poppy, *wild*, 308. Papaver *fomnifer*, F.

23. Larkfpur, 708.3. H. Delphinium *Ajacis*, F.
Marygold, *corn*, 182.1. Chryfanthemum *feget*. F.

24. Rofemary, 515. H. Rofmarinus *officinalis*, D.

25. Vine, 1613. H. Vitis *vinifera*, F.
Bindweed, *great*, 275.2. Convolvulus *ar-venfis*, F.
Feverfew, 187. Matricaria *parthenium*, F.
Woad, *wild*, 366.2. Refeda *luteola*, F.
Rocket, *bafe*, 366.1. Refeda *lutea*, F.
Archangel, *yellow*, 240.5. Galeopfis *gale-obdolon*, F.
Wheat, 386.1. Triticum *hybernum*, F.
Thermom. 20. The loweft this month.

27. *Clover mowed.*
Pennywort, *marfh*, 222. Hydrocotule *vul-garis*, F.
Meadow, *fweet*, 259. Spiræa *ulmaria*, F.

28. Oats *manured*, 389. Avena *fativa*, F.
Barley, 388. Hordeum *vulgare*, F.
Midfummer fhoots of apricot, oak, beech, elm.
SUCCORY, WILD, 172.1. Cichorium *inty-tus*, F.
Blue bottles, 198. Centaurea *cyanus*, F.

Knap-

3

June

28. Knapweed, *great*, 198. Centaurea *fca-biofa*, F.

30. *Currants ripe.*
    According to Dr. Hales, May and June heat is, at a medium, 28.5.

---

* The groves, the fields, the meadows, now no more
With melody refound. 'Tis filence all,
As if the lovely fongfters, overwhelm'd
By bounteous nature's plenty, lay intranc'd
In drowfy lethargy.

---

* I heard no birds after the end of this month, except the STONE CURLEW, 108.4. Charadrius Oedicnemus, whiftling late at night; the YELLOW HAMMER, 93.2. Emberiza flava; the GOLD-FINCH, 89.1. and GOLDEN CRESTED WREN, 79.9. Mota-cilla regulus, now and then chirping. I omitted to note down when the cuckow left off finging, but, as well as i remember, it was about this time. Ariftotle fays, that this bird difappears about the rifing of the dog ftar, i. e. towards the latter end of July.

VII. M O N T H.

Berries and pulpous fruits of various kinds,
The promife of the blooming fpring, now yield
Their rich and wholefome juices, meant t' allay
The ferment of the bilious blood.

July 2. Beech, 439. Fagus *fylvatica*, F.
Pearlwort, 345.2. Fagina *procumbens*, F.
Carrot, *wild*, 218. Daucus *carreta*, F.
Grafs, *dog*, 390.1. Triticum *repens, in ecr.*
Violet, *Calathian*, 274. Gentiana *pneu-menan.* F.

4. Silver weed, 256.5. Potentilla *anferina*, F.
Betony, 238.1. Betonica *officinalis*, F.
Nightfhade, *enchanters*, 289. Circæa *lute-tiana*, f.

X 2   Lavender,

July 6. Lavender, 512. Lavendula *spica*, F.
Parſley, *hedge*, Tordylium *anthriſcus*, F.
Gromill, 228.1. Lithoſpermum *officinale*,
F.
Furze, 475. Ulex *geniſta*, D.
Cow wheat, *eyebright*, 284.2. Euphraſia
odont. F.

7. Pinks, maiden, 335.1. Dianthus *deltoides*,
F.

8. Tanſey, 188.1. Tanacetum *vulgare*, f.
Bed-ſtraw, *lady's yellow*, 224. Galium
verum, F.
Sage, *wood*, 245. Teucrium *ſcorodonia*, F.
Spinach, 162. H. Spinacia *oleracia*, F.
Thermom. 22. *Loweſt this month.*

9. Angelica, *wild*, 208.2. Angelica *ſyl-
veſtris*, F.
Strawberries ripe.
Fennel, 217. Anethum *fœniculum*, F.

10. Beans, *kidney*, 884. H. Phaſeolus *vulgaris*,
podded.
Parſley, 884. H. Apium *petroſelinum*, F.
Sun dew, *round leaved*, 356.3. Droſera
rotundifol. F.
Sun dew, *long leaved*, 356.4. Droſera *lon-
gifol*. F.
Lilly, *white*, 1109. H. Lilium *candidum*, f.

11. Mullein, *hoary*, 288. Verbaſcum *phlo-
moid*. F.
Plantain, *great*, 314.1,2. Plantago *major*,
F.
WILLOW, SPIKED, of Theophr.
1699. H. Spiræa *ſalicifol*. F.
Jeſſamine, 1599. H. Jaſminum *officinale*,
F.
Reſt harrow, 332. Ononis *ſpinoſa*, F.
Hyſſop,

July

11. Hyffop, 516. H. Hyffopus *officinalis*, F.
Potatoes, 615.14. H. Solanum *tuberofum*, F.
Second fhoots of the maple.
Bell flower, *round leaved*, 277.5. Campanula, F.
LILLY, WHITE, 1109. H. Lilium *candidum*, F.
Rafberries ripe.
Figs yellow.

13. LIME TREE, 473. Tilia *Europæa*, F.
Knapweed, 198.2. Centaurea *jacea*, F.
Stonecrop, 269. Sedum *rupeftre*, F.
Grafs, *knot*, 146. Polygonum *aviculare*, F.
Grafs, *bearded dog*, 390.2. Triticum *caninum*, F.

15. *Thermom. 39. Higheft this month.*
16. Afparagus, 267.1. Afparagus *officinalis*, *berries.*
Mugwort, 190.1. Artemifia *vulgaris*, F.
18. Willow herb, *purple fpiked*, 367.1. Lythrum *falicaria*, F.
YOUNG PARTRIDGES.
Agrimony, *water hemp*, 187.1. Bidens *tripart.* F

- 20. Flax, *purging*, 362.6. Linum *catharticum*, F.
Arfmart, *fpotted*, 145.4. Polygonum *perficaria*, F.
Lilly, *martagon*, 1112. H. Lilium *martagon.*
HENS *moult.*
22. Orpine, 269. Sedum *telephium*, f.
Hart's tongue, 116. Afplenium *fcolopendra*, F.   Pen

July
22. Pennyroyal, 235. Mentha *pulegium*, F.
Bramble, 461.1. Rubus *fruticofus*. *Fruit red.*
Lauruftinus, 1690. H. Viburnum *tinus*, f.
24. Elecampane, 176. Inula *helenium*, F.
Amaranth, 202. H. Amaranthus *caudatus*, F.
27. Bindweed, *great*, 275.1. Convolvulus *fepium*, F.
28. Plantain, *great water*, 257.1. Alifma *plantago*, F.
Mint, *water*, 233.6. Mentha *aquatica*, F.
Willow herb, 311.6. Epilobium *paluftre*, F.
Thiſtle tree fow, 163.7. Sonchus *arvenſis*, F.
Burdock, 197.2. Arctium *lappa*, f.
Saxifrage, *burnet*, 213.1,2. Pimpinella *faxifraga*, F.
DEVIL'S BIT, 191.3. Scabiofa *fuccifa*, F.
30. Nightſhade, common, 288.4. Solanum *nigrum*, F.
DOVE, RING, 62.9. Columba *palumbus*, cooes.

VIII. MONTH.

Pour'd from the villages, a numerous train
Now fpreads o'er all the fields. In form'd array
The reapers move, nor fhrink for heat or toil,
By emulation urg'd. Others difpers'd,
Or bind in fheaves, or load or guide the wain
That tinkles as it paffes. Far behind,
Old age and infancy with careful hand
Pick up each ftraggling ear, &c.

Auguſt

1. Melilot, 331.1. Trifolium *officinale*, F.
   Rue, 874.1. Ruta *graveolens*, F.
   Soapwort, 339.6. Saponaria *officinalis*, F.
   Bedſtraw, *white, lady's*, 224.2. Galium
   paluſtre, F.
   Parſnep, *water*, 300. Siſymbrium *naſturt*.
   F.
   Oats almoſt fit to cut.
3. *Barley cut.*
5. Tanſy, 188.1. Tanacetum *vulgare*, F.
   Onion, 1115. H. Allium *cepa*, F.
7. Horehound, 239. Marrubium *vulgare*, F.
   Mint, *water*, 233.6. Mentha *aquat*. F.
   Nettle, 139. Urtica *dioica*, F.
   Orpine, 269.1. Sedum *telephium*, F.
   NUTHATCH, 47. Sitta *Europæa*,
   chatters.
8. *Thermom.* 20. *Loweſt to the 27th of this
   month.*
9. Mint, *red*, 232.5. Mentha *gentilis*, F.
   Wormwood, 188.1. Artemiſia *abſinthium*,
   F.
12. Horehound, *water*, 236.1. Lycopus *Eu-
    ropæus*, F.
    Thiſtle, *lady's*, 195.12. Carduus *marianus*,
    F.
    Burdock, 196. Arctium *lappa*, F.
    ROOKS *come to the neſt trees in the evening,
    but do not rooſt there.*
14. Clary, *wild*, 237.1. Salvia *verbenaca*, F.
    STONE CURLEW, 108. Charadrius
    oedicnemus, whiſtles at night.
15. Mallow, *vervain*, 252. Malva *alcea*, F.

GOAT

Auguſt

15. GOAT SUCKER, 26.1. Caprimulgus *Europæus, makes a noiſe in the evening, and young owls.*

16. *Thermom. 35. The higheſt to the 27th of this month.*

17. Orach, *wild,* 154.1. Chenopodium *album.*
ROOKS *rooſt on their neſt trees.*
GOAT SUCKER, *no longer heard.*

21. *Peas and wheat cut.*
Devil's bit, *yellow,* 164.1. Leontodon *autumnal.* F.

26. ROBIN RED BREAST, 78.3. Motacilla *rubecula, ſings.*
Goule, 443. Myrica *gale,* F. R.
Golden rod, *marſh,* 176.2. Senecio *paludoſus,* F.

29. Smallage, 214. Apium *graveolens,* F.
Teaſel, 192.2. Dipſacus *fullonum,* F.
Vipers come out of their holes ſtill.

IX. MONTH.

How ſweetly nature ſtrikes the raviſh'd eye
Thro' the fine veil with which ſhe oft conceals
Her charms in part, as conſcious of decay!

September

2. WILLOW HERB, *yellow,* 282.1. Lyſimachia *vulgaris,* F.
Traveller's joy, 258. Clematis *vitalba,* F.

---

* From the 27th of this month to the 10th of September i was from home, and therefore cannot be ſure that i ſaw the firſt blow of the plants during that interval.

Graſs

September

5. Grafs of Parnaffus, 355. Parnaffia *pa-luftris*, F.

10. *Catkins of the hafel formed.*
Thermom. 17. *The lowest from the* 10*th to the end of this month.*

11. *Catkins of the birch formed.*
Leaves of the Scotch fir fall.
Bramble still in blow, though some of the fruit has been ripe some time ; so that there are green, red, and black berries on the same individual plant at the same time.
Ivy, 459. Hedera *helix*, f.

14. *Leaves of the sycomore, birch, lime, mountain ash, elm, begin to change.*

16. Furze, 475. Ulex *Europæus*, F.
Catkins of the alder formed.
Thermom. 36.75. *The highest from the* 10*th to the end of this month.*
CHAFFINCH, 88. Fringilla *cælebs*, *chirps.*

17. *Herrings.*

20. FERN, FEMALE, 124.1. Pteris *aquilina*, *turned brown.*
Afh, *mountain*, 452.2. Sorbus *aucuparia*, F. R.
Laurel, 1549. H. Prunus *laurocerafus*, f. r.
Hops, humulus *lupulus*, 137.1. f. r.

21. SWALLOWS *gone. Full moon.*

23. *Autumnal æquinox.*

25. WOOD LARK, 69.2. Alauda *arborea*, *fings.*
FIELD FARE, 64.3. Turdus *pilaris*, *appears.*

Leaves

September

25. *Leaves of the plane tree, tawny---of the hasel, yellow---of the oak, yellowish green ---of the sycomore, dirty brown---of the maple, pale yellow---of the ash, fine lemon ---of the elm, orange---of the hawthorn, tawny yellow---of the cherry, red---of the hornbeam, bright yellow---of the willow, still hoary.*

27. BLACK BIRD *sings.*

29. THRUSH, 64.2. Turdus *musicus, sings.*

30. *Bramble, 467.1. Rubus *fruticosus,* F.

---

*Autumnal heat, according to Dr. Hales, at a medium, is 18.25.

X. MONTH.

Arise, ye winds, 'tis now your time to blow,
And aid the work of nature.   On your wings
The pregnant seeds convey'd shall plant a race
Far from their native soil.

October

1. Bryony, *black,* 262. Tamus *communis,* F. R.
Elder, *marsh,* 460.1. Viburnum *opulus,* F.R.
Elder, 461.1. Sambucus *nigra,* F. R.
Briar, 454.1. Rosa *canina,* F. R.
Alder, *black,* 465. Rhamnus *frangula,* F.R.
Holly, 466. Ilex *aquifolium,* F. R.
Barberry, 465. Berberis *vulgaris,* F. R.
Nightshade, *woody,* 265. Solanum *dulcamara.* F. R.

2. Thorn, *black,* 462.1. Prunus *spinosa,* F.R.
                                    CROW,

October
2. *CROW, ROYSTON, 39. 4. Corvus
   cornix, returns.
5. *Catkins of fallows formed.*
6. *Leaves of afp almoft all off---of chefnut,
   yellow---of birch, gold-coloured.
   Thermom. 26.50. Higheft this month.*
7. BLACK BIRD, 65.1. Turdus *merula,
   fings.
   Wind high; rooks fport and dafh about as
   in play, and repair their nefts.*
9. Spindle tree, 468.1. Euvonymus *Europæus*, F. R.
   *Some afh trees quite ftripped of their leaves.
   Leaves of marfh elder of a beautiful red, or
   rather pink colour.*
10. WOOD LARK *fings.*
    † RING DOVE *cooes.*
14. WOOD LARK *fings.*
    *Several plants ftill. in flower, as panfy,
    white behn, black nonefuch, hawkweed,
    buglofs, gentian, fmall ftitchwort, &c. in
    grounds not broken up.
    A great mift and perfect calm; not fo much
    as a leaf falls. Spiders webs innu-
    merable appear every where. Woodlark
    fings. Rooks do not ftir but fit quietly
    on their neft trees.*
16. GEESE, WILD, 1364. Anas, *anfer,
    leave the fens and go to the rye lands.*

---

* Linnæus obferves in the Syftema Naturæ, and the Fauna Suecica, that this bird is ufeful to the hufbandman, tho' ill treated by him.

† Ariftotle fays, this bird does not cooe in the winter, unlefs the weather happens to be mild.

October

    22. WOODCOCK, 104. Scolopax *rufticola*, returns.

       Some afh trees ftill green.

    24. LARK, SKY, 69.1. Alauda*arvenfis*, *fings.* Privet, 465.1. Liguftrum *vulgare*, F. R.

    26. *Thermom. 7. Lowaft this month.*

       Honeyfuckle, 458.1,2 *Lomicera periclymen. ftill in flower in the hedges, and mallow and feverfew.*

       WILD GEESE *continue going to the rye lands.*

Now from the north
Of Norumbega, and the Samoeïd fhore,
Burfting their brazen dungeons, arm'd with ice,
And fnow and hail, and ftormy guft, and flaw,
Boreas, and Cæcias, and Argeftes loud,
And Thrafcias rend the woods, and feas up-turn;
                       MILTON.

Here ends the Calendar, being interrupted by my going to London. During the whole time it was kept, the barometer fluctuated between 29.1. and 29.9. except a few days, when it funk to 28.6. and rofe to 30½.

A SIBI-

A Sibirian or Lapland Year.

June
23. Snow melts.
July 1. Snow gone.
9. Fields quite green.
17. Plants at full growth.
25. Plants in full blow.
August
2. Fruits ripe.
10. Plants shed their seeds.
18. Snow.

From this time to June 23, snow and ice ; so that by this account, plants, from the coming out of the ground to the ripening of their seeds, take but a month. And the spring, summer and autumn, are crouded into the space of 56 days. This account is taken from a treatise published in the Amæn. Academ. vol. iv. and agrees with one i have seen quoted out of Gmelin, who was in Sibiria many years.

THE

CALENDAR of FLORA.

By THEOPHRASTUS.

AT ATHENS, Latitude 37° 25′.

INTRODUCTION.

THE following Calendar was extracted chiefly from Theophraftus's Hiftory of plants, and put together in the beft manner i was able from imperfect materials. Any one who looks into the original, will fee that accuracy ought not to be expected; the manner of marking the times being often very indeterminate.

I am fenfible that objections may be made to many parts of this Calendar, but i thought it not worth while to give my reafons for what i have done, and thereby load a piece of mere curiofity with pompous quotations.

It has always feemed extraordinary to me, that when difciples of Linnæus have been fent into fo many parts of the world, in order to make difcoveries in natural hiftory, viz. Afia, Penfylvania, Lapland, Ægypt, Paleftine, Malabar, Surat, China, Java, Spain, America, Gotland, Italy, Apulia, Surinam, and St. Euftatia, that Greece fhould have been overlooked. It is true, Monfieur Tournefort was fent into the Levant by Lewis the Fourteenth to fearch for plants, and fpent fome years there; it is alfo as true, that he had all the knowledge and zeal neceffary for fuch a commiffion; but the country was too extenfive for one man to examine thoroughiy in that fpace of time. He rambled over moft of the Greek iflands, Armenia, and other parts of Afia; and though he enriched the royal gardens with many new plants, yet feveral muft have efcaped him for want of time, or a proper feafon.

It were to be wifhed, therefore, that fome perfons properly qualified, might be fent to Greece, and be enjoyned to make Attica, particularly, their place of refidence for a year at leaft. This might furnifh a Flora and Fauna Attica, that would

Y

would be extreemly curious to all lovers of natural
hiftory; and tend to clear up many paffages in
thofe authors, who firft opened that branch of
knowledge, as well as carried fome parts of it
much farther, than is generally known, or at leaft
acknowledged; and from whofe writings much
more benefit might ftill be reaped, were they
better underftood, efpecially in the medicinal way.

As the Englifh nation will have the honour of
firft making known to the world the true and
accurate proportions of the ancient Greek archi-
tecture, fo i hope it is referved for us to bring the
reft of Europe thoroughly acquainted with the nature of the foil, climate, productions, animals,
&c. of a country, whofe ancient glory fo much
refembles our own, and in a great meafure has
been the caufe of it, by furnifhing us with the
beft models of good fenfe, tafte, and juft fentiments
in every branch of human knowledge. We therefore ought in a particular manner to look upon
Attica, from whence, as Cicero fays, *Humanitas,*
doctrina, fruges, jura, leges ortæ, atque in omnes
terras diftributa putantur, with the veneration due
to a mother country. Should fuch a fceme take
place, i could name a perfon, perfectly well qualified, by his youth and abilities, and zealoufly inclined upon proper encouragement, to be one of
the party. France, Sweden*, and Ruffia have
fet us examples of this kind, and why this great
and flourifhing nation fhould not follow them, i
cannot fee. We have had our fhare in advancing
natural hiftory, it is true, but hitherto without any
public encouragement.

* Amongft many inftances of this fort, there is one that deferves
particular notice mentioned Amæn. Academ. p. 445. the author fays,
that Haffelquift was fent into Ægypt at the expence of his country-
men the Eaft Gothlanders, of the heads of the univerfity, and of the
Eaft India company, for the ftudy of natural hiftory; and ftaid above
a year at Cairo.

THE

CALENDAR of FLORA.

By THEOPHRASTUS.

Feb.

1. —* Violet, *early bulbous,* 1144. H. Leucoium
     vernum, λευκοιον, F.

   Wall flower, 291.2. Cheiranthus, *cheiri,*
     φλογιον, F.

   Cornel tree, 1536, H. Cornus, *mas,*
     κρανεια, L.

   Dogberry, 460. Cornus, *fanguinea,*
     θηλυκρανεια, L.

14. — Bay tree, 1688. H. Laurus *nobilis,*
     δαφνη, L.

   Alder, 442. Betula *alnus,* κληθρα, L.

   Abele, 446.3. Populus *alba,* λευκη, L.

   Elm, 468. Ulmus *campeftris,* πιελεα, L.

   Sallow, Salix, ιτεα, L.

   Poplar, *black,* 446.1. Populus *nigra,*
     αιγειρος, L.

   Plane tree, 1706. H. Platanus *orient.*
     πλατανος, L.

---

* This mark—after fome of the figures, denotes that the time is
only determined within certain limits.
   All the other marks mean the fame as in my own Calendar.

March

12 —   *Beginning of S P R I N G.

Fig tree, 1431. H. Ficus *carica*, ερινεος, L.

Alaternus, 1608.1. Rhamnus *alatern.* φιλυκη, L.

Hawthorn, 453.3. Cratægus *oxyacanth.* οξυακανθος, L.

Chrift's thorn, 1708. H. Rhamnus *paliurus*, παλιυρος, L.

Turpentine tree, 1577. H. Piftacia *terebin.* τερμινθος, L.

Chefnut-tree, 1382. H. Fagus *caftanea*, διος βαλανος, L.

Walnut tree, 1376. H. Juglans *regia*, καρυα, L.

Lilly of the valley, 264. Convallaria *Maialis*, οινανθη, F.

Narciffus, C. B 49. αγριον λειμωνια, F.

Daffodil, 1131. H. Narciffus *pfeudo-narc.* βυλβοκωδιον, F.

Corn flag, 1169.2. H. Gladiolus *communis*, F.

Hyacinth, 1162.31. Hyacinthus *comofus*, υακινθος, F.

Rofe, rofa, ροδον, F.

20. †Elder tree, 461.1. Sambucus *nigra*, ακτη, L.

---

* Between February 28 and March 12, the Ornithian winds blow, and SWALLOW appears.

† Between March 11 and 26, the *kite* and *nightingale* appear, that is in the leafing feafon. The appearance of the hawk is confonant to what Ariftotle fays, as quoted in the preface, but is determined upon a different kind of teftimony; which is a proof that this part of the Calendar at leaft is tolerably well ftated.

Fleawort,

March
20. Fleawort, 881. H. Plantago *pfyllium*,
κυνος↓, F.
Oak, 442. Quercus, robur, ſꝛus, L.
Fig tree, 1431. H. Ficus *carica*, συκη, L.
Oak, 1386. H. Quercus, *efculus*, φηγος, L.
Lime tree, 473. Tilia *Europæa*, φιλυρα, L.
Maple, 470.2. Acer *campeſtris*, ζυγια, L.
Apple tree, 451. Pyrus *malus*, μηλεα, L.
Ivy, 459. Hedera, *helix*, ιλος, L.
Beam tree, *white*, 453. Cratægus *aria*,
αρια, L.
26. Tree of life, 1408. H. Thuia *occident.*
θυεια, L.

April
4. — Succory, 172. Cichorium *intybus*, κιχοριον,
F.

May 12.   Beginning of S U M M E R.
15 — *Wheat harveſt.*
Turpentine tree, 1557. H. Piſtacia *te-
rebin*, τερμινθ℗, F. R.
Flower of Conſtantinople, 992.1. H.
Lychnis *Chalced.* λυχνις, F.
Rofe campion, 993.2. H. Lychnis *co-
ronar.* ſιℰ ανθℰ, F.
Afphodel, *yellow*, 1192.4. H. Afphodelus
luteus, αμαρακℰ, F.
Afh tree, 468. Fraxinus *excelſior*, μελια,
F. R.
Maple, 470.2. Acer *pfeudo-platanus*,
σφενδαμνℰ, F. R.
Pine, 1398. H. Pinus *ſylveſtris*, πιυς, F.
Fir tree, *common*, 1396.2. Pinus *abies*,
πευκη, F.
Y 3   Fir

June

20 — * Fir tree, *yew leaved*, 1394. Pinus *picea*,
ελαίη, F.

Yew tree, 445. Taxus *baccata*, μιλ⊕-, F. R.

Cornel tree, 1536. H. Cornus *mas*,
κρανεια, F. R.

Midsummer shoots of the oak.

*The fig, the vine, and the pomegranate,
shoot later.*

July

23. *Cuckow disappears.*

30. *Etesian winds blow.*

---

* Botanists doubt which of these two firs is the πευκη and which the ελαίη. Theophrastus says expressly that the πευκη flowers some days before the ελαίη, and therefore this question might be probably decided.

August

19 — Beginning of A U T U M N.

Lilly, Lilium, λειριον, F.

Crocus, 1173.3. Crocus *autumnal.* κροκ⊕-, F.

Dogberry, 460. Cornus *sanguinea*,
θηλυκρανεια, F. R.

Alder, 442. Betula *alnus*, κληθρα, F. R.

QUAIL, 58.6. Tetrao, *coturnix*, ορτυξ, departs.

Sept.

20 — CRANE, 95. Ardea, *grus*, γερανος, *departs.*

Autumn shoots of trees.

October

12 — Oak, 440. Quercus, *robur*, δρυς, F. R.

Chesnut,

October

12 — Chefnut, 1382. H. Fagus, *caſtanea*, δι$ς$
  $βαλανυς$, F. R.
  Chriſt's thorn, 1708. H. Rhamnus *paliur*.
  $παλ ιηους$, F. R.
  Hawthorn, 453.3. Cratægus *oxyacantha*,
  $οξυακανθος$, F. R.
  Holm oak, 1391. H. Quercus *coccifer*,
  $πρινος$, F. R.
  Alaternus, 1608.1. H. Rhamnus *alatern*.
  $φιλυκη$, F. R.

29 — Venice fumach, 1696. H. Rhus *cotinus*,
  $κοκκομηλεα$, F.
  Apple tree, 451. Pyrus *malus*, $μηλεα$, F. R.
  Beam tree, *white*, 453. Cratægus *aria*,
  $αρια$, F. R.
  Lime tree, 473. Tilia *Europæa*, $φιλυρη$,
  F. R.
  Box tree, 445. Buxus *fempervivens*, $πυξος$,
  F. R.

Beginning of W I N T E R.

Novem.

15 — Ivy, 459. Hedera *helix*, $κιτ\bar{l}ος$, F. R.
  Juniper, 444. H. Juniperus *communis*,
  $αρκ\bar{z}υθος$, F. R.
  Tree of life, 1408. H. Thuia *occident*.
  $θυεια$, F. R.
  Yew tree, 445. Taxus *baccata*, $μιλος$, F. R.
  Pear tree, 1450. Pyrus *communis*, $αχρας$,
  F. R.
  Arbutus, 1577.2. H. $αϑραχνη$, F. R.

Y 4   INDEX.

INDEX.

INDEX.

INDEX.

Pifum.

INDEX.

I N D E X.

INDEX.

INDEX.

INDEX.

INDEX:

Stitchwort,

Z

THE

SWEDISH PAN.

THE

SWEDISH PAN.

BY

NICOLAS HASSELGREN.

Upſal, 1749. Decem. 9.   !

Amænit. Academ. vol. 2.

§. I.

THE antients attributed the paſtoral life to *Pan*, thé care of flowers to *Flora*, hunting to *Diana*, and the cultivation of grain to *Ceres*. We, tho' acknowledging only one Deity, who governs all things, yet often uſe theſe names to denote the ſubjectwe undertake to treat upon: What word is now more known among botaniſts than the word *Flora*; by which they mean all thoſe plants, which grow within a cer-tain compaſs of ground ; as our Fauna Suecica

takes

takes in all thofe animals, which are natives of Sweden ? For a like reafon we have entitled this fmall tract the *Swedifh Pan* ; intending thereby to denote the five domeftic quadrupeds, which live upon plants growing in Sweden ; or the devouring army of *Pan*, which lays wafte the provinces of the *Swedifh Flora.* We choofe by this means to avoid a prolix definition, which is always difagreeable for the title of a book.

§. 2.

The paftoral life, by the teftimony of both facred, and prophane hiftory, is nearly as old as man himfelf; fo that i would willingly derive the knowledge, which i am going to deliver, from the moft ancient times. But altho' plants have been conftantly obvious to the eyes of every man; yet i am obliged to declare, that we have nothing delivered down to us in any book concerning the kinds of plants proper for the different kinds of cattle ; fo that i may be fure of not difgufting my reader with ftale matter new dreffed up. For the whole of what i prefent to him is new.—Our illuftrious prefident in his journey thro' Dalecarlia ann. 1734, made the firft attempt this way, as may be feen Flor.

Lapp.

Lapp. p. 158: where he fays thus. ' In my
' journey thro' Dalecarlia, when we had climbed
' up the mountains, and were got into Norway,
' my fellow travellers being tired, and afleep, i
' wandered about in a difmal wood, and per-
' ceived that the horfes eafily diftinguifhed
' wholefome from noxious food ; for being very
' hungry, they devoured all forts of plants, ex-
' cept the following ; *meadow fweet, valerian,*
' *lilly of the valley, angelica, loofe-ftrife, marfh-*
' *cinquefoil, cranes bill, hellebore, monks-hood,* and
' many fhrubs. This gave me a hint to re-
' commend to the curious, that they would fet
' about examining what plants fuch animals, as
' live on vegetables, viz. *the cow,* the *fheep,* the
' *goat,* the *deer,* the *horfe,* the *hog,* the *monkey*
' and their fpecies will not touch. An examina-
' tion which would not be without its ufe, were
' it properly made.' Notwithftanding this re-
commendation no enquiry was made, till our
prefident returned home from his travels thro'
forreign countries, and made a progrefs thro'
our own provinces. Afterwards profeffor Kalm,
that worthy difciple of fo great a mafter, follow-
ed his example ; fo that in his journey to Bahus
we find mention made of fome plants, which
cattle either eat, or refufe. Ann. 1747 and

1748 our prefident undertook with great diligence not only to make experiments himfelf,
but to excite his difciples, and auditors to do the
fame; of which number i was one. Thus at
laft many experiments were made, and repeated, efpecially by D. D. Hagftrom, Mag.
E. G. Liidbeck, E. Ekelund, J. G. Wahlbom,
L. Montin, F. Oldbers, J. C. Forfkahl, A.
Fornander; not to mention others, who ftrove,
as it were, to out-do one another in finding the
plants, which were fuitable to different animals.

§. 3.

The difficulty however of examining all the
Swedifh plants, and getting animals proper for
experiments, which ought all to be repeated,
has hindered us from being able to give a
compleat work on this fubject. But the greateft part, and the moft common vegetables of
Sweden being now determined by us; what is
wanting may be fupplied from time to time.
We hinted that animals proper for experiments,
which ought to be taken from among *cows,*
goats, fheep, horfes, and *fwine,* are difficult to be
found, for thefe reafons; firft, becaufe fome
plants are eaten by them in the fpring, which
they

they will not touch all the fummer ; when they are apt to grow rank in tafte, and fmell, and become ftalky and hard. Thus many people eat the *nettle* in the fpring ; but who could bear it afterwards ? Again, becaufe fome kinds of animals eat the flower, and will not eat the ftalks ; others eat the leaves and will not eat the ftalks. N. B. When they eat the leaves, we fay in general they eat the plant, otherwife there would be few. graffes they could be faid to eat. Œcon. Nat. Next, the animals ought not to be over hungry, when we make our experiments, if we intend to make them properly. For they will greedily devour moft kinds of plants at fuch a time, which they will abfolutely refufe at another. Thus when they come immediately out of the houfe, they are not fit to make experiments upon ; for then they are ravenous after every green thing that comes in their way. The beft method is to make the experiments when their bellies are almoft full, for they are hardly ever fo intirely. Moreover the plants ought not to be handled by fweaty hands ; fome animals will refufe the moft pleafing, and tafteful in that cafe. We ought to throw them on the ground, and if we find the animal refufes to eat them, we muft mix them

with

with others that we know they like ; and if they
ftill refufe them, we have a fure proof; efpecially if the fame be tryed with many individuals:

§. 4.

Our views do not extend beyond the Swedifh
plants, and that for the fake of our own œconomy.   Let forreigners look to that part which
concerns themfelves, and thus our work will be
confined within moderate bounds. We can produce above 2000 certain experiments, fome of
which were repeated ten times over, fome twice
as often.   If we take the *Flora Succia* Holm.
1745. and put to any herb the generical name,
adding the number, and fome epithet by way
of difference, our work will be very much
abridged.

§. 5.

It is manifeft that the vegetable world was intended for the fupport of the animal world; infomuch that altho' not a few animals are carnivorous, yet thefe animals which they devour
cannot fubfift without vegetables.   In this fpe-

3   culation

culation we behold with admiration the wisdom
of the Creator, which has made some vegetables
absolutely disagreeable to some animals that live
upon plants, while these plants are agreeable to
others. And there are plants, which are poi-
sonous to some animals, which are very wholesome to others, and on the contrary. This did
not happen by chance, but was contrived for
wise purposes. For if the Author of nature
had made all plants equally grateful to all kinds
of quadrupeds, it must necessarily have happened, that one species of them being remarkably increased, another species must have pe-
rished with hunger, before it could have got
into better pasture; the vegetables being con-
sumed over a large tract of ground. But as it
is ordained every species must by force leave
certain plants to certain animals, so that they
always find something to live upon, till they
meet with better pasture; in the like manner we
find it contrived in relation to the plants themselves, which do not all grow in the same countrey, and climate; but every plant has its place
appointed by the Creator, in which it grows
more abundantly, than any where else. From
hence we may observe, that those animals,
which chiefly live upon particular plants, chiefly
abound

abound in certain places. Thus the *lichen* or *liverwort*, Fl. 980. is found in greatest plenty on the cold alps, and therefore the *rhen deer*, which all winter live mostly upon this plant, are obliged to live there. The festuca, Fl. 94. which florishes and spreads most on dry pastures, draws the sheep thither, which above all things delight in that kind of grafs. The feeds of the *dwarf birch*, Fl. 777. which afford the best fort of food to the *rough-legg'd partridge*, and the *Norway rat*, Fn. 26. tempt them to dwell in these northern parts of the world. *Camels hay*, Mat. Med. 312. which above all plants, thrives on loose fand, draws the camel to choose thofe barren places, as they there find food most agreeable to them; not to mention many other fimilar inftances. Trees, whofe heads fhoot up fo high, that quadrupeds cannot eafily reach them, afford nourifhment for that reafon to more numerous tribes of infects, as the *fallow*, the *oak*, the *pear*, &c. The Creator, who moft wifely eftablifhed this law, has as it were imprinted it on the organs of animals, that they might not offend againft it thro' ignorance; and as every tranfgreffion has its punifhment allotted, fo alfo no offence againft the law of

nature

nature can efcape. Animals, which violate this law are punifhed by difeafes or death; and hence we behold with admiration that brutes, which were defigned to be guided by inftinct, can by no means whatever be prevailed upon to act againft it. If by chance it happens that any animal offends this way, and fuffers for it, we vulgarly fay it has taken poifon; fo that ignorant people wonder, not to fay murmur at the wife difpofition of the Creator, who has produced fo many noxious plants; but without fufficient reafon, for no one plant in the world is univerfally poifonous, but all things are good, as they came from the hands of the Creator. Phyficians often mention that this or that plant is deadly, becaufe its particles are of a nature apt to wound the fibres of the body or corrupt the juices. But this is only refpectively to the fpecies of animals, e. g. the *fun-fpurge*, Fl. 536. has a milky juice, which caufes blotches in our fkin and hurts our fibres, and therefore it is faid to be poifonous; yet the *moth*, Fn. 825. almoft entirely lives upon this plant, and prefers it both for tafte and nourifhment to all others, as it thrives beft upon it. Thus one animal leaves that, which to itfelf is poifonous, to another animal, which feeds upon it delicioufly.

Long-

Long-leaved water hemlock will kill a *cow,* whereas the *goat* browfes upon it greedily. *Monks-hood* kills a *goat,* but will not hurt a *horfe* ; and the *bitter almond* kills a *dog,* but is wholefome food for *man.* *Parfley* is 'deadly 'to *fmall birds* ; while *fwine* eat it fafely ; and *pepper* is mortal to *fwine,* and wholefome to *poultry.* *Thus every creature has its allotted portion.* Animals diftinguifh the noxious from the falutary by fmell and tafte. Younger animals have thefe fenfes more acute, and therefore are more nice in diftinguifhing plants. An empty ftomach will often drive animals to feed upon plants, that were not intended for them by nature. But whenever this has happened they become more cautious for the future, and acquire a certain kind of experience; e. g. *the monks-hood,* which grows near Fahluna, is generally left untouched by all the animals, that are accuftomed to thefe places ; but if forreign cattle are brought thither and meet with this vegetable, they venture to take too large a quantity of it, and are killed [b]. The cattle that have

[b] The fame thing has been told me by the countrey people in Herefordfhire in relation to *meadow-faffron,* which grows in plenty in fome parts of that county. Gmelin, Flor. Sibirica, p. 76. fays that cattle eat the leaves of the *hellebore,* 40. when they firft fpring out of the ground, and are thereby killed.

been

been reared in the plains of Schonen, and Weſtrogothia, commonly fall into a dyſentery when they come into the woodland parts, becauſe they feed upon ſome plants, which cattle uſed to thoſe places have learned to avoid. In the ſpring, when the *water hemlock* is under water, ſo that the cows cannot ſmell it, they dye in heaps ^c. But when the ſummer comes on and

---

^c This affair is of ſo much conſequence to the farmer, that i think it right to tranſcribe a paſſage out of Linnæus upon this ſubject.

"When I arrived, ſays he, at Tornea, the inhabitants complained of a terrible diſeaſe, that raged among the horned cattle, which upon being let into the paſtures in the ſpring dyed by hundreds. They deſired that i would conſider this affair, and give my advice what was to be done in order to put a ſtop to this evil. After a proper examination i thought the following circumſtances worth obſerving.

1. That the cattle dyed as ſoon as they left off their winter fodder, and returned to grazing.

2. That the diſeaſe diminiſhed as the ſummer came on, at which time, as well as in the autumn, few dyed.

3. That this diſtemper was progagated irregularly, and not by contagion.

4. That in the ſpring the cows were driven into a meadow near the city, and that they chiefly dyed there.

5. That the ſymptoms varied much, yet agreed in this, that the cattle, upon grazing indiſcriminately on all ſorts of herbs, had their bellies ſwelled, were ſeized with convulſions, and in a few days expired with horrible bellowings.

6. That

and has dryed the ground, they are very care-
full not to touch it. It is alſo true, that all
vegetables prohibited by nature to particular
animals are not equally pernicious; and therefore
though through neceſſity and hunger they eat
them,

6. That no man dared to flea the recent carcaſes, as they
found by experience, that not only the hands of ſuch as
attempted it, but their faces too had been inflamed, and
mortified, and that death had enſued.

7. The people enquired of me, whether there were any
kinds of poiſonous ſpiders in that meadow, or whether the
water which had a yellowiſh tint was not noxious.

8. That it was not a murrain was clear, becauſe the diſtemper was not contagious, and becauſe that diſtemper is
not peculiar to the ſpring. I ſaw no ſpiders but what are
common all over Sweden; and as to the water, the ſediment
at the bottom, that cauſed the yellowneſs, was nothing but
what came from iron.

9. I was ſcarcely got out of the boat, which carried me
over the river into the meadow, before i gueſſed the real
cauſe of the diſeaſe. For i there beheld the *long-leaved*
water hemlock. My reaſons for gueſſing this were as follow.

10. Becauſe in that meadow, where the cattle firſt fell ill,
this poiſonous plant grows in great plenty, chiefly near the
banks of the river. In other places it was ſcarce.

11. The leaſt attention will convince us that brutes ſhun
whatever is hurtfull to them, and diſtinguiſh poiſonous
plants from ſalutary by natural inſtinct; ſo that this plant is
not eat by them in the ſummer, and autumn, which is the
reaſon that in thoſe ſeaſons few cattle dye, viz. only ſuch as
either accidentally, or preſſed by extreme hunger, eat of it.

12. But

them, yet they do not immediately dye; but it is certain that they cannot have from thence good and proper nourifhment.

§. 6.

The end of this kind of knowledge is not

12. But when they are let into the paftures in fpring, partly from their greedinefs after frefh herbs, and partly from the emptinefs and hunger which they have undergone during a long winter, they devour every green thing which comes in their way. It happens moreover that herbs at this time are fmall, and fcarcely fupply food in fufficient quantity. They are befides more juicy, are covered with water, and fmell lefs ftrong, fo that what is noxious is not eafily difcerned from what is wholefome. I obferved likewife, that the radical leaves were always bitten, the others not; which confirms what I have juft faid.

13. I faw this plant in an adjoining meadow mowed along with grafs for winter fodder; and therefore it is not wonderfull, that fome cattle, tho' but a few, fhould dye of it in winter.

14. After i left Tornea i faw no more of this plant till i came to the vaft meadows near Limmingen, where it appeared along the road, and when i got into the town i heard the fame complaints, as at Tornea, of the annual lofs of cattle with the fame circumftances.

15. It would therefore be worth while to eradicate carefully thefe plants, which might eafily be done, as they grow in marfhy grounds; and are not hard to find, as they grow by the fides of pools or rivers. Or if this could not be done, the cattle fhould not be fuffered to go into fuch places, at leaft during the fpring. For i am perfuaded, that later in the year they can diftinguifh this plant by the fmell alone.

A a   bare

bare curiofity, although were this the cafe every part of knowledge, which fets forth the ftupendous works of the Creator, is never to be looked upon as of no confequence. On the other hand we do not pretend to gain any medicinal advantages from thefe fpeculations, namely, to be able from hence to conclude, that this or that plant is noxious to man, becaufe it is fo to this or that brute animal. Nor do we for that reafon approve of Wepfer's experiments upon dogs, and other animals, as if any knowledge can be thence gained in regard to man. No, the end we aim at is merely œconomical.

α. From thefe experiments we may know whether certain paftures afford good nourifhment for this or that fpecies of animals. We fee e. g. *keifers* wafte away in enclofures, where the *meadow-fweet* grows in abundance, and covers the ground fo that they can fcarce make their way through it ; the countrey people are amazed, and imagine that the pafture is too rich for them; not dreaming that the *meadow-fweet* affords them no nourifhment. Whereas the *goat*, which is bleating on the other fide of the hedge, is not fuffered to go in, though he longs to be browfing upon this plant, which to him is a moft delicate and nourifhing food.

β. From

β. From thefe experiments we may almoft be fure by affinity and analogy, whether mea-dows or paftures are falutary or noxious to par-ticular animals; e. g. long experience has taught us that our *fheep* take up poifon in marfhy grounds, though no one till lately knew what was the particular poifon. Yet the *fpiderwort* 267. the *moufe-ear fcorpion grafs* 149. the *mer-cury* 823. the *fun-dew* 257,8. the *hairy wood grafs* 287. the *leffer fpearwort* 458. the *butter-wort* 21. have evidently fufpicious marks[c]. I will therefore propofe a new experiment. The *andromeda* Fl. Virgin. 160. is known to be a moft rank poifon to fheep in Virginia. The *andromeda,* called by the people of New York *dwarf laurel,* Cold. Act. Upfal. 1743. p. 123. is very fatal to the fheep in New York. Thefe two plants are of a different fpecies, but of the fame natural genus, and therefore have the fame vertues. Amongft us, efpecially in the northern parts, the wild *rofemary, andromeda*

[c] There is great reafon to think that what makes low grounds fo noxious to fheep is not the moifture, but the plants that grow there. For it is obferved by fhepherds that the great danger to fheep is immediately after a frefh fpring of grafs, which i imagine is owing to their licking up the young and tender fhoots of poifonous plants, along with their proper food, not being able to diftinguifh them.

335. grows every where in marſhy grounds, which being of the ſame natural genus with the foregoing, we may reaſonably conclude that it deſtroys our ſheep. To this we may add, that it is on account of three other ſpecies of *andromeda* 336,7,8. which grow on the Lapland mountains, that the ſheep there never are healthy; and laſtly although the *ciſtus ledon* 341. is not a ſpecies of *andromeda*, yet being of the ſame natural claſs, it is not unlikely but that this plant is far from affording good nouriſhment to ſheep. This conjecture gives our ſhepherds an unexpected opportunity of making experiments with their ſheep; and indeed they cannot omit to do it without being juſtly blameable, ſince on this the health of their whole flock depends. It is particularly to be noted upon this occaſion, that the botany of America, a countrey ſo far disjoyned from us, gives a hint for conſidering things of the greateſt uſe, of which the antients did not ſo much as dream.

᛬. From hence the œconomiſt may truly judge of his meadows, and know that ſome are vaſtly preferable to others for certain animals. For although cattle, preſſed by neceſſity and hunger, will feed upon vegetables leſs gratefull to them; yet it is not to be doubted but that
they

they are not equally well nourifhed by thefe as by others. Thus the Dalecarlians are obliged in a fcarcity of wheat to fupport themfelves by *bread* made of the *bark* of the *pine*; yet it does by no means follow from hence that this affords proper nourifhment. We fee that *horfes* in time of war, when preffed by extreme hunger, will eat *dead hedges*, but we cannot hence conclude, that wood is good food for them.

ſ. The induſtrious farmer may judge from hence, when he fows his meadows with hay feeds for pafture, that it is not indifferent what kinds of feeds he choofes, as the vulgar think. For fome are fit for *horfes*, others for *cows*, &c. *Horfes* are nicer in choofing than any of our cattle; *filiquofe* and *filiculofe* plants particularly are not relifhed by them. *Goats* feed upon a greater variety of plants than any other cattle, but then they chiefly hunt after the extremities and flowers. *Sheep* on the contrary pafs by the flowers and eat the leaves. Not to mention the different difpofition in different animals as to grazing near the ground or not. The countreyman who underftands thefe things, and knows how in confequence to difpofe of his grounds, and affign each kind of cattle to its propereft food, muft neceffarily have them more healthy

A a 3 and

and fat, than he who is deftitute of thefe principles.   The good œconomift will obferve the
fame of his hay.   For although many herbs,
when dry, are eat, which when green would
be refufed, it does not follow from hence that
they yield good nourifhment.   Much might be
added concerning the propenfion of cattle to
this or that plant, which the compafs of this
fmall tract will not admit of; e. g. that *fheep*
above all things delight in the *feftuca* 95. and
grow fatter upon it than any other kind of
grafs ;   that *goats* prefer certain plants,   but
being led by an inftinct peculiar to themfelves,
they fearch more after variety, and do not long
willingly ftick to any one kind of food whatever;
that *geefe* are particularly fond of the feeds of
the *feftuca*, Fl. 90 ; that *fwine* greedily hunt
after the roots of the *bull-rufh* 40. while they
are frefh, but will not touch them when dry.
Hence it appears that it is in vain to contrive
engines to extract the roots of the *bull-rufh* out
of the water, and dry them for the ufe of thefe
animals in winter.   Becaufe thefe animals fpoil
the meadows, where the *fcorzonera* grows, in
order to come at its root, which they delight
in ; and alfo the fields, to get at the roots of
clowns-all-heal, the hufbandman imagines they
do

do good to his fields by ploughing the ground and eating the roots of *couch-grafs*, whereas they never touch them, but when preffed by the utmoft neceffity [d].

§. 7.

To give a view of my defign in a few words. I have difpofed the plants mentioned in the Flora Suecica according to their numbers ; and to be as fhort as poffible, it was neceffary to add the generical name with a fhort and incompleat

---

[d] In the fame way with us it is a notion that prevails commonly that *cows* eat the *crow-foot* that abounds in many meadows, and that this occafions the butter to be yellow, from whence i fuppofe it is generally known by the name of the *butter-flower*. But this i believe is all a miftake, for i never could obferve that any part of that plant was touched by *cows* or any other cattle. Thus Linnæus obferves, Fl. Lapp. p. 195. that it was believed by fome people that the *marfh-marygold* made the butter yellow, but he denies that cows ever touch that plant. Yet he thinks that all kinds of pafture will not give that yellownefs, and then obferves that the beft and yelloweft butter he knows, and which is preferred by the dealers in thofe parts to all other butter, was made where the *cow-wheat* grew in greater plenty than he ever faw any where elfe. This fhews how very incurious the countrey people are in relation to things they are every day converfant with, and which it conccrns them fo much to know.

epithet,

epithet, which however may be illuftrated out of the Flora itfelf. I have diftinguifhed the cattle againft every plant into five columns. The firft of which contains *oxen.* The fecond *goats.* The third *fheep.* The fourth *horfes.* The fifth *fwine.* By the mark (1) i have de-noted thofe plants which are eaten; by the mark (o) thofe which are not eaten; by both together thofe which are fometimes eaten, fome-times refufed; or are eaten when cattle are more ufed to them, and are more hungry, otherwife not.

§. 8.

Upon the firft view of this fubject the reader will perceive, that it is not treated compleatly, fo that every Swedifh plant is pointed out, and by what animals it is eaten. What generally happens upon breaking up old pafture lands, viz. that for the firft years it cannot be cleanfed from all ufelefs weeds, and be laid down fine like a garden, but will here and there have rough tumps and hard clods, unlefs we will let it lye fallow for a very long time; the fame or fomething like it has happened upon this oc-cafion.

I am

I am apt to believe however that the reader will be better pleafed that I have opened this new, fcene, than if I had waited longer in order to gain farther light. For fince there are many people here curious in botany and œconomy, i hope they will all lend a helping hand, that i may one day be enabled to give a more compleat edition of this piece [e].

[e] After this in the original follows a long table of experiments, of which i fhall only give a fmall fpecimen ; as the whole would increafe the bulk but not the value of this piece to fuch readers as this tranflation is intended for, fince they would neither know the plants by the names the author has given them, nor by any i could put in their room. However i fhall for curiofity give a fpecimen, and add the general refult of his experiments, juft as he has marked it at the end of his table ; which is as follows. ' Thus·far,' fays he, ' we have given 2314 experiments. From thefe it appears ' that

Oxen eat	276	refufe	218	plants
Goats	449		126	
Sheep	387		141	
Horfes	262		212	
Swine	72		171	

' And thus thefe animals leave untouched 886 plants.
' Thefe animals will not eat any kind of *mofs*.
' The goats are very fond of the *algæ*.
' Some of them greedily devour the *fungi*, others will ' not tafte them. But we recommend farther trials in relation to thefe matters.'
Then follows an account of fome trials made by Dr. O. Hagftrom to the fame purpofe in relation to *rhen deer*, but

but as they no ways concern us, i have omitted to mention them.

N. B. For the table i have chosen not to take such plants as occurred first in my author, but to select the grasses of our own countrey, and have given English names to them of my own invention, the reason of which will appear in the following observations.

	O.	G.	S.	H.	Sw.
Spring grass	1	1	1	1	-
Mat grass	10	1	1	1	0
Canary grass, *reed*	1	1	1	1	0
Cat's-tail, *meadow*	1	1	0	1	0
Fox-tail, *meadow*	10	1	1	1	10
———— *flote*	1	1	1	1	0
Millet grass	1	1	1	-	-
Bent grass, *silky*	-	1	0	1	-
———— *fine*	1	1	-	1	-
Hair grass, *small leaved*	1	1	1	1	-
———— *water*	1	-	1	1	-
Meadow, *creeping*	1	1	1	1	0
———— *annual*	1	1	1	1	1
———— *great*	1	1	1	1	1
———— *narrow leaved*	1	1	1	1	1
———— *common*	1	1	1	1	1
Cock's-foot grass, *rough*	0	1	1	1	0
Dogs-tail grass, *crested*	-	-	1	-	-
———— *blue*	-	1	1	1	0
Fescue grass, *flote*	0	1	1	1	10
———— *purple*	1	1	1	1	-
———— *sheep's*	1	1	11	1	-
Brome grass, *field*	1	1	1	1	-
———— *spiked*	-	1	1	1	-
Oat grass, *meadow*	1	1	1	1	-
———— *bearded*	-	10	-	-	-

2

Ob-

Obſervations on GRASSES.

Obſervations on GRASSES.

AS the foregoing treatiſe contains ſome obſervations on graſſes [f], that are quite new,
and as this affair is of the utmoſt importance to
the huſbandman, i ſhall ſubjoyn ſome obſervations of my own relating to the ſame ſubject.

It is wonderfull to ſee how long mankind has
neglected to make a proper advantage of plants
of ſuch importanee, and which in almoſt every
countrey are the chief food of cattle.   The farmer for want of diſtinguiſhing, and ſelecting
graſſes for ſeed, fills his paſtures either with
weeds, or bad, or improper graſſes ; when by
making a right choice, after ſome trials he might
be ſure of the beſt graſs, and in the greateſt
abundance that his land admits of.   At preſent
if a farmer wants to lay down his land to graſs,

[f] *By graſſes are meant all thoſe plants, which have a round,
jointed and hollow ſtem, ſurrounded at each joint with a ſingle
leaf, long, narrow and pointed, and whoſe ſeeds are contained in
chaffy huſks.   It appears by this definition, which is Ray's, that
all the kinds of grain, as wheat, oats, barley, &c. are properly
graſſes, and that the broad, the white, the hop, &c. clovers are
not graſſes, though ſo frequently called by that name.*

what

what does he do ? he either takes his feeds indifcriminately from his own foul hayrick, or fends
to his next neighbour for a fupply.   By this
means, befides a certain mixture of all forts of
rubbifh, which muft neceffarily happen ; if he
chances to have a large proportion of good feeds,
it is not unlikely, but that what he intends for
dry land may come from moift, where it grew
naturally, and the contrary ᵍ.   This is fuch a
flovenly

ᵍ *Since the firft edition of thefe tracts i have had feveral opportunities of obferving inftances of this flovenly kind of hufbandry,
and its effects.   Inftead of covering the ground in one year with
a good turf, i have feen it filled with weeds not natural to it,
and which never would have fprung up, if they had not been
brought there.*

*Arguments are never wanting in fupport of ancient cuftoms,
and i am no ftranger to the arguments, fuch as they are, which
prejudice and indolence have made ufe of on this occafion.*

*1. Some fay then, that if you manure your ground properly,
good graffes will come of themfelves.   I own they will.   But
the queftion is how long it will be before that happens, and why
be at the expence of fowing what you muft afterwards try to kill
by manuring ?   which muft be the cafe, as long as people fow all
kinds of rubbifh under the name of hay feeds.   Again, if the beft
way is to let the ground take its chance, why is the farmer at
the expence of procuring the feeds of the white, and broad clover, which come up in almoft all parts of England fpontaneoufly ?
but if this is allowed not to be the beft way in relation to clover
of any kind, what reafon can be in nature, why grafs feeds only
ought not to be fown pure ?*

2. Others

flovenly method of proceeding, as one would think could not poffibly prevail univerfally; yet this is the cafe as to all graffes except the dar-nel grafs, and what is known in fome few counties by the name of the Suffolk grafs; and this latter inftance is owing, i believe, more to the foil than any care of the hufbandman. Now would the farmer be at the pains of fe-parating once in his life half a pint, or a pint of the different kinds of grafs feeds [h], and take

care

2. *Others fay, that it is better to have a mixture of different feeds. I will fuppofe this to be true. But cannot a mixture be had though the feeds be gathered, and feparated? and is not a mixture by choice more likely to be proper, than one by chance? efpe-cially after a fufficient experience has been had of the particular virtues of each fort, the different kinds of cattle each grafs is moft adapted to, the different grounds where they will thrive beft, &c. all which cicumftances are now in general wholly un-known, though of the utmoft confequence.*

3. *It is faid by fome, that weeds will come up along with the grafs. No doubt of it. Can any one imagine that grafs feeds fhould be exempted above from what happens to every other kind of feed. But i will venture to fay, that not near the quantity of weeds will fpring up which they imagine, if it be fown very thick. Men muft be very much put to it, when they make fuch objections as this laft, or indeed any of the others. I am almoft inclined to fay with a great writer, ' It is a fimple thing to ' take much pains to anfwer fimple objections.'*

[h] *I have had frequent experience how eafy it is to gather the feeds of graffes, having employed children of ten or eleven years*

old

care to fow them feparately; in a very little time he would have wherewithal to ftock his farm properly, according to the nature of each foil, and might at the fame time fpread thefe feeds feparately over the nation by fupplying

old feveral times, who have gathered many forts for me without making any miftakes, after i had once fhewn them the forts i wanted.

I have procured thus the creeping bent, the fine bent, the fheep's fefcue, the crefted dog-tail, &c. in fufficient quantities to begin a ftock, but for want of a proper opportunity of cultivating them myfelf, or meeting with any one who had zeal enough to beftow a proper care on them, my collections of this kind hitherto have only proved that the fcheme is in itfelf feafible.

This very year 1761, a little boy by my direction gathered as much of the crefted dog-tail in 3 hours by the fide of a road, as when fhed, yielded upon weighing above a quarter of a pound averdupois, perfectly free from hufks. As this feed is fmall the fkillfull will eafily judge how far fuch a quantity would go if properly employed.

My very eftimable and ingenious friend Mr. Aldworth, who was witnefs of the fact which i laft mentioned, at my defire or-dered a fmall part of a meadow, near his feat at Stanlake, which had better graffes and lefs mixed than the reft, to be left unmowed till the feeds were fit for gathering. This piece yielded upon threfhing and fifting a full bufhel by meafure of almoft pure feed of the crefted dog-tail. In cafe any one fhould be in-clined to follow this example, i think it highly neceffary to ob-ferve that care muft be taken to mow the grafs before it fheds; that it be mowed very early in the morning before the dew is off the ground, and that it ought not be fpread as in making hay, but left as it falls from the fcythe a fufficient time, and then gently turned over.

the

the feed-fhops. The number of graffes fit for the farmer is, i believe, fmall; perhaps half a dozen, or half a fcore are all he need to culti- vate; and how fmall the trouble would be of fuch a tafk, and how great the benefit, muft be obvious to every one at firft fight. Would not any one be looked on as wild who fhould fow *wheat, barley, oats, rye, peas, beans, vetches, buck-wheat, turneps* and weeds of all forts to- gether? yet how is it much lefs abfurd to do what is equivalent in relation to graffes? does it not import the farmer to have good hay and grafs in plenty? and will cattle thrive equally on all forts of food? we know the contrary. Horfes will fcarcely eat hay, that will do well enough for oxen and cows. Sheep are parti- cularly fond of one fort of grafs, and fatten upon it fafter, than on any other in Sweden, if we may give credit to Linnæus. And may they not do the fame in England? How fhall we know till we have tryed? Nor can we fay that what is valuable in Sweden may be inferior to many other graffes in England; fince it ap- pears by the Flora Suecica that they have all the good ones that we have. But however this may be i fhould rather choofe to make experi- ments, than conjectures.

B b

I now

I now propofe to add a few obfervations on fome of our graffes, as far as i have been able to make any with fome appearance of probability ; but as there has reigned hitherto the greateft confufion in the Englifh names of thefe moft valuable plants, and as they have never been properly ranged but by Linnæus, i fhall firft, in imitation of that great author in his Flora Suecica, give new generical names with trivial ones to diftinguifh the fpecies of all our Englifh graffes [i]. I mean all thofe which are found in that author ; as for the reft, fince fome are omitted by him, their names may be eafily fupplyed when their genera are fettled by the learned [k]. It happens very luckily, that our common people know fcarce any of the graffes by names, as far as i could ever find by converfing with farmers, hufbandmen, &c. fo that fomething may be done to remove this confufion, if a lift of names be fettled and agreed

---

[i] Mr. Hudfon having thought proper to adopt my names with fome alterations ; and having cleared up many of the fpecies of graffes in a better manner than has been done before ; i have referred throughout to his Flora Britannica, which is likely to be in the hands of all who are curious in botany.

[k] This has fince been done in fome meafure in the aforementioned Flora Britannica.

on

on by fuch as are likely to have influence fufficient in thefe matters.   As to my own lift, it
is only meant as a hint for others to work upon.

In giving names i have had two things in
view.   Firft to retain as much as poffible fuch
as have hitherto been ufed for fome fpecies of the
genus.   Secondly, where that could not be done,
to give fuch as are of eafy and familiar pronun-
ciation to our common people, and at the fame
time approach as near as poffible to the Latin
names in found where they could not be in-
terpreted.   This was done for the fake of the
learned for the more eafy recolle&ting the botanical name.   Thus i have called the *aira hair*-
grafs, the *bromus brome*-grafs, &c. in others i
have merely tranflated the Latin name, as
alopecurus *fox-tail* grafs, cynofurus *dog-tail*
grafs, &c.

After thefe preliminary obfervations i hope
it will not be neceffary to make any apology for
the liberty i have taken.   I am certain that till
names properly adapted to the purpofe be invented, we have little chance of feeing any general reformation made in this part of hufbandry; and even after this without fome perfon
properly qualified to dire&t the countrey people, and fhew them the graffes with their names,

nothing

nothing will come of that moft ufeful doctrine delivered in the foregoing treatife of Haffelgren [1]. But it is to be hoped that gentlemen at leaft will not be fo incurious as to remain ignorant of what imports them fo much to know. Nor is the mere botanift lefs concerned in the fuccefs of this fcheme, for there is great reafon to think that many of the graffes are not thoroughly fettled, varieties perhaps being put for different fpecies [m]; now this uncertainty can never be better cleared up than by fowing the fame kind of feeds on different foils.

[1] Many people having expreffed a defire that i fhould have plates of fome of the profitable graffes added to this piece, that moft excellent man, the late Mr. Price of Foxley, whofe extraordinary character i fhall always revere, and do intend to give a fketch of on fome future occafion, kindly condefcended to employ his pencil, which in the opinion of the beft judges was equal to things of a much fuperior nature, in making me feveral drawings from the plants themfelves, and a very able hand has fupplied the reft and engraved them all.

[m] Thus Gmelin Flor. Lapp. mentions four of the meadow graffes which he fays have for a long time perplexed botanifts of great reputation. And the editor of Ray's Synopfis, p. 402. doubts whether five graffes which are put down as different by Petiver be not only varieties of a grafs mentioned before. I have many fpecimens of this grafs in my collection differing in color, ftature and outward afpect, which yet moft likely are of the fame fpecies.

A Table

A Table of Englifh G R A S S E S.

G E N U S 1.

VERNAL grafs, *Tab.* 1. Anthoxanthum *Odoratum* *H. 10. R. 398.1.

G E N U S 2.

MAT grafs   Nardus *Stricta*
H. 20. R. 393.2.

G E N U S 3.

Manured   CANARY grafs Phalaris *Canariensis*
H. 20. R. 394.

Sea   CANARY   Phalaris *Arenaria*
H. 21. R. 398.4.

Reed   CANARY   Phalaris *Arundinacea*
H. 21. R. 400.1.

Ribband   CANARY   Phalaris *ibid. b. ibid.*

G E N U S 4.

Green   PANIC grafs   Panicum *Viride*
H. 21. R. 393.1.

Loofe   PANIC   Panicum *Crufgalli*
H. 22. R. 394.2.

Cock's-foot PANIC   Panicum *Sanguinale*
H. 22. R. 399.2.

Creeping   PANIC   Panicum *Dactylon*
H. 22. R. 399.1.

*N. B. H refers to the Flora Britannica of Mr. Hudfon.

G E N U S 5.

Meadow CAT's-TAIL grafs Phleum *Pra-tenfe* H. 22. R. 398.1.

Branched CAT's-TAIL Phleum *Paniculatum* H. 23.

Bulbous CAT's-TAIL Phleum *Nodofum* H. 23. R. 398.3

G E N U S 6.

Meadow FOX-TAIL grafs, *Tab.* 2. Alopecurus *Pratenfis* H. 23. R. 396.1.

Field FOX-TAIL Alopecurus *Myofuroides* H. 23. R. 397.

Bulbous FOX-TAIL Alopecurus *Bulbofus* H. 24. R. 397.3.

Flote FOX-TAIL Alopecurus *Geniculatus* H. 24. R. 396.2.

G E N U S 7.

FEATHER grafs Stipa *Pennata* H. 24. R. 393.3.

G E N U S 8.

Smooth COCK's-FOOT grafs Dactylis *Cynofuroides* H. 25. R. 393.4.

Rough COCK's-FOOT Dactylis *Glomeratus* H. 25. R. 400.2.

G E N U S 9.

MILLET grafs Milium *Effufum* H. 25. R. 402. 1.

G E N U S 10.

Silky	BENT grafs	Agroſtis *Spica venti*
	H. 26. R. 405.17.	
Brown	BENT	Agroſtis *Canina*
	H. 26.	
Red	BENT	Agroſtis *Rubra*
	H. 26. R. 394.4.	
Creeping	BENT	Agroſtis *Stolonifera*
	H. 27. R. 402. 2.	
Marſh	BENT	Agroſtis *Paluſtris*
	H. 27. R. 404.11.	
Fine	BENT *Tab. 3.*	Agroſtis *Capillaris*
	H. 27. R. 402.4.	
Wood	BENT	Agroſtis *Sylvatica*
	H. 28. R. 404.13.	
Small	BENT	Agroſtis *Minima*
	H. 28. R. appendix.	

G E N U S 11.

Creſted	HAIR grafs	Aira *Criſtata*
	H. 28. R. 396.3.	
Purple	HAIR	Aira *Cærulea*
	H. 29. R. 404.8.	
Water	HAIR	Aira *Aquatica*
	H. 29. R. 402.3.	
Turfy	HAIR	Aira *Cefpitofa*
	H. 29. R. 403.5.	

B b 4   *Mountain*

Mountain	HAIR	*Tab.* 4.	Aira *Flexuofa*

H. 30. R. 407.8,9.

Small-leaved	HAIR		Aira *Setacea*

H. 30.

Grey	HAIR		Aira *Canefcens*

H. 30. R. 405.16.

Early	HAIR		Aira *Præcox*

H. 31. R. 407.10.

Silver	HAIR	*Tab.* 5.	Aira *Caryophillea*

H. 31. R. 407.7.

G E N U S 12.

MELIC grafs   Melica   *Nutans*

H. 31. R. 403.6.

G E N U S 13.

Middle	QUAKING grafs	Briza *Media*

H. 32. R. 412.1.

Small	QUAKING	Briza *Minor*

H. 32. R. 412.2.

G E N U S 14.

Water	MEADOW grafs	Poa *Aquatica*

H. 32. R. 411.13.

Common	MEADOW	Poa *Trivialis*

H. 33. R. 409.2.

Great	MEADOW	*Tab.* 6.	Poa *Pratenfis*

H. 33. R. 409. 3.

Creeping	MEADOW	Poa *Compreffa*

H. 33. R. 409.5.

Narrow-

Narrow-leaved MEADOW   Poa *Angustifolia*
H. 34. R. 409. 4.

Bulbous   MEADOW   Poa *Bulbosa*
H. 34. R. 411.12.

Hair-leaved MEADOW   Poa *Setacea*
H. 34.

Annual   MEADOW   *Tab.* 7.   Poa *Annua*
H. 34. R. 408 1.

Wood   MEADOW   Poa *Nemoralis*
H. 34.

Sea   MEADOW   Poa *Maritima*
H. 35. R. 410.7.

Hard   MEADOW   Poa *Rigida*
H. 35. R. 410.8.

Spiked   MEADOW   Poa *Loliacea*
H. 35. R. 395.4.

          G E N U S 15.

Sheep's   FESCUE grafs, *Tab.* 8. Feftuca *Ovina*
H. 36. R. 410.9.

          FESCUE   Feftuca *Vivipara*
ibid. *b.*

Hard   FESCUE   Feftuca *Duriuscula*
H. 36. R. 413.4.

Purple   FESCUE   *Tab.* 9.   Feftuca *Rubra*
H. 36.

Barren   FESCUE   Feftuca *Bromoides*
H. 37. R. 415.13.

                      Wall

Wall	FESCUE	Feſtuca *Myurus*
	H. 37. R. 411.16.	
Tall	FESCUE	Feſtuca *Elatior*
	H. 37. R. 411.15.	
Small	FESCUE	· Feſtuca *Decumbens*
	H. 38. R. 408. 11.	
Flote	FESCUE *Tab.* 10.	Feſtuca *Fluitans*
	H. 38. R. 412.17.	
Spiked	FESCUE	Feſtuca *Loliacea*
	H. 38.	
Wood	FESCUE	Feſtuca *Sylvatica*
	H. 38. R. 394.	

G E N U S 16.

Field	BROME grafs	Bromus *Secalinus*
	H. 39. R. 413.5. 414.7,8.	
Corn	BROME	Bromus *Arvenſis*
	H. 39. R. 414.9.	
Upright	BROME	Bromus *Erectus*
	H. 39.	
Wall	BROME	Bromus *Ciliatus*
	H. 40. R. 413.2.	
Barren	BROME	Bromus *Sterilis*
	H. 40. R. 412.1.	
Tall	BROME	Bromus *Giganteus*
	H. 40. R. 415.11.	
Wood	BROME	Bromus *Ramoſus*
	H. 40. R. 415.10.	

Spiked

Spiked	BROME	Bromus *Pinnatus*
	H. 41. R. 392.	

GENUS 17.

Naked	OAT grafs	Avena *Nuda*
	H. 41. R. 389. *b.*	
Bearded	OAT	Avena *Fatua*
	H. 41. R. 389.7.	
Meadow	OAT	Avena *Pratenfis*
	H. 42. R. 405.1.	
Rough	OAT	Avena *Pubefcens*
	H. 42. R. 406.2.	
Tall	OAT	Avena *Elatior*
	H. 42. R. 406.4.	
Yellow	OAT	Avena *Flavefcens*
	H. 42. R. 407.5.	

GENUS 18.

Common	REED grafs	Arundo *Phragmites*
	H. 43. R. 401.1.	
Branched	REED	Arundo *Calamagroftis*
	H. 43. R. 401.2.	
Small	REED	Arundo *Epigeios*
	H. 43. R. 401.3.	
Sea	REED	Arundo *Arenaria*
	H. 43. R. 393.1.	

GENUS 19.

Perennial	DARNEL grafs	Lolium *Perenne*
	H. 44. R. 395.2,	

Annual

Annual   DARNEL   Lolium *Temulentum*
H. 44. R. 395.1.
    G E N U S 20.
    LYME graſs   Elymus *Arenarius*
H. 44. R. 390.3.
    G E N U S 21.
Common   WHEAT graſs   Triticum *Repens*
H. 45. R. 390.1.
Bearded   WHEAT   Triticum *Caninum*
H. 45. R. 390.2,
Sea   WHEAT   Triticum *Junceum*
H. 45. R. 391.5.
    G E N U S 22.
    BARLEY graſs Hordeum *Murinum*
H. 46. R. 392.3.
    G E N U S 23.
    RYE graſs   Secale *Villoſum*
H. 46. R. 392.4.
    G E N U S 24.
Creſted   DOG's-TAIL, graſs*Tab.* 11.Cynoſurus
Criſtatus H. 47. R. 398.2. 399.3.
Rough   DOG's-TAIL Cynoſurus *Echinatus*
H. 47. R. 397.5.
Blue   DOG's-TAIL   Cynoſurus *Cæruleu:*
H. 47. R. 399.4.
Bearded   DOG's-TAIL   Cynoſurus *Paniceus*
H. 47. R. 396.4.
                G E-

G E N U S 25.

SOFT grafs   Holcus *Lanatus*

H.   R. 404.14:

Genus the firft. VERNAL. *Tab.* 1.

This grafs grows very commonly on dry hills, and likewife on found rich meadow land. It is one of the earlieft graffes we have, and from its being found on fuch kinds of paftures as fheep are fond of, and from whence excellent mutton comes, it is moft likely to be a good grafs for fheep paftures. It gives a grateful odor to hay.

ADDITION. *This grafs i have found on all kinds of grounds, from the moft fandy and dry to the moft ftiff and moift, and even in bogs. It is very plentiful in the beft meadows about London, viz. towards Hampftead and Hendon. It is very eafy to gather, as i have found by experience; as it fheds its feeds upon the leaft rubbing.*

Genus the fixth. *Meadow* FOX-TAIL .*Tab.* 2.

This grafs as well as the foregoing is found in great plenty in our beft meadows about London, and i believe makes very good hay. Linnæus fays that it is a proper grafs to fow on grounds that have been drained.

ADDITION. *I am informed that the beft*

                                       hay

hay which comes to London is from the meadows, where this grafs abounds. I saw this spring a meadow not far from Hampstead, which confisted of this grafs chiefly with some of the vernal grafs and the corn brome grafs. This grafs is fcarce in many parts of England, particularly Herefordshire, Berkshire and Norfolk. It might be gathered at almoft any time of the year from hay ricks, as it does not shed its feeds without rubbing, which is the cafe of but few graffes.

Water FOX-TAIL.

This is alfo found in the meadows about town, that are found but lye under water in the winter, and perhaps might be proper to fow on fuch grounds.

Genus the tenth. *Marsh* BENT.

ADDITION. *This grafs grows very common-ly in moift grounds and ditches in many parts of England, where i have been. I shall say more of it under article Flote* FESCUE *grafs.*

Fine BENT. *Tab.* 3.

This grafs i have always found in great plenty on the beft sheep paftures, as on Malvern hills and on all the high grounds in Herefordshire, that are remarkable for good mutton.

ADDITION. *I may add on Bagshot heath and the beft sheep paftures in Berkshire, Oxfordshire and Norfolk.*

Genus the eleventh. *Mountain* HAIR. *Tab.* 4.

The fame may be faid of this grafs as of the foregoing. It grows in great plenty on Bagfhot heath.

Silver HAIR. *Tab.* 5.

This alfo is found on the fame kind of pafture as the two foregoing.

Genus the fourteenth. *Great* and *narrow-leaved*
MEADOW. *Tab.* 6.

Thefe graffes are common in our beft meadow grounds, and i believe make good pafture and hay.

ADDITION. *I have found them frequently on banks by the road fide, and near ditches, even where they were not to be found in the adjoyning meadows, and paftures.*

Annual MEADOW. *Tab.* 7.

This grafs makes the fineft of turfs. It grows every where by way fides, and on rich found commons. It is called in fome parts the Suffolk grafs. I have feen whole fields of it in High Suffolk without any mixture of other graffes, and as fome of the beft falt butter we have in London comes from that county, it is moft likely to be the beft grafs for the dairy. I have feen a whole park in Suffolk covered with this grafs, but whether it affords good venifon i cannot tell, having never tafted of any from it. I fhould rather
think

think not, and that the beſt paſture for ſheep
is alſo the beſt for deer. However this wants
trial. I remarked on Malvern hill ſomething
particular in relation to this graſs. A walk that
was made there for the convenience of the water
drinkers, in leſs than a year was covered in
many places with it, tho' i could not find one
ſingle plant of it beſides in any part of the hill.
This was no doubt, owing to the frequent
treading, which above all things makes this
graſs floriſh, and therefore it is evident that
rolling muſt be very ſerviceable to it.

ADDITION. *It has been objeɛ̄ted that this
graſs is not free from bents, by which word is meant
the flowering ſtems. I anſwer that this is moſt
certainly true, and that there is no graſs without
them. But the flowers and ſtems do not grow ſo
ſoon brown as thoſe of other graſſes, and being
much ſhorter they do not cover the radical leaves ſo
much, and therefore this graſs affords a more agreeable turf without mowing than any other whatever
that i know of.*

Sheeps FESCUE. Tab. 8.

This is the graſs ſo much eſteemed in Sweden for ſheep.

Gmelin, Flor. Sibir. ſays that the Tartars
chooſe to fix during the ſummer in thoſe places
where there is the greateſt plenty of this graſs;

becauſe

becaufe it affords a moft wholefome nourifhment
to all kinds of cattle, but chiefly fheep; and he
obferves that the fepulchral monuments of the
antient Tartars are moftly found in places that
abound with this grafs, which fhews, adds he,
that it has long been valued amongft them.

I have among my graffes a fpecimen of it, but
do not remember where i found it. I am certain it is not common in any of the places where
i have been. Perhaps upon examination it may
be found on places famous for our beft mutton,
as Banftead Downs, Church-Stretton in Shrop-
fhire, fome parts of Wales &c.

ADDITION. *I have fince found this grafs in*
great plenty in many parts of England and Wales;
indeed on all the fineft fheep paftures in Hereford-
fhire, Berkfhire, Oxfordfhire, Norfolk &c. The
reafon why i thought it not common was, that it
is an early grafs, and had fhed its feeds, before i
ufually made my fearches in thofe places where it only
grows. I muft alfo obferve that, contrary to what
Linnæus fays, either the fheep or fome other animals
do eat the flowering ftems of this grafs, for upon
Banftead Downs there was nothing to be feen but
the radical leaves of it, unlefs amongft the bufhes
near the hedges, where it was guarded from the
fheep.

C c   Genus

Genus the fifteenth. *Purple* FESCUE. *Tab.* 9.

ADDITION. *This grafs i have always found along with the fine* BENT *and filver* HAIR-GRASS, *particularly on Banftead Downs in great plenty in a place inclofed in order to keep the fheep out. From hence i am inclined to think that this is the chief grafs all over the Downs, but as the flowering ftems in the other parts were intirely gone, unlefs along the hedges, i could not be certain.*

Flote FESCUE. *Tab.* 10.

I have no knowledge of the qualities of this grafs from my own experience, but fhall quote fomething concerning it out of a piece publifhed in the Amæn. Academ. vol. 3. entitled Plantæ Efculentæ. The author fays there, artic. 90. that the feeds of this grafs are gathered yearly in Poland, and from thence carried into Germany and fometimes into Sweden, and fold under the name of manna feeds. Thefe are much ufed at the tables of the great on account of their nourifhing quality and agreeable tafte. It is wonderfull, adds the author, that amongft us thefe feeds have hitherto been neglected, fince they are fo eafily collected and cleanfed.

ADDITION. *Mr. Dean, a very fenfible farmer at Rufcomb, Berkfhire, affured me that a fold always lying under water of about four acres,*

that

that was occupied by his father when he was a boy, was covered with a kind of grafs, that maintained five farm-horfes in good heart from April to the end of harveft without giving them any other kind of food, and that it yielded more than they could eat. He at my defire brought me fome of the grafs, which proved to be the flote FESCUE *with a mixture of the marfh* BENT; *whether this laft contributes much towards furnifhing fo good pafture for horfes i cannot fay. They both throw out roots at the joynts of the ftalks, and therefore likely to grow to a great length. In the index of dubious plants at the end of Ray's Synopfis, there is mention made of a grafs under the name of Gramen caninum fupinum longiffimum, growing not far from Salifbury* 24 *feet long. This muft by its length be a grafs with a creeping ftalk; and that there is a grafs in Wiltfhire growing in watery meadows fo valuable, that an acre of it lets from* 10 to 12 *pounds, i have been informed by feveral perfons. Thefe circumftances incline me to think it muft be the flote fefcue; but whatever grafs it be, it certainly muft deferve to be inquired after.*

There is a clamminefs on the ear of the flote fefcue when the feeds are ripe that taftes like honey, as i have often found, and for this reafon perhaps they are called manna feeds.

C ç 2　　　　　　*Linnæus*

Linnæus Flor. Suec. art. 95. *says, that the bran of this grafs will cure horfes troubled with bots, if kept from drinking for fome hours.*

Genus the feventeenth. *Yellow* OAT.

This grafs is found in great pleaty in fome grounds where the fheep's FESCUE, *the fine* BENT, *and the crefted* DOG-TAIL *grow, and therefore likely to be good for fheep. It is alfo not uncommon in good meadows.*

Genus the nineteenth. *Perennial* DARNEL.

This grafs is well known, and cultivated all over England; and it is to be hoped the fuccefs we have had with it will in time encourage our farmers to take the fame pains about fome others that are no lefs valuable, and are full as eafy to be feparated. It makes a moft excellent turf on found rich land where it will remain.

If i may judge by the venifon i have eat out of a paddock, that was chiefly filled with this grafs, i would by no means recommend it for parks. I know it will be faid that venifon is never good out of a paddock, that the deer muft have room to range, trees to browfe on, &c. I grant there is fome reafon for faying this, but i believe in general it is more owing to want of proper food, viz. good grafs, than merely to confinement; for paddocks are generally made

by

OBSERVATIONS ON GRASSES. 389

by converting fome rich fpot near the houfe,
that has conftantly been manured, and of courfe
is full of graffes fitter for the dairy or the ftable
than for deer, which hardly ever is the cafe of
large parks. No man will, i fuppofe, pretend
to make good pork from a hog fed with
grains inftead of peas, tho' he has the liberty of
choofing as much ground as he pleafes, and
where he pleafes.

This grafs is called in many counties *rye* grafs.
It were to be wifhed that the old name might
prevail, becaufe there is a genus of grafs, viz. the
22d. known by the name of *rye* all over the
kingdom, of which genus there is a fpecies that
ought to bear the fame generical name.

ADDITION. *I have fince eaten venifon out
of a large park, where there was much of this
grafs, and it was no better than that out of the
paddock. I fhould be apt to think from hence that
this grafs would not be proper for fheep, as i have
always obferved that the fame kind of ground which
yeilds good venifon yields alfo good mutton. For
what particular ufes it is good, wants to be tryed,
whether for the dairy, for fatting cattle, or for
horfes. Many are tempted by the facility of procuring the feed of this grafs to lay down grounds
near their houfes, where they want to have a fine*

turf

turf with it ; for which purpose unless the soil be very rich a worse grass cannot be sown, as it will certainly die off in a very few years intirely.

Genus the twenty fourth. *Crested* DOG-TAIL. *Tab.* 11.

This grass i imagine is proper for parks. I know one where this abounds, that is famous for excellent venison. It may perhaps be as good for sheep.

ADDITION. *That it is good for sheep i have since found by experience. The best mutton i have tasted, next to that which comes from hills where the purple and sheep's fescue, the fine bent, and the silver hair grasses abound, having been from sheep fed with it.*

It makes a very fine turf upon dry sandy or chalky soils, as i have seen in many parts of Berkshire, but unless swept over with the scythe, its flowering stems will look brown ; which is the case of all grasses, which are not fed by variety of animals. For that some animals will eat the flowering stems is evident by commons, where scarcely any parts of grasses appear but the radical leaves.

Order of coming into ear of the above mentioned grasses.

Annual MEADOW

Meadow FOX-TAIL

VERNAL

VERNAL

Great MEADOW

Narrow-leaved MEADOW

Crested DOG-TAIL

Sheep's FESCUE

Purple FESCUE

Fine BENT

Marsh BENT

Silver HAIR

Yellow OAT

Flote FESCUE

The whole time from the beginning of May till about the middle of June.

Ει—κεν και σμικρον επι σμικρω καλαθειο
Και θαμα τυθ' ερδοις, ταχα κεν μεγα και το γενειο.

Hesiod.

F I N I S.

Tab. 1.

Vernal Grass.

R. Price delin.   Meadow Fox-tail Grass.

Alopecurus pratensis

R. Price delin.

Fine Bent Grass.

Mountain Hair Grass.

E. Bree delin.

Silver Hair-Grass.

Tab. 6.

Great-Meadow Grass.

Price delin.

Tab. 7

Annual Meadow Grass.

Tab. 8.

Tab. 10.

Flote Fescue Grass.

J. Miller del. et sc.

Crested Dogs tail Grass.

R. Rice delin.

cynosurus cristatus

www.ingramcontent.com/pod-product-compliance
Lightning Source LLC
Chambersburg PA
CBHW032303280326
41932CB00009B/676